Lecture Notes in Artificial Intelligence　10002

Subseries of Lecture Notes in Computer Science

LNAI Series Editors

Randy Goebel
  University of Alberta, Edmonton, Canada
Yuzuru Tanaka
  Hokkaido University, Sapporo, Japan
Wolfgang Wahlster
  DFKI and Saarland University, Saarbrücken, Germany

LNAI Founding Series Editor

Joerg Siekmann
  DFKI and Saarland University, Saarbrücken, Germany

More information about this series at http://www.springer.com/series/1244

Nardine Osman · Carles Sierra (Eds.)

Autonomous Agents and Multiagent Systems

AAMAS 2016 Workshops, *Best Papers*
Singapore, Singapore, May 9–10, 2016
Revised Selected Papers

 Springer

Editors
Nardine Osman
Campus de la UAB
IIIA-CSIC
Bellaterra
Spain

Carles Sierra
Campus de la UAB
IIIA-CSIC
Bellaterra
Spain

ISSN 0302-9743   ISSN 1611-3349   (electronic)
Lecture Notes in Artificial Intelligence
ISBN 978-3-319-46881-5   ISBN 978-3-319-46882-2   (eBook)
DOI 10.1007/978-3-319-46882-2

Library of Congress Control Number: 2016952511

LNCS Sublibrary: SL7 – Artificial Intelligence

Printed on acid-free paper

This Springer imprint is published by Springer Nature
The registered company is Springer International Publishing AG
The registered company address is: Gewerbestrasse 11, 6330 Cham, Switzerland

Preface

AAMAS is the leading scientific conference for research in autonomous agents and multiagent systems, which is annually organized by the non-profit organisation the International Foundation for Autonomous Agents and Multiagent Systems (IFAAMAS). The AAMAS conference series was initiated in 2002 by merging three highly respected meetings: the International Conference on Multi-Agent Systems (ICMAS); the International Workshop on Agent Theories, Architectures, and Languages (ATAL); and the International Conference on Autonomous Agents (AA).

Besides the main program, AAMAS hosts a number of workshops, which aim at stimulating and facilitating discussion, interaction, and comparison of approaches, methods, and ideas related to specific topics, both theoretical and applied, in the general area of autonomous agents and multiagent systems. The AAMAS workshops provide an informal setting where participants have the opportunity to discuss specific technical topics in an atmosphere that fosters the active exchange of ideas.

This book compiles the best papers of the AAMAS 2016 workshops. In total, AAMAS 2016 ran 16 workshops. To select the best papers, the organizers of each workshop were asked to nominate two papers from their workshop and send those papers, along with the reviews they received during their workshop's review process, to the AAMAS 2016 workshop co-chairs. The AAMAS 2016 workshop co-chairs then studied each paper carefully, in order to assess its quality and whether it was suitable to be selected for this book. One paper was selected from each workshop, although not all workshops were able to contribute. The result is a compilation of 11 papers selected from 11 workshops, which we list below.

- The 18th International Workshop on Trust in Agent Societies (Trust 2016)
- The 7th International Workshop on Optimization in Multiagent Systems (OptMAS 2016)
- The Third International Workshop on Exploring Beyond the Worst Case in Computational Social Choice (EXPLORE 2016)
- The Second International Workshop on Issues with Deployment of Emerging Agent-Based Systems (IDEAS 2016)
- The 17th International Workshop on Multi-Agent-Based Simulation (MABS 2016)
- The 4th International Workshop on Engineering Multiagent Systems (EMAS 2016)
- The 14th International Workshop on Adaptive Learning Agents (ALA 2016)
- The 9th International Workshop on Agent-Based Complex Automated Negotiations (ACAN 2016)
- The First International Workshop on Agent-Based Modelling of Urban Systems (ABMUS 2016)
- The 21st International Workshop on Coordination, Organization, Institutions and Norms in Agent Systems (COIN 2016), with a special joint session with the 7th International Workshop on Collaborative Agents Research and Development: CARE for Digital Education (CARE 2016)

- The 15th International Workshop on Emergent Intelligence on Networked Agents (WEIN 2016)

We note that a similar process was carried out to select the most visionary papers of the AAMAS 2016 workshops. While best papers follow the style of more traditional papers, visionary papers are papers with novel ideas that propose a change in the way research is currently carried out. The selected visionary papers may be found in the Springer LNAI 10003 book.

Revised and selected papers of the AAMAS workshops have been published in the past (see Springer's LNAI Vol. 7068 of the AAMAS 2011 workshops). Despite not publishing such books regularly for the AAMAS workshops, there has been a clear and strong interest on other occasions. For instance, publishing the "best of the rest" AAMAS workshops volume has been discussed with Prof. Michael Luck, who was enthusiastic concerning AAMAS 2014 in Paris. This book, along with Springer's LNAI 10003 volume, aims at presenting the best and most visionary papers of the AAMAS 2016 workshops. The aim of publishing these books is essentially to better disseminate the most notable results of the AAMAS workshops and encourage authors to submit top-quality research work to the AAMAS workshops.

July 2016   Nardine Osman
                                                                                      Carles Sierra

Organization

AAMAS 2016 Workshop Co-chairs

Nardine Osman   Artificial Intelligence Research Institute, Spain
Carles Sierra   Artificial Intelligence Research Institute, Spain

AAMAS 2016 Workshop Organizers

Trust 2016

Jie Zhang   Nanyang Technological University, Singapore
Robin Cohen   University of Waterloo, Canada
Murat Sensoy   Ozyegin University, Turkey

OptMAS 2016

Archie Chapman   University of Sydney, Australia
Pradeep Varakantham   Singapore Management University, Singapore
William Yeoh   New Mexico State University, USA
Roie Zivan   Ben-Gurion University of the Negev, Israel

EXPLORE 2016

Haris Aziz   NICTA and University of New South Wales, Australia
Felix Brandt   Technische Universität München, Germany
David Manlove   University of Glasgow, UK
Nicholas Mattei   NICTA and University of New South Wales, Australia

IDEAS 2016

Adam Eck   University of Nebraska-Lincoln, USA
Leen-Kiat Soh   University of Nebraska-Lincoln, USA
Bo An   Nanyang Technological University, Singapore
Paul Scerri   Platypus LLC, USA
Adrian Agogino   NASA, USA

MABS 2016

Luis Antunes   University of Lisbon, Portugal
Luis Gustavo Nardin   Center for Modeling Complex Interactions, USA

EMAS 2016

Matteo Baldoni   University of Turin, Italy
Jörg P. Müller   Technische Universität Clausthal, Germany

| Ingrid Nunes | Universidade Federal do Rio Grande do Sul, Brazil |
| Rym Zalila-Wenkstern | University of Texas at Dallas, TX, USA |

ALA 2016

Daan Bloembergen	University of Liverpool, UK
Tim Brys	Vrije Universiteit Brussels, Belgium
Logan Yliniemi	University of Nevada, Reno, USA

ACAN 2016

Katsuhide Fujita	Tokyo University of Agriculture and Technology, Japan
Naoki Fukuta	Shizuoka University, Japan
Takayuki Ito	Nagoya Institute of Technology, Japan
Minjie Zhang	University of Wollongong, Australia
Quan Bai	Auckland University of Technology, New Zealand
Fenghui Ren	University of Wollongong, Australia
Chao Yu	Dalian University of Technology, China
Reyhan Aydogan	Ozyegin University, Turkey

ABMUS 2016

Pascal Perez	University of Wollongong, Australia
Lin Padgham	RMIT, Australia
Kai Nagel	Technische Universität Berlin, Germany
Ana L.C. Bazzan	Universidade Federal do Rio Grande do Sul, Brazil
Mohammad-Reza Namazi-Rad	University of Wollongong, Australia

COIN 2016, with a special joint session with CARE 2016

Samhar Mahmoud (COIN)	King's College London, UK
Stephen Cranefield (COIN)	University of Otago, New Zealand
Fernando Koch (CARE)	Samsung Research Institute, Brazil
Tiago Primo (CARE)	Samsung Research Institute, Brazil
Andrew Koster (CARE)	Samsung Research Institute, Brazil
Christian Guttmann (CARE)	UNSW, Australia, IVBAR, and Karolinska Institute, Sweden

WEIN 2016

Satoshi Kurihara	University of Electro-Communications, Japan
Hideyuki Nakashima	Future University-Hakodate, Japan
Akira Namatame	National Defense Academy, Japan

Contents

On the Trustworthy Fulfillment of Commitments

Edmund H. Durfee$^{(\boxtimes)}$ and Satinder Singh

Computer Science and Engineering, University of Michigan, Ann Arbor, MI, USA
{durfee,baveja}@umich.edu

Abstract. An agent that adopts a commitment to another agent should act so as to bring about a state of the world meeting the specifications of the commitment. Thus, by faithfully pursuing a commitment, an agent can be trusted to make sequential decisions that it believes can cause an intended state to arise. In general, though, an agent's actions will have uncertain outcomes, and thus reaching an intended state cannot be guaranteed. For such sequential decision settings with uncertainty, therefore, commitments can only be probabilistic. We propose a semantics for the trustworthy fulfillment of a probabilistic commitment that hinges on whether the agent followed a policy that would be expected to achieve an intended state with sufficient likelihood, rather than on whether the intended state was actually reached. We have developed and evaluated algorithms that provably operationalize this semantics, with different tradeoffs between responsiveness and computational overhead. We also discuss opportunities and challenges in extending our proposed semantics to richer forms of uncertainty, and to other agent architectures besides the decision-theoretic agents that have been our initial focus of study. Finally, we consider the implications of our semantics on how trust might be established and confirmed in open agent systems.

1 Motivation

In open systems occupied by multiple (human and/or artificial) agents, where in order to best achieve their goals the agents need to rely on each other, issues of trust come to the fore. The many important challenges regarding trust include how to build trust, how to maintain trust, how to utilize trust, how to detect when trust is misplaced, how to propagate reputations about trustworthiness, and how to incentivize trustworthiness. In this paper, we consider the case where agents have incentive to be trustworthy, and where they will do everything in their power to merit the trust of other agents, but where uncertainty inherent in the environment, and the agents' uncertainty about the environment, mean that an agent sometimes cannot, or even should not, achieve outcomes that other agents might be relying upon.

Specifically, we ask the question of whether an agent that has made a (social) commitment to another agent, and has acted in good faith with respect to the commitment, can be said to have fulfilled the commitment even if the outcomes of its actions fail to reach a state that the commitment was intended to bring about. By acting in good faith, has the agent earned trust despite not delivering the

© Springer International Publishing AG 2016
N. Osman and C. Sierra (Eds.): AAMAS 2016 Ws Best Papers, LNAI 10002, pp. 1–13, 2016.
DOI: 10.1007/978-3-319-46882-2_1

intended outcome? For instance, consider a physician who is treating a patient for some condition: There is a (perhaps implicit) commitment by the doctor to improve that condition, but the treatments administered might not be effective for the patient, or the doctor might even abandon treatment of the condition to address more consequential conditions instead. Has the doctor violated the trust of the patient and failed to meet the commitment?

To answer such questions about what it means for a computational agent to be trustworthy in its fulfillment of social commitments, we have been developing a decision-theoretic formulation for framing and studying the semantics of commitments in settings where the agents' environment, and/or what the agent knows about the environment, can be uncertain. To jump to the punchline of this paper, our investigations so far have led us to advocate a commitment semantics that focuses on whether the agent's choices of actions were consistent with the trustworthy fulfillment of its commitments (e.g., whether the physician followed proper standards of patient care), rather than on whether the state of the world reached by the agent's actions, coupled with the other partially-known ongoing processes and factors in the environment, had the intended outcome (e.g., whether the patient's condition was cured).

For reasons of publication restrictions we cannot here present a deeper technical treatment of our work, so our goal in this paper is to summarize the background, context, justification, and implications of adopting our suggested semantics for the trustworthy fulfillment of commitments, for consideration by the community. In what follows, we first briefly examine some of the relevant past literature on computational models of commitment, with a particular focus on commitments in uncertain, probabilistic worlds.[1] We then (Sect. 3) present a decision-theoretic formulation of the problem, highlighting the representation of the agent's uncertainty about rewards, and how the fact that pursuing commitments is a sequential process means that the agent might want to change its course of actions sometime between when the commitment is made and when the conditions it is trying to achieve could come about. This formulation then allows us to more formally state the semantics for trustworthy commitment achievement in the face of uncertain rewards that we advocate, and to summarize computational strategies for realizing those semantics (Sect. 4) for reward uncertainty and beyond. In Sect. 5, we speculate on how the semantics might apply to other, non-decision-theoretic agent architectures, and in Sect. 6 we consider the broader implications of our semantics on the problem of establishing trust.

2   Computational Models of Commitment

Munindar Singh provides a comprehensive overview of computational research into characterizing commitments using formal (modal and temporal) logic [17],

---

[1] The material presented in Sects. 2 and 3 has appeared in similar form in an unpublished symposium paper [7], and summaries of the algorithms presented in Sect. 4 appeared in an extended abstract at AAMAS12 [20].

drawing on a broad literature (e.g., [2,4–6,11,16]). In brief, these formulations support important objectives such as provable pursuit of mutually agreed-upon goals, and verification of communication protocols associated with managing commitments. When commitments are uncertain to be attained, they can have associated conventions and protocols for managing such uncertainty (e.g., [8,19, 22]). For example, by convention an agent unable to keep a commitment must inform dependent agents.

Dropping commitments too readily, however, obviates their predictive value for coordination. The logical formulations above explicitly enumerate the conditions under which an agent is permitted to drop a local component of a mutual goal, where these conditions usually amount to either (1) when the agent believes its local component is unachievable; (2) when the agent believes that the mutual goal is not worth pursuing any longer; or (3) when the agent believes some other agents have dropped their components of the mutual goal. However, while logically reasonable, these conditions do not impose a commitment semantics on an agent's local decisions. For example, to avoid the first condition, should an agent never take an action that would risk rendering is local component unachievable? What if every action it can take has some chance of rendering the local component unachievable? For the second condition, should it really be allowed to unilaterally abandon the mutual goal and renege on other agents just because it has recognized it can achieve a slightly more preferred goal?

To tighten predictability, commitments can be paired with conditions under which they are sure to hold [1,13,17,18]. For example, an agent could commit to providing a good or service conditioned on first receiving payment. Of course, this representation also admits to weakening commitments to the point where they are worthless, such as committing to achieving a local component of a mutual goal under the condition that no better local goal arises in the meantime! Sandholm and Lesser [15] noted difficulties in enumerating such conditions, and verifying they hold in decentralized settings. Their leveled-commitment contracting framework associates a decommitment penalty with each commitment to accommodate uncertainty but discourage frivolous decommitment. The recipient of a commitment, however, will generally be unable to know the likelihood that the commitment will be fulfilled, because it will lack knowledge of the internals of the agent making the commitment, including how likely it is that uncertain action outcomes or evolving local goals will make paying the decommitment penalty the only/better choice.

An alternative means to quantify uncertainty is to explicitly make probabilistic commitments, where an agent provides a probability distribution over possible outcomes of the commitment, including how well it will be fulfilled (if at all) and when [3,21,23]. Xuan and Lesser [23] explain how probabilistic commitments can improve joint planning by allowing agents to suitably hedge their plans to anticipate possible contingencies, including anticipating even unlikely outcomes and planning for consequent changes to probabilities of reaching commitment outcomes. A more myopic (hence more tractable) variation on this approach was developed for the DARPA Coordinators program [10], where only as circumstances unfolded would the agents update probabilistic predictions about future outcomes, and then exchange updates and reactively compute new plans. These prior approaches however treat commitment probabilities fundamentally as predictions about how whatever plan an agent has chosen to follow will affect other agents. In contrast, our treatment of commitments in uncertain settings is not only to provide predictive information to the recipient of a commitment about what might happen, but also to impose prescriptive semantics on the provider of a commitment to guide its behavior into a good faith effort in making those predictions come true.

3 Problem Formulation

Our initial strategy for capturing intuitive, everyday notions of commitment semantics that account for and respond to model uncertainty is to map these notions into a principled, decision-theoretic framework for agent use. Here, we present a reward-uncertainty-centered formulation that we use most in this paper, though later we briefly generalize this to other forms of model uncertainty. In our initial formulation, we restrict our attention to the class of problems with the following properties. (1) A single intelligent agent interacts with a single human user (operator). (2) The agent's actions influence what is possible for the user to achieve but not vice-versa (though, because the user also derives reward from the agent's actions, the user's preferences might influence what the agent *should* do). (3) The agent has an accurate[2] controlled Markov process model of its environment dynamics defined by a multidimensional state space, an action space, and a transition probability function. The state space $\Phi = \Phi_1 \times \Phi_1 \times \cdots \times \Phi_n$ is the cross product of n discrete-valued state variables. The transition probability $T(\phi'|\phi, a)$ is the probability of the next state being ϕ' given the agent took action a in state ϕ. (4) The agent has uncertainty over its reward function expressed via a prior distribution μ_0^b over possible built-in reward functions $R_1^b, R_2^b, \ldots, R_n^b$, where each R_i^b maps $\Phi \to \mathbb{R}$. Each reward function R_i^b captures both the designed-rewards for the agent (e.g., a large negative reward for exceeding power or memory constraints), and the uncertain rewards that can arise over time in the environment. From the perspective of the single human-user in this problem, these multiple sources of reward are "built-in" and the uncertainty over them is summarized into the distribution over $\{R_i^b\}$. The agent obtains samples of the true built-in reward-function as it acts in the world and thus can update its distribution over $\{R_i^b\}$ during execution.

Finally, (5) the user has her own goals and acts in the world, and the agent's actions may **enable** the user to obtain higher reward than she would without the agent's help. This is where the notions of commitment and trust come into play.

---

[2] Because the model is assumed accurate, the agent can be assumed to only formulate policies (and thus commitments) that it is capable of executing. Permitting inaccurate models (where an agent might make a commitment it is inherently incapable of fulfilling) is outside the scope of the focus of this paper on trustworthy fulfillment of commitments.

Consider an agent that could make either of two commitments to an operator: commitment ξ, where it commits to producing an analysis within 2 min with probability at least 0.95, and commitment ξ' where it commits to producing the analysis in 1 min but with probability only 0.5 (e.g., its faster analysis tool works in fewer cases). Commitment ξ enables the operator's optimal policy to prepare for the analysis output with associated enablement-utility $U(\xi)$, while commitment ξ' induces an optimal policy where the operator begins doing the analysis herself (as a backup in case the agent fails) with lower utility $U(\xi')$. Depending on the degree of cooperativeness of the agent, solving the agent's sequential decision problem might require taking into account these enablement-utility (U) values to the user of candidate enablement-commitments. If the agent adopts a commitment to the user, the user becomes a "trustor" of the agent and the agent a "trustee" of the user.

Some special cases of this formulation help motivate our commitment semantics:

Bayes-MDP. In this special case, the agent is not enabling user actions (no U's and hence no need for commitments), but the agent is uncertain about which of the built-in rewards $\{R_i^b\}$ applies. The agent thus faces a standard Bayesian-MDP problem (a particular kind of partially-observable MDP, or POMDP, where partial observability is only with respect to the true reward function in $\{R_i^b\}$). One can define an extended belief-state MDP in which the belief-state of the agent at time t is the joint pair (ϕ_t, μ_t^b) where μ_t^b is the posterior belief of the agent over $\{R_i^b\}$ after the first $t - 1$ observations about reward as it acts in the world. The Bayes-optimal *policy* is a mapping from belief-states to actions[3] that maximizes the expected cumulative reward for the agent. Exact algorithms (applicable only to small problems) and approximate algorithms (with increased applicability) exist to solve the belief-state MDP for (near-Bayes-optimal) policies and we exploit them as one component in our research [12].

Commitment-Only. In this case, there are enablement-actions but the built-in reward function is known to be R^b. Because of stochastic transitions, the agent could find itself in unlikely states from which it cannot enable the user, and thus commitments are in general only probabilistic. Because the agent can only control its actions, and not their outcomes, we assert that, in uncertain worlds, *the decision-theoretic semantics of what it means for an agent to faithfully pursue a probabilistic commitment is that it adheres to a policy that meets the commitment with a probability at least as high as the probability associated with the commitment.* Given that its rewards are fixed (in this special case) the

---

[3] Recall that a policy is defined over *all* (belief) states, and so covers every possible contingency that could arise during execution. We refer to a particular sequence of states and (policy-dictated) actions that might be experienced as a *trajectory*. Note that a policy thus differs from a *plan*, which is typically defined in terms of a specific (nominal) trajectory. Hence, a plan can fail (stimulating plan repair or replanning) when unintended action outcomes or external events cause a deviation from the plan's nominal trajectory. In contrast, a policy never "fails" because it specifies actions for every state (and thus for every possible trajectory).

agent will at the outset commit to a policy that maximizes some function of its expected reward and the user's enablement utility, and follow that policy unswervingly. In a cooperative setting (including when a single agent is making a commitment to another facet of itself), the function could simply sum these. In a self-interested setting, the agent's reward could predominate (the user is helped only as a side-effect of the agent's preferred policy), or in a setting where the agent is subordinate the user's utility could be preeminent.

Commitment in the face of Uncertain Rewards. This special case has been the main focus of our work, where there is uncertainty over the agent's rewards ($\{R_i^b\}$), and there is the possibility of enablement (U). The departure from the previous commitment-only case is that now the agent learns about its built-in reward function as it acts in the world. As in the previous case, in general commitments are only probabilistic because transitions are stochastic, so the agent has limitations on its ability to help the user attain the enablement utility U despite its best efforts. Compounding this problem, the evolving model of the reward function might also tempt the agent toward redirecting its efforts away from the enablement. What can we expect of an agent in terms of making sequential decisions that live up to a commitment when it is faced with such limitations and temptations? For example, perhaps the agent's modified beliefs about rewards would tempt it to change its behavior in a way that actually improves the chances of achieving the intended conditions of the commitment, in a "win-win" way. But would changing its policy even then violate the trust of the user?

4   Commitment Semantics

We argue that a semantics for commitments in sequential-decision settings with stochastic transitions, as was mentioned in the previous section, should be as follows: *The semantics of what it means for an agent to faithfully pursue a probabilistic commitment is that it adheres to a policy that in expectation meets the commitment.* Remember that "in expectation" in this context means that the probability of meeting the commitment is at least as high as the probability specified by the probabilistic commitment. So, if the commitment was to reach an intended state with probability 0.9, the agent would need to follow a policy that in expectation would reach the state at least 90 % of the time, while if the commitment probability was only 0.1 the agent could follow a policy that in expectation would reach the state only 10 % of the time. Thus, "in expectation" does not mean "as likely has possible." Nor does it mean "more likely than not" (better than a 50 % chance). Instead, it means "at least as likely as promised by the commitment."

This semantics sounds straightforward enough, though as the sections that follow will show it is not always trivial to operationalize. Before considering algorithms for implementing the semantics, however, we first briefly consider how this semantics departs from prior semantics for computational commitments.

4.1   Relationship to Other Commitment Semantics

Probably the most thorough and precise computational semantics for commitments is that of Munindar Singh and his colleagues. In that vein of work, commitments are expressed in terms of expressions over state variables, describing what state(s) the agent(s) making the commitment promises to bring about, possibly conditioned on other agents achieving other aspects of the state. However, as we have discussed, in environments with stochastic transitions agents cannot commit to assuredly achieving particular states because outcomes of actions are not fully under their control. Agents however do have control over the actions they take, and hence our semantics focuses not on states of the world *but rather on the actions agents have control over*. Agents commit to acting in ways that, with sufficiently high probability, will lead to outcomes that other agents care about.

In this regard, then, our commitment semantics shares similarities with work on joint policies in cooperative sequential decision frameworks like Decentralized (Partially-Observable) Markov Decision Processes. In Dec-(PO)MDP solutions, agents' joint policies dictate a particular policy for each agent to follow, where the policy of each agent is (approximately) optimized with respect to the policies to be followed by the others. Thus, optimal joint behavior is achieved when agents precisely execute their assigned policies. Our commitment semantics similarly restrict agents' policy choices, but differ from Dec-POMDPs in that our semantics are agnostic about cooperation (we treat the reason why agents adopt commitments as orthogonal to what the commitments that have been adopted mean) and only require that an agent pursue a policy that in expectation will achieve the commitment: If there are multiple such policies, then the agent is free to select from among them. This is exactly the kind of flexibility that we seek to exploit when an agent is acting sequentially under reward uncertainty.

Our commitment semantics also hearkens back to some of the earliest work on agent commitments, which focused not on (social) commitments between agents, but rather on commitments an agent makes to its internal behavior as part of a meta-control strategy. The work by Kinny and Georgeff [9] considered the degree to which an agent should question continuing to pursue a plan in an uncertain world, where they explored strategies by which an agent might be "cautious" (reconsidering what plan it should follow every step of the way) or "bold" (pursuing its current plan until it is either finished, or is impossible to continue). Like that work, our semantics for commitment concentrates on commitments to action policies rather than outcomes, but unlike that work we view a (in our case social) commitment as a constraint on possible physical action policy choices rather than as a meta-construct for controlling reasoning effort.

4.2   Semantics-Respecting Algorithms

Of the algorithms we now summarize, the first can arguably be seen as being "bold" because it presses on with a policy without being responsive to changing circumstances, and thus avoids the overhead of questioning whether and how to respond to circumstances every step of the way. The second is "cautious" because it preplans for every foreseeable change to circumstances. As a result, it is extremely responsive, but incurs high reasoning costs. The third is a compromise between the first two, striving to be responsive enough without incurring excessive overhead.

Mean Reward (MR). This algorithm most simply and directly implements our commitment semantics so that an agent can be trustworthy in fulfilling the commitment. Given a commitment and a distribution over the true reward function, the agent finds its Bayes-optimal policy that meets the probabilistic commitment. Specifically, at the outset, the agent formulates a commitment-constrained policy that is optimal for its initial reward belief-state, which equates [14] to an optimal policy for the distribution's Mean Reward (MR). The agent then pursues this policy without deviation, ignoring temptations and opportunities that arise during execution as it improves its understanding of the true reward function in its environment. Thus, the MR algorithm implements a "bold" strategy for commitment attainment using our semantics: The agent adheres to a policy that meets the commitment, and never reconsiders it. This satisfies our commitment semantics, and incurs computational cost only for computing an optimal policy given a single (mean) reward function; its downside is that it will not take advantage of serendipity, when new information about rewards would have allowed it to achieve higher reward while still meeting (or even exceeding) the probabilistic expectations of the commitment.

Extended Belief State (EBS). This algorithm implements the most "cautious" of strategies by modeling all possible ways in which the agent's beliefs about the reward might change over its sequential actions, and developing a policy that accounts for every single one of them (while still meeting or exceeding the probabilistic commitment). The Extended Belief State approach adds directly into the state model a representation of the agent's beliefs about the reward function. Thus, as the agent models possible trajectories, it considers not only its choices of actions and their stochastic outcomes on the physical state, but also the possible reward observations it might make and the consequent posterior beliefs about the reward function it might have. The branching associated with action choices, action outcome stochasticity, and uncertainty over reward observations exponentially enlarges the number of trajectories the agent needs to explore, incurring high computational overhead. However, once the EBS policy has been derived, it is guaranteed to be optimal, not only being responsive to all possible evolving models of the environment's rewards, but even leading the agent to acting in ways that anticipate and exploit expected future reward observations.

Commitment-Constrained Iterative Mean Reward (CCIMR). This algorithm is a compromise between the previous algorithms, seeking to gain some of the computational benefits of MR while permitting some degree of responsiveness like EBS, all while being trustworthy in adhering to the commitment semantics. Conceptually, the algorithm works with a space of policies Π_ξ that all satisfy the commitment ξ. If this space is empty, then the agent cannot make a commitment, but otherwise our commitment semantics allow the agent to commit to following *any* of these policies, as they are all equally satisfactory given commitment ξ. The crux of our Commitment-Constrained Iterative Mean Reward (CCIMR) algorithm, then, is to use a reward observation reactively (unlike EBS that proactively anticipates them) to compute a new posterior mean reward. It then selects from the current Π_ξ the policy that optimizes expected reward under the new reward beliefs and pursues that one. Note, though, that Π_ξ will shrink over time: as a particular policy has been followed to the current time, policies that would have chosen different actions in the states up until that time must be removed from Π_ξ. (A policy that appends the first half of one element of Π_ξ with the second half of another element might not itself be an element of Π_ξ, and so mustn't be allowed.)

While this gives the conceptual basis of our CCIMR algorithm, a key aspect of this algorithm is that it does *not* explicitly enumerate and manipulate the commitment-constrained set of policies Π_ξ, as this set can be exceedingly large. Instead, we have developed a linear programming approach that explicitly captures constraints, including not just those associated with the commitment(s) but also those associated with the policy pursued so far, so that the agent can construct, at any given time, only the optimal element of the (possibly shrunken) space of policies Π_ξ. This means CCIMR is solving a number of optimal policy calculations that is linear in time (one for each new mean reward, which at most happens once per time step), whereas MR only performs one optimal policy calculation (the initial MR policy), and EBS computes one optimal policy but for an exponentially-larger (belief) state space. CCIMR thus represents a compromise in terms of computation. Meanwhile, because it is responsive to changing reward beliefs, it is guaranteed to achieve rewards no worse than MR, while achieving rewards no better than EBS (because EBS is not only responsive but proactive).

Evaluation. Again, the technical details of the algorithms just described, including formal proofs about CCIMR being lower-bounded by MR and upper-bounded by EBS, and a proof that CCIMR conforms to our commitment semantics, are excluded from this paper due to publication restrictions. Similarly, we cannot present detailed empirical results for these algorithms. In brief, though, our experiments have shown that CCIMR can often allow an agent to achieve rewards close to what EBS permits (and significantly better than MR), and that scaling a problem to more states and longer time horizons can cause the time needs of EBS to explode while CCIMR's time needs increase more manageably.

4.3   Semantics with Other Kinds of Uncertainty

The work we've done so far has emphasized the need to account for and respond to an agent's uncertain rewards. However, uncertainty can arise in other decision model components too. For example, an agent can apply machine learning techniques to resolve uncertainty about its transition model: by maintaining statistics about the effects of actions in various states, it improves its ability to predict the probabilities of action outcomes and thus to formulate good policies. Making commitments in the face of transition uncertainty unfortunately appears to be qualitatively different from the reward uncertainty case. A key observation is that, when uncertainty is only over rewards, then the agent can *always* faithfully pursue its commitment by, in the worst case, turning a blind eye to what it learns about rewards and simply following its initial commitment-fulfilling policy throughout. That is, what it learns about rewards has no effect on what states of the world it can probabilistically reach, but just in how happy it is to reach them. In contrast, an agent with transition uncertainty can learn, during execution, that states it thought likely to be reached when it made its commitment are in fact unlikely, and *vice versa*. Hence, in contrast to reward uncertainty where a committed agent was obligated to pursue one of the initial commitment-constrained policies (limiting its later choices), with transition uncertainty it could be argued that a faithful agent might be *required* to shift to a policy outside this initial set under some changes to its updated beliefs. If unchecked, this latitude renders commitment semantics meaningless. The question of what constitutes trustworthy pursuit of a commitment by a decision-theoretic agent, in the face of transition uncertainty, is an open problem that we are starting to tackle.

5   Implications for Non-Decision-Theoretic Agents

By framing the question of trustworthy pursuit of commitments despite uncertainty in a decision-theoretic setting, we have been able to exploit useful aspects of a decision-theoretic framework, such as explicit models of rewards and transitions, and of uncertainty over these. However, decision-theoretic approaches have weaknesses too, and in particular the power of these approaches generally comes at a steep computational cost. As a result, these techniques are often applied to only small problems, or (for particular classes of problems) approximation techniques are used to find good, but not necessarily optimal, solutions. Other agent architectures, such as those based on Belief-Desire-Intention concepts, can often be fruitfully applied to problems where the richness of the decision-theoretic approach is not needed and where the computational costs cannot be afforded. The question then arises as to whether our proposed semantics generalizes to other architectures based on more classical notions of plans and goals. While at this point we can only speculate about this, our initial thinking is that they can, and we now delve briefly into initial thoughts as to how.

In essence, mapping our commitment semantics to an agent using classical plans and goals would mean that such an agent is committing not to achieving particular goals (conditions in the world) but rather it is committing to executing one out of a set of plans. Therefore, before making a commitment, the agent would need to have identified a non-empty set of plans to commit to. Compared to the decision-theoretic setting, where we could summarize the space of commitment-satisfying policies based on a small number of parameters, it is less clear how (without incorporating new annotations to elements of a plan library) we could do the same in a more classical setting, but assuming such a set is specified (through enumeration if in no other way) then an agent can commit to executing one of the plans in that space, where each plan is executable when particular preconditions it depends upon are met.

The operational semantics for pursuing other goals that could conflict (depending on how they are pursued) with the goal(s) of the committed-to plans could then be patterned after the semantics we've outlined. For example, the semantics could dictate that an agent is not allowed pursue a plan for another goal if that plan would violate the preconditions for the element of the space of committed-to plans that is currently being followed. This would be like MR: the agent commits to a particular plan for the commitment, and it must follow that plan (in that it cannot take actions that preclude following the plan). The exception, however, is whereas the MR policy would associate an action for all eventualities that could arise, a typical plan will have a single nominal trajectory. If the world state deviates from this trajectory then the plan fails, triggering possible repairs or adoption of alternative plans. It is possible, however, that no recourse is possible. Again, based on our semantics, the agent still met its commitment because it followed the plan as promised.

It could be that, during pursuit of its plan, the agent acquires new or different goals, whose satisfaction would be incompatible with a plan it had committed to. The challenge then is determining whether it is possible to change its commitment plan so that it can pursue its new goal(s), while still being trustworthy regarding its commitment. Like CCIMR, the agent could instead commit to pursuing one plan out of a set of plans, and as its goals change could dynamically select from among the subset whose preconditions are still met. If the different plans are differentially susceptible to failure, then a commitment to the set of plans is only as strong as the most failure-prone of the set. This in turn suggests the need for some sort of "reliability" ordering over plans. Strategies for determining such orderings could be based on probabilistic knowledge (gravitating back towards decision-theoretic ideas), or could be based on a form of adversarial analysis to find the worst-case outcome of a plan given a purposely adversarial environment.

6 Conclusions

In this paper, we argue in favor of an operational semantics for commitments based on what an agent can control—its own actions. Thus, fulfilling a commitment corresponds to pursuing an action policy, beginning at the time the commitment was made, that has sufficient likelihood of coercing the world into an intended state. In this semantics, by "acting in good faith" an agent fulfills its commitment even if the intended state is not reached. We have summarized algorithms, based on these semantics, that operationalize foundational concepts about when an agent is permitted to drop a committed-to goal, and more importantly that guide agents' decisions to act in good faith until such a goal is met or dropped. These algorithms represent potential starting points in a broader exploration of the semantics and utilization of commitments to coordinate sequential decision-making agents in highly-uncertain environments, and we have speculated as to the transferability of these notions to agents other than decision-theoretic agents.

As advertised at the beginning of this paper, our emphasis has been on how an agent that is abiding by its commitments should constrain its behaviors (the space of action policies it considers) to act in good faith on the commitment. If we connect back to a human example of this, where a doctor is trustworthy if she follows standards of care even if a particular patient does not do well, then interesting questions arise as to how external parties, rather than the agent itself, can actually confirm trustworthiness. In the US, questions of medical trust often rely on an unbiased expert stepping through the decision making of a doctor to assess that appropriate sequential decisions were being made. In open systems where trust needs to be earned, interesting questions arise as to how easy it would be to know whether to bestow trust on an agent, where the outcomes of the decisions are observable but the decisions, and the processes used to reach the decisions, are not. Perhaps notions of certification play a more significant role for this form of trust, where a certifying body has evaluated and approved the decision-making processes of an agent. These are potentially interesting topics for future consideration.

Acknowledgments. Inn-Tung (Anna) Chen, Stefan Witwicki, Alexander Gutierrez, and Qi Zhang contributed to various aspects of the ideas and algorithms described in this paper. We also benefited from detailed discussions about commitments with Munindar Singh and Scott Gerard, and from the questions and suggestions of the anonymous reviewers. This work was supported in part by the Air Force Office of Scientific Research under grant FA9550-15-1-0039.

References

1. Agotnes, T., Goranko, V., Jamroga, W.: Strategic commitment and release in logics for multi-agent systems (extended abstract). Technical report IfI-08-01, Clausthal University (2007)
2. Al-Saqqar, F., Bentahar, J., Sultan, K., El-Menshawy, M.: On the interaction between knowledge and social commitments in multi-agent systems. Appl. Intell. **41**(1), 235–259 (2014)
3. Bannazadeh, H., Leon-Garcia, A.: A distributed probabilistic commitment control algorithm for service-oriented systems. IEEE Trans. Netw. Serv. Manage. **7**(4), 204–217 (2010)
4. Castelfranchi, C.: Commitments: from individual intentions to groups and organizations. In: Proceedings of the International Conference on Multiagent Systems, pp. 41–48 (1995)
5. Chesani, F., Mello, P., Montali, M., Torroni, P.: Representing and monitoring social commitments using the event calculus. Auton. Agent. Multi-Agent Syst. **27**(1), 85–130 (2013)

6. Cohen, P.R., Levesque, H.J.: Intention is choice with commitment. Artif. Intell. **42**(2–3), 213–261 (1990)
7. Durfee, E.H., Singh, S.: Commitment semantics for sequential decision making under reward uncertainty. In: Papers from the AAAI Fall Symposium on Sequential Decision Making for Intelligent Agents (AAAI Technical report FS-15-06) (2015)
8. Jennings, N.R.: Commitments and conventions: the foundation of coordination in multi-agent systems. Knowl. Eng. Rev. **8**(3), 223–250 (1993)
9. Kinny, D.N., Georgeff, M.P.: Commitment and effectiveness of situated agents. In: Proceedings of the 1991 International Joint Conference on Artificial Intelligence (IJCAI-91), pp. 84–88 (1991)
10. Maheswaran, R., Szekely, P., Becker, M., Fitzpatrick, S., Gati, G., Jin, J., Neches, R., Noori, N., Rogers, C., Sanchez, R., Smyth, K., Buskirk, C.V.: Look where you can see: predictability & criticality metrics for coordination in complex environments. In: International Joint Conference on Autonomous Agents and Multiagent Systems (AAMAS) (2008)
11. Mallya, A.U., Huhns, M.N.: Commitments among agents. IEEE Internet Comput. **7**(4), 90–93 (2003)
12. Poupart, P., Vlassis, N., Hoey, J., Regan, K.: An analytic solution to discrete Bayesian reinforcement learning. In: Proceedings of International Conference on Machine Learning (ICML 2006), pp. 697–704 (2006)
13. Raffia, H.: The Art and Science of Negotiation. Harvard University Press, 79 Garden St. (Belknap Press) (1982)
14. Ramachandran, D., Amir, E.: Bayesian inverse reinforcement learning. In: International Joint Conference on Artificial Intelligence (IJCAI), pp. 2586–2591 (2007)
15. Sandholm, T., Lesser, V.R.: Leveled commitment contracts and strategic breach. Games Econ. Behav. **35**, 212–270 (2001)
16. Singh, M.P.: An ontology for commitments in multiagent systems. Artif. Intell. Law **7**(1), 97–113 (1999)
17. Singh, M.P.: Commitments in multiagent systems: some history, some confusions, some controversies, some prospects. The Goals of Cognition. Essays in Hon. of C. Castelfranchi, pp. 1–29 (2012)
18. Vokrínek, J., Komenda, A., Pechoucek, M.: Decommitting in multi-agent execution in non-deterministic environment: experimental approach. In: 8th International Joint Conference on Autonomous Agents and Multiagent Systems (AAMAS 2009), pp. 977–984 (2009)
19. Winikoff, M.: Implementing flexible and robust agent interactions using distributed commitment machines. Multiagent Grid Syst. **2**(4), 365–381 (2006)
20. Witwicki, S., Chen, I.T., Durfee, E., Singh, S.: Planning and evaluating multiagent influences under reward uncertainty (extended abstract). In: Proceedings of the International Joint Conference on Autonomous Agents and Multiagent Systems (AAMAS), pp. 1277–1278 (2012)
21. Witwicki, S., Durfee, E.: Commitment-based service coordination. Int. Jour. of Agent-Oriented Softw. Eng. **3**(1), 59–87 (2009)
22. Xing, J., Singh, M.P.: Formalization of commitment-based agent interaction. In: Proceedings of the 2001 ACM Symposium on Applied Computing (SAC), pp. 115–120 (2001)
23. Xuan, P., Lesser, V.R.: Incorporating uncertainty in agent commitments. In: Jennings, N.R., Lespérance, Y. (eds.) ATAL 1999. LNCS (LNAI), vol. 1757, pp. 57–70. Springer, Heidelberg (2000). doi:10.1007/10719619_5

Evaluating the Efficiency of Robust Team Formation Algorithms

Chad Crawford, Zenefa Rahaman, and Sandip Sen[(✉)]

University of Tulsa, Tulsa, USA
{chad-crawford,zenefa-rahaman,sandip-sen}@utulsa.edu

Abstract. Selecting a minimal-cost team from a set of agents, with associated costs, to complete a given set of tasks is a common and important multiagent systems problem. Some degree of fault-tolerance in such teams is often required which enables the team to continue to complete all tasks even if a subset of the agents are incapacitated. A k-robust team is one that is capable of completing all assigned tasks when any k team members are not available. The corresponding decision problem of selecting a k-robust team that costs no more than a desired cost threshold has been shown to be NP-Complete. We present and experimentally evaluate, for varying problem sizes and characteristics, heuristic and evolutionary approximation approaches to find optimal-cost k-robust teams which can be used for large problems. We present a Linear Programming approximation algorithm that produces optimal results for small problem sizes and prove that it is a $2\ln(m+k) + O(\ln m)$-factor approximation of the optimal solution, where m is the number of tasks to be completed. We also present three heuristic algorithms and an evolutionary computation approach which scales up to larger problems. Another advantage of the evolutionary scheme is that it can approximate the Pareto-frontier of teams trading off robustness and cost.

Keywords: Robust teams · Approximation algorithms · Weighted set multicover

1 Introduction

Team formation is a critical activity in multiagent systems, particularly in cooperative settings. Teams are often formed in a distributed setting where demands of the situation necessitates otherwise self-interested agents to join together in cooperative teams or coalitions [19]. A significant amount of work in the cooperative game theory and in the multiagent systems community on coalition formation addresses this scenario. These approaches seek fair payoff distribution schemes between team members to incentivize agents joining and staying in stable coalitions.

Teams can be also formed in a centralized manner with prior knowledge of the capabilities and expertise requirement in the domain as well as the price or cost of including each agent in the team. A centralized decision maker is

© Springer International Publishing AG 2016
N. Osman and C. Sierra (Eds.): AAMAS 2016 Ws Best Papers, LNAI 10002, pp. 14–29, 2016.
DOI: 10.1007/978-3-319-46882-2_2

provided requirements for fulfilling a set of tasks in a domain, where each task has certain resource and/or capability requirements, using a set of available agents with given capabilities and resource capacities. Typically the emphasis in such a scenario (e.g., forming a team of robots to explore inhospitable environments) is to guarantee a degree of certainty of outcomes while minimizing cost. Many real life scenarios can be framed as an instance of this team formation problem, e.g., choosing team of first responders, surveillance and reconnaissance missions with unmanned vehicles, robotics assembly tasks, assisting disabled patients with chores at their homes, etc.

The problem of selecting a minimal cost team of agents with the necessary capabilities to achieve a given set of tasks can be posed as an optimization problem. Recently, a variant of this problem has been studied which examines the robustness of such teams. Robustness is defined by the number of team members, k, that may be lost without compromising the ability of the rest of the team members achieving all tasks [17]. The loss of team members is prevalent particularly with robot teams, where robots may become physically incapacitated or isolated, lose power or connectivity, get disoriented, or be impaired by software errors. Such incapacitated members can no longer contribute to completing team tasks and can therefore limit the effectiveness of the team. The corresponding Task-Oriented Robust Team Formation (TORTF) optimization problem can have variants: (A) given a cost budget, finding the team which is robust against the loss of the largest number of agents, i.e., a k-robust team with the maximal k value, (B) given a desired robustness level k, finding a k-robust team of minimal cost, and (C) a dual-objective constraint optimization problem with a pareto-frontier of solutions trading off team cost and team robustness. Though the corresponding decision problems are NP-complete, Okimoto et al. present an exact algorithm for solving variant C and evaluates it on small problem sizes [17]. The TORTF problem can be mapped into the Weighted Set Multicover (SMC) problem, which has been widely studied in the theoretical computer science literature. A variety of exact algorithms have been proposed for the SMC [15], all of which understandably are of exponential complexity and hence cannot be used for large problem sizes.

In this paper we present our work on developing and evaluating approximation algorithms for variation B of the TORTF optimization problem, i.e., the problem of generating the minimal-cost k-robust team. We present a suite of approximation algorithms for this problem: three greedy heuristic algorithms, a genetic algorithm based optimization approach and a Linear Programming based approximation for the SMC problem and prove that it is a $2\ln(m+k)+O(\ln m)$-factor approximation. The genetic algorithm variant, NSGA-II [3], is designed to solve Multi-Objective Optimization problems and hence can be used to address variant C of the TORTF problem. We evaluate the relative efficiencies of these optimization techniques on a testbed of TORTF problems, varying the number of agents, the number of tasks, the tasks/agent ratio, the cost distributions of the agents, etc. We present an in-depth analysis of the experimental results, including scalability considerations, and present guidelines for choosing an algorithm given problem characteristics.

2   Problem Definition

Each agent in a TORTF scenario is capable of doing a subset of the needed tasks. A team is a set of agents that can complete a task iff any of its members can complete it. Each agent has an associated cost for adding that agent to the team. The goal of TORTF is to find a team of minimal cost such that even if any k agents are removed from the team, the team retains the capability of completing all assigned tasks. In practical team formation scenarios, there are often cases where some members may be incapacitated and may not be able to complete some or many of the tasks required of them. In those scenarios, other agents are expected to step up and complete the tasks in their place.

A TORTF problem can be specified as the tuple $(\mathcal{A}, \mathcal{T}, c, \alpha, k)$, where $\mathcal{A} = \{a_1, \ldots, a_n\}$ is a set of agents, $\mathcal{T} = \{t_1, \ldots t_m\}$ is a set of tasks, $c : \mathcal{A} \to \mathbb{R}^+$ is the cost function assigning a cost to each agent, and $\alpha : \mathcal{A} \to 2^{\mathcal{T}}$ is the function that lists the subset of tasks that an agent can complete. Unlike some other task assignment problems, there are no time/resource constraints, and hence an agent is expected to complete all tasks that it is capable of doing.

Furthermore, if $S \subseteq \mathcal{A}$ is a team of agents, then the total cost of forming the team is $c(S) = \sum_{a \in S} c(a)$.

Definition 1 (Efficiency). *[17] defines a team $S \subseteq \mathcal{A}$ to be **efficient** if and only if the team members as a group can complete all tasks:*

$$\bigcup_{a \in S} \alpha(a) = \mathcal{T}.$$

We will prefer to use the term robust *or* effective *to describe this property, since we are also interested in the efficiency of the algorithms in this paper.*

Definition 2 (k-robustness). *A team, $S \subseteq \mathcal{A}$, is **k-robust**, where $k \in \{0, \ldots, n-1\}$, if and only if it is efficient when any k agents are removed from the team:*

$$\forall S' \subseteq S, |S'| \leq k \Rightarrow S - S' \text{is efficient}.$$

Furthermore,

$$\text{k-robust}(S) = \max\{k | S \text{ is k-robust}\}$$

is robustness of a team – the maximum number of agents which can be removed from the team without violating efficiency. We define the robustness of a team for a single task to be the number of team members that can perform the task:

$$\text{k-robust}_j(S) = |\{a_i \in S | t_j \in \alpha(a_i)\}|$$

Computing k-robust(S) can be done in $O(n)$ time, as explained in [17]. The procedure computes the number of agents that can complete each task in $\mathcal{T}$; the k-robustness is then the minimum number of agents assigned to some task minus 1. We examine two optimization problems: (a) Find the least-cost k-robust team, and (b) compute the Pareto frontier of teams that minimize cost and maximize k.

3   Related Work

Team formation is a critical problem for multiagent domains that require agent cooperation. Research on team formation has been focused on applications such as robotics [6], engineering projects [20] or business projects [22]. Deciding an optimal team for a project can also have different types of constraints, for example, social ties or compatibility between pairs of agents [7]. Another approach by [10] examines teams that collaborate to vote to make decisions. They compare teams of informed but not diverse voters with more uninformed but diverse voters and found that diverse teams are more effective. Optimal voting rules for selecting a diverse team are proposed in [10] which can overcome a uniform team of well-informed agents. One factor that needs to be accounted for in team formation is the possibility that some agents will not be able to contribute to the group after the team is selected due to unforeseen circumstances.

Several papers focus on coalitional skill games, for example, Bachrach and Rosenschein [11] uses a simple model of cooperation among agents. Each agent has skills and each task requires a set of skills; it is only possible to complete the tasks if the coalition's agents cover the set of required skills for the task. Bachrach *et al.* [9] focuses on Coalition Structure Generation (CSG), which partitions a set of agents into groups to maximize the sum of the values of all coalitions. Finding an optimal coalition structure is NP-hard.

The k-robustness problem is an agent-based formulation of the weighted set multicover problem. The set cover problem was one of the original 21 problems to be proven NP-complete by Karp [5], and the natural greedy approximation was proven to be within a factor of H_n (the partial sum of the first n terms of the Harmonic series) for the unweighted problem in [4,8] and for the weighted problem in [2]. Furthermore, it has been proven that there cannot exist an efficient approximation better than $\ln n$ for the set cover [12] (the aforementioned greedy mechanism has this factor since $H_n = \ln n + O(1)$). The weighted set multicover problem is proven to be NP-hard [17,21].

A number of exact algorithms have been developed to solve the weighted set multi-cover problem [13–15,17]. The algorithm developed in [17] calculates the entire Pareto frontier of solutions using a branch-and-bound approach. However, this algorithm is unusable for even moderately large number of agents or tasks. The fastest exact algorithm discussed in [15] uses a dynamic programming approach to build multiset covers that builds up a solution from combinations of multisets. This algorithm runs in $O((k+2)^n)$ time, which is the fastest known optimal algorithm that we know of.

The natural greedy algorithm for weighted set cover yields an H_n-factor approximation. Similar approximations have been found for the unweighted/weighted set multicover problems [21]. The approximation factor is derived by showing that the "prices" assigned to tasks by the greedy algorithm satisfy the dual of the integer programming formulation of the problem, where the dual represents feasible lower bounds on the true cost of the optimal allocation. Since the greedy approximation satisfies the dual and since the dual of the LP relaxation is within a factor of H_n of the integer solution, the greedy approximation is also within a factor of H_n.

4   Approximations of the TORTF Problem

We now present the approximation approaches for the TORTF problem that we evaluate in this paper. We assume that for each of these algorithms, for the given k, a k-robust team exists. It is simple to verify existence: since a k robust team will also be L-robust for any $L \leq k$, then a k-robust team exists if and only if k-robust$(\mathcal{A}) \geq k$.

4.1   Greedy Algorithms

We first describe a set of greedy approaches to approximate solutions to a TORTF problem.

Greedy Heuristic 1: We present (see Algorithm 1) the naive greedy approach as one method for selecting a robust team G. This algorithm has been studied extensively for the weighted set multi-cover problem, and has been proven to be an H_n-factor approximation of the optimal solution [21]. This algorithm and its derivative, Heuristic 2, run in $O(n^2)$ time.

Heuristic 1 selects the agent with minimum *price*, which is the cost of the agent per needed task it can complete. In other words, the greedy algorithm iteratively selects the cheapest agent given the number of additional tasks that they can do and will help the team achieve the specified level of robustness. This process is repeated until the team is k-robust.

Algorithm 1. Greedy Heuristic 1
1: **procedure** AGENT-TEAM$(\mathcal{A}, \mathcal{T}, c, \alpha, k)$
2:     $G \leftarrow \emptyset$
3:     **while** k-robust$(G) < k$ **do**
4:         $C \leftarrow \{t_j \in \mathcal{T} \mid $ k-robust$_j(G) < k\}$
5:         Choose $a^* \leftarrow \arg\min\limits_{a \in \mathcal{A}} \frac{c(a)}{|\alpha(a) \cap C|}$
6:         $G \leftarrow G \cup \{a^*\}$
7:     **return** G

Greedy Heuristic 2: This modification of the first greedy approach focuses on tasks which can be completed by the fewest number of agents. Unlike the last method, which considered the entire set $\mathcal{A}$ when choosing the best agent, this mechanism only considers agents that can perform the task t^*, which corresponds to the task with the fewest number of unselected agents that can complete it. Our motivation behind this approach is to minimize losses on the most restrictive choices. As the first greedy heuristic progresses, it will need to find k agents to complete t^*. However, as more and more agents are selected, the number of unselected agents capable of completing t^* becomes smaller. To alleviate this issue, this variation of the greedy heuristic selects t^* to cover immediately and continues to make similarly greedy choices subsequently (see Algorithm 2 for the complete algorithm).

Algorithm 2. Greedy Heuristic 2

1: **procedure** AGENT-TEAM$(\mathcal{A}, \mathcal{T}, c, \alpha, k)$
2:     $G \leftarrow \emptyset$
3:     **while** k-robust$(G) < k$ **do**
4:         $C \leftarrow \{t_j \in \mathcal{T} \,|\, \text{k-robust}_j(G) < k\}$
5:         $t^* \leftarrow \underset{t \in C}{\arg\min} |a \in \mathcal{A} \setminus G : t \in \alpha(a)|$
6:         $TA \leftarrow \{a \in \mathcal{A} \setminus G : t^* \in \alpha(a)\}$
7:         Choose $a^* \leftarrow \underset{a \in TA}{\arg\min} \frac{c(a)}{|\alpha(a) \cap C|}$
8:         $G \leftarrow G \cup \{a^*\}$
9:     **return** G

Greedy Heuristic 3: In this heuristic, agents are selected based on their marginal utility. The marginal utility is the difference between the benefit of a team with that agent and without the agent. The algorithm (see Algorithm 3) greedily selects agents at each turn, always choosing the agent that maximizes marginal utility given the previously selected set of agents. Let $\tau(G) = \{t_j \in \mathcal{T} : \text{k-robust}_j(G) < k\}$ is the set of *uncovered* tasks not k-covered by the already selected set of agents G. The marginal utility for a not yet selected agent a, given the currently selected set of team members G, is approximated as

$$u(a, G) = \sum_{t \in \alpha(a)} \binom{z_t(\mathcal{A} \setminus G) - 1}{r_t(G)} \cdot \bar{c}_t(G \cup \{a\})$$

$$- \left(c(a) + \sum_{t \in \alpha(a)} \binom{z_t(\mathcal{A} \setminus G) - 1}{r_t(G) - 1} \cdot \bar{c}_t(G \cup \{a\}), \right) \quad (1)$$

where z_t is the number of agents available to complete an uncovered task t and r_t is the additional robustness needed for that task $(k - \text{k-robust}_t(G))$ given the set of agents G chosen so far. The function $\bar{c}$ is the sum of the average costs per uncovered task of agents that can complete t:

$$\bar{c}_t(G) = \sum_{a:a \in \mathcal{A} \setminus G \text{ and } t \in \alpha(a)} \frac{c(a)}{|\alpha(a) \cap \tau(G)|}. \quad (2)$$

The first term in the expression for u is the average potential cost when a is not added to the team with respect to task t, i.e., it is the "average" cost of r_t

---

Algorithm 3. Greedy Heuristic 3

1: **procedure** AGENT-TEAM($\mathcal{A}, \mathcal{T}, c, \alpha, k$)
2:      $G \leftarrow \emptyset$
3:      **while** k-robust$(G) < k$ **do**
4:          Choose $a^* \leftarrow \arg\max\limits_{a_i \in \mathcal{A} \backslash G} u(a_i, G)$
5:          $G \leftarrow G \cup \{a^*\}$
6:      **return** G

---

randomly selected agents who can complete the task. The second term computes how much potential cost is added if we first select a and then select the rest of the team. The marginal utility of adding the agent to the team is then the sum of the difference between these two terms, over all the tasks that this agent can do.

4.2   Genetic Algorithm

The team formation problem can be framed as a multiple-objective optimization problem: maximizing k and minimizing cost. While previous algorithms compute the solution for only one k, knowing solutions for other k might help find better teams at k-robustness. We apply a multi-objective genetic algorithm to compute the entire Pareto frontier of solutions to the TORTF problem. That is, this GA will not be given a single k value to optimize, but will instead attempt to learn team allocations to ensure k-robustness for any k.

We adapt the implementation of the Nondominated Sorting Genetic Algorithm (NSGA-II) [3]. The NSGA-II algorithm tracks both a parent and child population. To optimize solutions on the Pareto frontier, NSGA-II adds a preprocessing step to each generation: the population is broken into non-dominating fronts, sorted by the domination relation. Another metric further sorts the solutions inside each front based on their diversity; this encourages the GA to select solutions across the entire Pareto frontier. The first N solutions among this group are put inside the *parent population*. The following M solutions compose the *child population*, and are generated using GA operators on the parent population. We are interested in solving the general optimization problem, but solutions for one k value may help inform solutions for other k values, assuming that the best teams with varying robustness would share some overlap in members. The NSGA-II algorithm is ideal since it is designed to find diverse solutions across the Pareto frontier.

NSGA-II is much slower than the heuristic and linear programming approaches. The time complexity of the preprocessing step is $O(2N^3)$, where N is the size of the chromosome pool. While this is faster than the naive approach to sorting the pool by multiple objectives, it runs significantly longer than the other algorithms presented.

Chromosomes in our GA are represented as bitstrings; if $b = b_1, \ldots, b_n$ is a bitstring, then agent $a_i \in \mathcal{A}$ belongs to the corresponding team iff $b_i = 1$. Our algorithm uses Tournament selection with $p = 0.65$: when generating the pool of chromosomes for crossover, it randomly selects two chromosomes from the parent pool and places the better chromosome in the new pool with probability p, otherwise it adds the worse chromosome. Crossover is uniform: each bit has an equally likely probability of being copied from the first or second parent. The probability of crossover occuring is 95 %, otherwise a parent is copied directly to the child pool. Bitwise mutation is performed next: a randomly chosen bit is flipped with a mutation probability of 10 % per chromosome in the newly generated child pool. We use a parent pool size of 150 and a child pool size of 200, and run experiments for 1500 generations.

4.3   Linear Programming Approach

The team formation problem can be formulated as an integer programming problem as follows:

$$\text{MINIMIZE} \qquad \sum_{i=1}^{n} c(a_i) \cdot x_i$$

$$\text{SUBJECT TO} \qquad \sum_{i:t_j \in \alpha(a_i)} x_i \geq \quad k+1 \quad j = 1, \ldots, m$$

$$x_i \in \quad \{0, 1\}$$

The variable vector x represents our choice of including agents in the team; if $x_i = 1$, then agent $a_i \in \mathcal{A}$ belongs to our team, and otherwise they do not. In the LP relaxation of the integer program, we allow the integral vector x to assume real values with $0 \leq x_i \leq 1$. This is an exact solution to the fractional weighted set multicover; that is, if we could choose "fractions" of agents to solve some tasks, then this would be an optimal team. To compute the solution to the LP relaxation, we use the linear programming package PuLP [16]. As algorithm times are not compared in this paper (since we implemented NSGA-II in a different language from the others) there was no difference in choosing PuLP over other state-of-the-art LP solvers.

To translate the LP relaxation into a team formation solution, we order agents by $a^{(1)}, \ldots, a^{(n)}$ such that $x^{(1)} \geq \cdots \geq x^{(n)}$. The team chosen is the smallest cutoff point c such that the team $\{a^{(1)}, \ldots, a^{(c)}\}$ is k-robust. However there is no guarantee that this ordering may provide an optimal solution. We are interested in finding an approximation bound on this method, and use a randomized rounding mechanism which has been used for a similar proof to the set cover problem [18,24]. Consider the random algorithm for solving the team formation problem that performs the following during each iteration of the algorithm: For each agent a_i that does not yet belong to our team, place a_i in the team with probability x_i, where x is the solution vector to the linear relaxation of the integer program. Our method will perform about as well as this random algorithm, since it selects the most likely agents to be chosen in the random method.

Theorem 1. *The randomized rounding method is a $2\ln(m+k)+O(\ln m)$-factor approximation of the TORTF problem with probability $\frac{(m-1)^k}{m^k}$.*

Proof. Let OPT_f to be the optimal cost of the fractional set k-cover, and OPT to be the optimal cost of the integral set k-cover. Our proof will show the randomized rounding algorithm produces a probably approximate factor approximation of the integral cover by showing that it will have an expected upper bound cost and a high probability of being completed within a certain number of steps of the randomized rounding algorithm.

Let x be the solution vector to the linear relaxation. The randomized round algorithm constructs a team in an iterative manner: for each iteration, we add agent a_i to our team with probability x_i where x_i is the value found via the LP relaxation method. The expected upper bound on the cost of members added in a team for a single iteration of the algorithm is

$$E[c(\text{new members})] = \sum_{i=1}^{n} P(a_i \text{ added to team}) \, c(a_i) = \sum_{i=1}^{n} x_i \, c(a_i) = OPT_f.$$

Hence, at each iteration, the expected cost of the team being formed increases by OPT_f. After T iterations, the expected cost of the constructed team will be $T \cdot OPT_f$. Since $OPT_f \leq OPT$, $T \cdot OPT_f \leq T \cdot OPT$; if the team produced is k-robust, then it would be a T-factor approximation. We choose a T relative to m that is large enough such that the approximation factor is (relatively) competitive and the likelihood of the team being k-robust is also high.

The probability of a $t \in T$ not being 1-robust after the first iteration, given that the associated probabilities of adding one of the p agents that can complete t is $x_1, \ldots, x_p$ is expressed as:

$$P(\text{robustness of } t \text{ does not increase}) = (1 - x_1) \cdots (1 - x_p). \tag{3}$$

An upper bound on this probability can be found using the constraint $x_1 + \cdots + x_p \geq k + 1$:

$$(1 - x_1) \cdots (1 - x_p) \geq e^{-x_1} \cdots e^{-x_p} = e^{-x_1 - \cdots - x_p} \geq e^{-k}. \tag{4}$$

Suppose q agents in our team cover t; let the probabilities of the uncovered agents being selected by $x_1, \ldots, x_{p-q}$ (we arbitrarily reorder x for simplicity). Since each $x_i \leq 1$,

$$k - 1 \leq x_1 + \cdots + x_p - 1 \leq x_1 + \cdots + x_p - x_i$$

Therefore, removing any arbitrary q agents will guarantee that $x_1 + \cdots + x_{p-q} \geq k - q$, and the associated probability of a team increasing robustness for t when already q-robust is e^{-k+q}.

Now, suppose that we run this greedy method for $\frac{2}{k} \ln m$ rounds; then, the likelihood of not covering task t is $(e^{-k})^{2/k \ln m} = \frac{1}{m^2}$. The probability of any task being uncovered is $m \cdot \frac{1}{m^2} = \frac{1}{m}$. Furthermore, suppose that when a team reaches $(q-1)$-robustness, we run the algorithm for $\frac{2}{k-q}\ln n$ iterations. Then, the probability of a task being uncovered during this series of iterations is $n(e^{-k+q})^{2/(k-q)\ln m} = \frac{1}{m}$. Run this algorithm for $q = 0, 1, \ldots, k$; the probability of having any tasks uncovered during any of these steps becomes

$$\prod_{q=0}^{k-1} \frac{m-1}{m} = \left(\frac{m-1}{m}\right)^k. \tag{5}$$

The total number of iterations is

$$\sum_{q=0}^{k-1} \frac{2}{k-q} \ln m = 2\left(1 + \frac{1}{2} + \cdots + \frac{1}{k}\right) \ln m \tag{6}$$

$$= 2H_k \ln m. \tag{7}$$

Since $H_k = \ln k + O(1)$, the total number of iterations for this algorithm is approximately $2\ln(m+k) + O(\ln m)$. Therefore, with probability $\frac{(m-1)^k}{m^k}$, this algorithm will approximately be a factor $2\ln(m+k) + O(\ln m)$ of OPT_f.

The likelihood of the randomized rounding algorithm being within this factor is largest for large m and small k. These cases are more relevant to our interests, since we usually do not a huge robustness when forming teams, but we are interested in cases when dealing with a large number of tasks.   □

5   Results and Discussion

To test our approximation algorithms, we compare their average cost performance on varying datasets. These datasets are constructed to reflect realistic scenarios in selecting a robust team. As we will show, each algorithm is able to perform marginally better than the others in different scenarios.

5.1   Datasets

We constructed several sample datasets to represent realistic team formation scenarios.

Uniform Cost, Uniform Tasks: Agent cost is uniformly distributed from 1 to 1000, and the number of tasks an agent can do are uniformly distributed from 1 to m. This dataset is similar to that used in [17].

We consider other datasets where the number of tasks are normally distributed. For the following three datasets, the number of tasks is normally distributed on $N(18\frac{m}{n}, 5)$. The mean was chosen because the systems using this value would have a maximal k-robustness of 5 to 14, depending on the configuration. A high maximal robustness guarantees that there are a large number of k-robust teams for sufficiently small k.

Uniform Cost, Normal Tasks: In this dataset, cost is uniformly distributed from 1 to 1000. It considers the scenario in which each agent can perform approximately the same number of tasks, but their costs may vary widely. For example, a business hiring contract workers to complete a project will select from a pool of workers that can complete approximately the same number of tasks. However, the amount that each worker wants to be paid may not be a function of how many tasks they can complete, so there may be no correlation between the two.

Constant Cost, Normal Tasks: The cost is kept constant at $c(a) = 1$. This is equivalent to the unweighted variant of the set multicover problem. The cost of hiring different team members may not be roughly the same in certain scenarios. Therefore, it is more important to minimize the size of the team required to achieve robustness rather than reducing cost.

Proportional Cost, Normal Task: The cost for each agent is determined by the number of tasks they can perform. Let $T(a) = |\alpha(a)|$; the cost for each agent is sampled uniformly from $N(2 \cdot T(a), 2)$. This corresponds to many scenarios where agents are valued based on how many tasks they can complete. For example, when forming a team of robots, the cost of adding a member would depend on what tasks they complete. If each task is equally challenging to complete, then the cost of an agent should be directly proportional to the number of tasks they can complete. The challenge of this problem is that forming teams is "approximately additive;" that is, the cost of hiring 4 agents to perform n tasks is approximately equal to the cost of hiring one agent to do those tasks. Therefore, teams with the same k-robustness should have approximately the same cost. The optimization problem will be taking advantage of the noise factor that appears in sampling an agent's cost from a normal distribution.

5.2　Results

We compare the algorithms across multiple metrics. Since we are not aware of any other state-of-the-art approximation algorithms for solving the TORTF problem or set multicover, we only compare the algorithms presented in this paper. Figure 1 compares the average costs of teams computed by each algorithm for each dataset and for varying numbers of agents. The cost of teams increases with the number of agents available for the three normally distributed datasets, since the number of tasks assigned to each agent is inversely proportional to the number of agents in the system. The maximimal k-robustness of teams in these datasets stays approximately the same regardless of the number of agents or tasks, and the number of teams with a particular k-robustness should stay the same as well. Therefore, the relative performances of each algorithm for an agent population size reveal how each algorithm performs with more agents available in situations where the number of teams avaiable is approximately equally dense. When the number of tasks is uniformly distributed, the average cost decreases since agents that can perform more tasks are more likely to appear. The average cost of the best teams found by each algorithm does not change as significantly

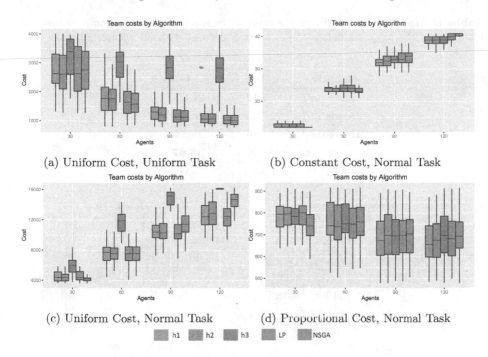

(a) Uniform Cost, Uniform Task   (b) Constant Cost, Normal Task

(c) Uniform Cost, Normal Task   (d) Proportional Cost, Normal Task

h1   h2   h3   LP   NSGA

Fig. 1. Distribution of costs per algorithm performed on 60 instances (for each number of agents) on multiple datasets with $m = 110$ and $k = 4$.

for the proportional cost dataset. Since every k-robust team should have similar cost, the small decrease is understandable. What decrease does occur is due to having more cost-efficient agents to choose from.

Surprisingly, the performance of the heuristic algorithms for different k values is not significantly different, as shown in Fig. 2. One point to note is that the variance in performance of the algorithms decrease, i.e., they perform more consistently, for larger values of k. This is because the number of at least k-robust teams decreases as the value of k increases. Table 1 compares the performances of the algorithms presented in this paper against that of an integer program solver in the PuLP package [16], which we were able to run only on very small problem sizes, on the proportional cost/normal task dataset for few agents and tasks. Average error is the average difference between the algorithmic solution and percent correct is the percentage of solutions that achieved optimal cost. This comparison measures the approximation quality of the algorithms for smaller problem sizes. While the linear program and heuristic algorithms achieve the highest percentage of optimal teams, NSGA-II consistently finds teams with near-optimal cost.

Greedy Heuristic 1 selects the agent with minimum cost per task. As Fig. 1 shows, Heuristic 1 performs well in all datasets and over all agent sizes. The greedy decisions made by Heuristic 1 makes it likely to choose some optimal

Table 1. Algorithm cost performance against the optimal solution, computed on 60 instances of the proportional cost/normal task dataset with 30 agents, 20 tasks and $k = 2$.

Algorithm	Avg. error	% Correct
Heuristic 1	7.12	21.67
Heuristic 2	7.05	26.67
Heuristic 3	4.36	28.33
Linear program	4.76	**36.67**
NSGA-II	**0.03**	5.00

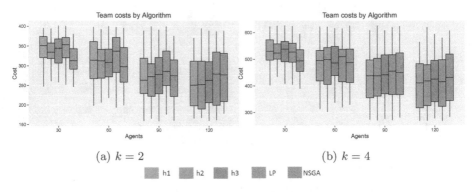

(a) $k = 2$ (b) $k = 4$

h1   h2   h3   LP   NSGA

Fig. 2. Distribution of costs per algorithm performed on 60 instances (for each number of agents) of the proportional cost/normal task dataset for varying k.

agents, and it has the strictest known approximation bound on the heuristics we compare. For smaller number of agents, its performance was not optimal, but it outperforms all other algorithms for larger agent sizes. In particular, Heuristic 1 generates the most cost-effective team on average when there are a large number of agents, since it is guaranteed to generate at most a H_n-factor approximation. In comparison to NSGA-II, Heuristic 1 found optimal-cost teams at a much higher rate. This is due to the construction of the proportional cost dataset and the fact that the heuristics we implemented choose agents with minimum cost per task. For example, if costs were exactly equal to the number of tasks that an agent can perform, then Heuristic 1 will always assign certain optimal agents the minimum price. Let $O \subseteq \mathcal{A}$ be the optimal team, and let C be the set of tasks that are not k-covered by the current greedy team G. If there is an agent $a^* \in O$ such that $\alpha(a^*) \subseteq C$, then its cost will be $c(a^*)/|\alpha(a^*)| = 1$, the minimum cost possible. Therefore, the greedy algorithm will always have a preference towards choosing optimal teams.

Like Heuristic 1, Heuristic 2 performs moderately well on all datasets. For a smaller number of agents, heuristic 2 performs better than Heuristic 1. In cases with constant or proportional cost, Heuristic 3 performs competitively with the other greedy heuristics. Among the heuristics and linear program performances, Heuristic 3 has the minimum cost difference with the optimal solution (see Table 1). On datasets using uniform cost, Heuristic 3 vastly under-performs the other algorithms, which suggests that marginal utility calculations fail to work when agent costs have high variance or are uncorrelated with the number of tasks the agent performs.

The linear programming approach that we use is the most consistent in its performance: when compared against the other algorithms presented, it often performs among the top 3. Table 1 also shows that this approach can often find optimal solutions in a dataset where there are many near-optimal teams. Since the approximation factor on the linear program is similar to that of the greedy algorithm, it is not surprising that their performances are similar.

The NSGA-II algorithm performed best with a smaller number of agents across all datasets, as indicated in Fig. 1. We observed that its relative perfor-mance was not affected by the number of tasks. Since the size of the search space for the GA increases exponentially only with the number of agents in the problem increasing, this is not a surprising trend. Moreover, since GAs search locally about existing solutions to make improvements, NSGA-II often finds near-optimal results, as shown in Table 1. Since the NSGA-II algorithm com-putes the entire Pareto frontier of solutions, it runs much slower than the greedy approximation and the linear program. Therefore, NSGA-II should be used in scenarios with fewer agents or when multiple values of k need to be computed.

6 Conclusions

We present and experimentally compare a number of approximation algorithms for producing efficient k-robust team for the team formation problem. Our heuristic methods are based on a naive greedy algorithm that is proven to be a H_n-factor of the optimal solution. We also present a linear programming relax-ation of the optimal, but costly, integer programming formulation, which has approximately the same approximation factor as Heuristic 1. These methods are compared to an NSGA-II based genetic algorithm approach that approximates the Pareto frontier of solutions to the team formation problem instead of finding only an optimal team for a single k value.

Results indicate that the NSGA-II method performs near-optimally for smaller number of agents, but the heuristic and linear programming mechanisms scale up better in terms of cost-effectiveness. The NSGA-II method takes much longer to run compared to the other heuristics but its run time does not depend on the number of tasks, so it is best to use with a large number of tasks or when multiple robustness levels need to be compared. Heuristic and linear program-ming techniques are a better fit for large problems involving many agents and tasks.

The team formation problem is a re-expression of the weighted set multi-cover problem, which has been studied extensively in literature. This formulation is applicable to scenarios where team members are at risk of not completing tasks, but does not account for time or resource constraints. To study more realistic scenarios, we may want to examine cases where an agent can only complete a fraction of a task, or have an associated probability of being able to complete a task. Another possible extension would be to restrict the number of tasks that an agent can be assigned to complete. This would map to real-life scenarios where team members may be capable of completing many tasks, but time and/or resource constraints restrict them from completing all of them.

References

1. Bansal, Nikhil, Pruhs, Kirk: Weighted Geometric Set Multi-cover via Quasi-uniform Sampling. In: Epstein, Leah, Ferragina, Paolo (eds.) ESA 2012. LNCS, vol. 7501, pp. 145–156. Springer, Heidelberg (2012). doi:10.1007/978-3-642-33090-2_14
2. Chvatal, V.: A greedy heuristic for the set-covering problem. Math. Oper. Res. 4(3), 233–235 (1979). INFORMS
3. Deb, K., Pratap, A., Agarwal, S., Meyarivan, T.: A fast and elitist multiobjective genetic algorithm: NSGA-II. IEEE Trans. Evol. Comput. 6(2), 182–197 (2002). IEEE
4. Johnson, D.S.: Approximation algorithms for combinatorial proble. In: Proceedings of the Fifth Annual ACM Symposium on Theory of computing, pp. 38–49. ACM (1973)
5. Karp, R.M.: Reducibility among combinatorial problems. In: Miller, R., Thatcher, J., Bohlinger, J. (eds.) Complexity of Computer Computations. The IBM Research Symposia Series, pp. 85–103. Springer, US (1972). doi:10.1007/978-1-4684-2001-2_9
6. Kitano, H.: RoboCup rescue: a grand challenge for multi-agent systems. In: 2000 Proceedings Fourth International Conference on MultiAgent Systems, pp. 5–12 (2000). doi:10.1109/ICMAS.2000.858425
7. Lappas, T., Liu, K., Terzi, E.: Finding a team of experts in social networks. In: Proceedings of the 15th ACM SIGKDD International Conference on Knowledge Discovery and Data Mining, KDD 2009, pp. 467–476. ACM, New York (2009). doi:10.1145/1557019.1557074
8. Lovász, L.: On the ratio of optimal integral and fractional covers. Discrete Math. 13(4), 383–390 (1975)
9. Bachrach, Y., Kohli, P., Kolmogorov, V., Zadimoghaddam, M.: Optimal coalition structure generation in cooperative graph games. In: Proceedings of the Twenty-Seventh AAAI Conference on Artificial Intelligence, AAAI 2013, pp. 81–87. AAAI Press (2013). http://dl.acm.org/citation.cfm?id=2891460.2891472
10. Marcolino, L.S., Jiang, A.X., Tambe, M.: Multi-agent team formation: diversity beats strength?. In: Proceedings of the Twenty-Third International Joint Conference on Artificial Intelligence, pp. 279–285. AAAI Press (2013)
11. Bachrach, Y., Rosenschein, J.S.: Coalitional skill games. In: Proceedings of the 7th International Joint Conference on Autonomous Agents and Multiagent Systems-Volume 2, pp. 1023–1030. International Foundation for Autonomous Agents and Multiagent Systems (2008)
12. Feige, U.: A threshold of $\ln n$ for approximating set cover. J. ACM (JACM) 45(4), 634–652 (1998). ACM
13. Hua, Q.-S., Wang, Y., Yu, D., Lau, F.C.M.: Set multi-covering via inclusion-exclusion. Theoret. Comput. Sci. 410(38), 3882–3892 (2009). Elsevier

14. Hua, Q.-S., Yu, D., Lau, F.C.M., Wang, Y.: Exact algorithms for set multicover and multiset multicover problems. In: Algorithms and Computation, pp. 34–44. Springer (2009)
15. Hua, Q.-S., Wang, Y., Yu, D., Lau, F.C.M.: Dynamic programming based algorithms for set multicover and multiset multicover problems. Theor. Comput. Sci. **411**(26), 2467–2474 (2010). Elsevier
16. Mitchell, S., OSullivan, M., Dunning, I.: PuLP: a linear programming toolkit for python. In: The University of Auckland, Auckland, New Zealand, http://www.optimization-online.org/DB_FILE/2011/09/3178. pdf (2011)
17. Okimoto, T., Schwind, N., Clement, M., Ribeiro, T., Inoue, K., Marquis, P.: How to form a task-oriented robust team. In: Proceedings of the 2015 International Conference on Autonomous Agents and Multiagent Systems, pp. 395–403. International Foundation for Autonomous Agents and Multiagent Systems (2015)
18. Raghavan, P., Tompson, C.D.: Randomized rounding: a technique for provably good algorithms and algorithmic proofs. Combinatorica **7**(4), 365–374 (1987). Springer
19. Shehory, O., Kraus, S.: Methods for task allocation via agent coalition formation. Artif. Intell. **101**(1–2), 165–200 (1998). doi:10.1016/S0004-3702(98)00045-9
20. Chen, S.-J., Lin, L.: Modeling team member characteristics for the formation of a multifunctional team in concurrent engineering. IEEE Trans. Eng. Manage. **51**(2), 111–124 (2004). doi:10.1109/TEM.2004.826011
21. Vazirani, V.V.: Approximation Algorithms. Springer Science & Business Media (2013)
22. Wi, H., Oh, S., Mun, J., Jung, M.: A team formation model based on knowledge and collaboration. Expert Syst. Appl. **36**(5), 9121–9134 (2009). doi:10.1016/j.eswa.2008.12.031
23. Zzkarian, A., Kusiak, A.: Forming teams: an analytical approach. IIE Trans. **31**(1), 85–97 (1999). doi:10.1023/A:1007580823003
24. Chakrabarty, D.: Approximation via Randomized Rounding. University of Pennsylvania (2010). http://research.microsoft.com/cn-us/um/people/dechakr/Courses/CIS800/Notes/lec7.pdf

Social Welfare in One-Sided Matching Mechanisms

George Christodoulou[1], Aris Filos-Ratsikas[2],
Søren Kristoffer Stiil Frederiksen[3], Paul W. Goldberg[2], Jie Zhang[2(✉)],
and Jinshan Zhang[1]

[1] Department of Computer Science, University of Liverpool, Liverpool, UK
{gchristo,jinshan.zhang}@liv.ac.uk
[2] Department of Computer Science, University of Oxford, Oxford, UK
{aris.filos-ratsikas,paul.goldberg,jie.zhang}@cs.ox.ac.uk
[3] Department of Computer Science, Aarhus University, Aarhus, Denmark
ssf@cs.au.dk

Abstract. We study the Price of Anarchy of mechanisms for the well-known problem of one-sided matching, or house allocation, with respect to the social welfare objective. We consider both ordinal mechanisms, where agents submit preference lists over the items, and cardinal mechanisms, where agents may submit numerical values for the items being allocated. We present a general lower bound of $\Omega(\sqrt{n})$ on the Price of Anarchy, which applies to *all* mechanisms. We show that two well-known mechanisms, Probabilistic Serial, and Random Priority, achieve a matching upper bound. We extend our lower bound to the Price of Stability of a large class of mechanisms that satisfy a common proportionality property, and show stronger bounds on the Price of Anarchy of all *deterministic* mechanisms.

1 Introduction

One-sided matching (also called the house allocation problem) is the fundamental problem of assigning items to agents, such that each agent receives exactly one item. It has numerous applications, such as assigning workers to shifts, students to courses or patients to doctor appointments. In this setting, agents are often asked to provide *ordinal preferences*, i.e. preference lists, or rankings of the items. We assume that underlying these ordinal preferences, agents have numerical

George Christodoulou, Paul W. Goldberg and Jinshan Zhang were supported by the EPSRC grant EP/K01000X/1. Paul W. Goldberg was supported by COST Action IC1205. Aris Filos-Ratsikas and Jie Zhang were supported by the ERC Advanced Grant 321171 (ALGAME). Aris Filos-Ratsikas and Søren K.S. Frederiksen acknowledge support from the Danish National Research Foundation and The National Science Foundation of China (under the grant 61061130540) for the Sino-Danish Center for the Theory of Interactive Computation, within which part of this work was performed and support from the Center for Research in Foundations of Electronic Markets (CFEM), supported by the Danish Strategic Research Council.

© Springer International Publishing AG 2016
N. Osman and C. Sierra (Eds.): AAMAS 2016 Ws Best Papers, LNAI 10002, pp. 30–50, 2016.
DOI: 10.1007/978-3-319-46882-2_3

values specifying how much they value each item [18]. In game-theoretic terms, these are the agents' von Neumann-Morgenstern utility functions [27] and the associated preferences are often referred to as *cardinal preferences*.

A *mechanism* is a function that maps agents' valuations to matchings. However, agents are rational strategic entities that might not always report their valuations truthfully; they may misreport their values if that results in a better matching (from their own perspective). Assuming the agents report their valuations strategically to maximize their utilities, it is of interest to study the *Nash equilibria* of the induced game, i.e. strategy profiles from which no agent wishes to unilaterally deviate.

A natural objective for the designer is to choose the matching that maximizes the *social welfare*, i.e. the sum of agents' valuations for the items they are matched with, which is the most prominent measure of aggregate utility in the literature. Given the strategic nature of the agents, we are interested in mechanisms that maximize the social welfare *in the equilibrium*. We use the standard measure of equilibrium inefficiency, the *Price of Anarchy* [22], that compares the maximum social welfare attainable in any matching with the *worst-case* social welfare that can be achieved in an equilibrium.

We evaluate the efficiency of a mechanism with respect to the Price of Anarchy of the induced game. We study both deterministic and randomized mechanisms: in the latter case the output is a probability mixture over matchings, instead of a single matching. We are interested in the class of *cardinal* mechanisms, which use cardinal preferences, and generalize the ordinal mechanisms.

Note that our setting involves no monetary transfers and generally falls under the umbrella of *approximate mechanism design without money* [24]. In general settings without money, one has to fix a canonical representation of the valuations. A common approach in the literature is to consider the *unit-sum* normalization, i.e. each agent has a total value of 1 for all the items. We obtain results for unit-sum valuations, and extend most of these to another common normalization, *unit-range*.

1.1   Our Results

In Sect. 3 we bound the inefficiency of the two best-known mechanisms in the matching literature, *Probabilistic Serial* and *Random Priority*. In particular, for n agents and n items, the Price of Anarchy is $O(\sqrt{n})$. In Sect. 4 we complement this with a *matching* lower bound (i.e. $\Omega(\sqrt{n})$) that applies to *all* cardinal (randomized) mechanisms. As a result, we conclude that these two *ordinal* mechanisms (ones that compute matchings that only depend on preference orderings) are optimal. These results suggest that it does not help a welfare maximizer to ask agents to report more than the ordinal preferences.

We separately consider *deterministic* mechanisms and in Sect. 4 prove that their Price of Anarchy is $\Omega(n^2)$, even for cardinal mechanisms. This shows that randomization is necessary for non-trivial worst-case efficiency guarantees.

In Sect. 5, we extend our results to more general solutions concepts as well as the case of incomplete information. Finally, in Sect. 6, we prove that under a mild "proportionality" property, our lower bound of $\Omega(\sqrt{n})$ extends to the *Price of Stability*, a more optimistic measure of efficiency [3], which strengthens the negative results even further. Additionally, we discuss how our results extend to the other common normalization in the literature, *unit-range* [2,15,28].

1.2 Discussion and Related Work

The one-sided matching problem was introduced in [18] and has been studied extensively ever since (see [1] for a recent overview). Over the years, several different mechanisms have been proposed with various desirable properties related to truthfulness, fairness and economic efficiency with Probabilistic Serial [1,7–9] and Random Priority [1,2,4,9,15,23] being the two prominent examples.

As mentioned earlier, in settings without money, one needs to represent the valuations in some canonical way. A common approach is the *unit-sum* normalization, i.e. each agent has a total value of 1 for all the items. Intuitively, this normalization means that each agent has equal influence within the mechanism and her values can be interpreted as "scrip money" that she uses to acquire items. The unit-sum representation is standard for social welfare maximization in many settings without money including fair division, cake cutting and resource allocation [10,11,15,16] among others. Moreover, without any normalization, non-trivial Price of Anarchy bounds cannot be achieved by any mechanism.

The objective of social welfare maximization for one-sided matching problems has been studied before in the literature, but mainly for truthful mechanisms [2, 15]. Our lower bounds are more general, since they apply to *all* mechanisms, not just truthful ones. In particular, our lower bound on the Price of Anarchy of all mechanisms generalizes the corresponding bound for truthful mechanisms in [15]. Note that Random Priority is truthful (truth-telling is a dominant strategy equilibrium) but it has other equilibria as well; we observe that the welfare guarantees of the mechanism hold for all equilibria, not just the truthtelling ones. Similar approaches have been made for truthful mechanisms like the second price auction in settings with money.

While given our general lower bound, proving a matching upper bound for Random Priority is enough to establish tightness, it is still important to know what the welfare guarantees of Probabilistic Serial are, given that it is arguably the most popular one-sided matching mechanism. The mechanism was introduced by [9] and since then, it has been in the center of attention of the matching literature, with related work on characterizations [17,20], extensions [19], strategic aspects [21] and hardness of manipulation [6]. Somewhat surprisingly, the Nash equilibria of the mechanism were only recently studied. Aziz et al. [5] prove that the mechanism has pure Nash equilibria while Ekici and Kesten [14] study the *ordinal* equilibria of the mechanism and prove that the desirable properties of the mechanism are not necessarily satisfied for those profiles.

Another, somewhat different recent branch of study considers ordinal measures of efficiency instead of social welfare maximization, under the assumption that agents' preferences are only expressed through preference orderings over items. Bhalgat et al. [8] study the approximation ratio of matching mechanisms, when the objective is maximization of *ordinal social welfare*, a notion of efficiency that they define based solely on ordinal information. Other measures of efficiency for one-sided matchings were also studied in Krysta et al. [23], where the authors design truthful mechanisms to approximate the size of a maximum cardinally (or maximum agent weight) Pareto-optimal matching and in Chakrabarty and Swamy [12] where the authors consider the rank approximation as the measure of efficiency. While interesting, these measures of efficiency do not accurately encapsulate the socially desired outcome the way that social welfare does, especially since an underlying cardinal utility structure is part of the setting [9,18,27,28]. Our results actually suggest that in order to achieve the optimal welfare guarantees, one does not even need to elicit this utility structure; agents can only be asked to report preference orderings, which is arguably more appealing.

Finally, we point out that our work is in a sense analogous to the literature that studies the Price of Anarchy in item-bidding auctions (e.g. see [13,26] and references therein) for settings without money. Furthermore, the extension of our results to very general solution concepts (coarse correlated equilibria) and settings of incomplete information (Bayes-Nash equilibria) is somehow reminiscent of the *smoothness* framework [25] for games. While our results are not proven using the smoothness condition, our extension technique is similar in spirit.

2 Preliminaries

Let $N = \{1, \ldots, n\}$ be a finite set of agents and $A = \{1, \ldots, n\}$ be a finite set of indivisible items. An *allocation* is a matching of agents to items, that is, an assignment of items to agents where each agent gets assigned exactly one item. We can view an allocation μ as a permutation vector $(\mu_1, \mu_2 \ldots, \mu_n)$ where μ_i is the unique item matched with agent i. Let O be the set of all allocations. Each agent i has a valuation function $u_i : A \to \mathbb{R}$ mapping items to real numbers. Valuation functions are considered to be well-defined modulo positive affine transformations, that is, for item $j : j \to \alpha u_i(j) + \beta$ is considered to be an alternative representation of the same valuation function u_i. Given this, we fix the canonical representation of u_i to be *unit-sum*, that is $\sum_j u_i(j) = 1$, with $u_i(j) \geq 0$ for all i, j. Equivalently, we can consider valuation functions as *valuation vectors* $u_i = (u_{i1}, u_{i2}, \ldots, u_{in})$ and let V be the set of all valuation vectors of an agent. Let $\mathbf{u} = (u_1, u_2, \ldots, u_n)$ denote a typical *valuation profile* and let V^n be the set of all valuation profiles with n agents.

We consider *strategic agents* who might have incentives to misreport their valuations. We define $\mathbf{s} = (s_1, s_2, \ldots, s_n)$ to be a pure strategy profile, where s_i is the *reported* valuation vector of agent i. We will use $\mathbf{s}_{-i}$ to denote the strategy profile without the ith coordinate and hence $\mathbf{s} = (s_i, \mathbf{s}_{-i})$ is an alternative way to denote a strategy profile. A *direct revelation mechanism* without money is a function $M : V^n \to O$ mapping *reported* valuation profiles to matchings. For a randomized mechanism, we define M to be a random map $M : V^n \to O$. Let $M_i(\mathbf{s})$ denote the restriction of the outcome of the mechanism to the i'th coordinate, which is the item assigned to agent i by the mechanism. For randomized mechanisms, we let $p_{ij}^{M,\mathbf{s}} = \Pr[M_i(\mathbf{s}) = j]$ and $p_i^{M,\mathbf{s}} = (p_{i1}^{M,\mathbf{s}}, \ldots, p_{in}^{M,\mathbf{s}})$. When it is clear from the context, we drop one or both of the superscripts from the terms $p_{ij}^{M,\mathbf{s}}$. The utility of an agent from the outcome of a deterministic mechanism M on input strategy profile $\mathbf{s}$ is simply $u_i(M_i(\mathbf{s}))$. For randomized mechanisms, an agent's utility is $\mathbb{E}[u_i(M_i(\mathbf{s}))] = \sum_{j=1}^n p_{ij}^{M,\mathbf{s}} u_{ij}$.

A subclass of mechanisms that are of particular interest is that of *ordinal mechanisms*. Informally, ordinal mechanisms operate solely based on the *ordering* of items induced by the valuation functions and not the actual numerical values themselves, while cardinal mechanisms take those numerical values into account. Formally, a mechanism M is *ordinal* if for any strategy profiles $\mathbf{s}, \mathbf{s}'$ such that for all agents i and for all items j, ℓ, $s_{ij} < s_{i\ell} \Leftrightarrow s'_{ij} < s'_{i\ell}$, it holds that $M(\mathbf{s}) = M(\mathbf{s}')$. A mechanism for which the above does not necessarily hold is *cardinal*. Equivalently, the strategy space of ordinal mechanisms is the set of all permutations of n items instead of the space of valuation functions V^n. A strategy s_i of agent i is a *preference ordering* of items $(a_1, a_2, \ldots, a_n)$ where $a_\ell \succ a_k$ for $\ell < k$. We will write $j \succ_i j'$ to denote that agent i prefers item j to item j' according to her true valuation function and $j \succ_{s_i} j'$ to denote that she prefers item j to item j' according to her strategy s_i. When it is clear from the context, we abuse the notation slightly and let u_i denote the truthtelling strategy of agent i, even when the mechanism is ordinal. Note that agents can be indifferent between items and hence the preference order can be a weak ordering.

Two properties of interest are *anonymity* and *neutrality*. A mechanism is anonymous if the output is invariant under renamings of the agents and neutral if the output is invariant under relabeling of the objects.

An *equilibrium* is a strategy profile in which no agent has an incentive to deviate to a different strategy. First, we will focus on the concept of *pure Nash equilibrium*, formally

Definition 1. *A strategy profile $\mathbf{s}$ is a pure Nash equilibrium if $u_i(M_i(\mathbf{s})) \geq u_i(M_i(s'_i, s_{-i}))$ for all agents i, and pure deviating strategies s'_i.*

In Sect. 5, we extend our results to more general equilibrium notions as well as the setting of incomplete information, where agents' values are drawn from known distributions.

Let $S_{\mathbf{u}}^M$ denote the set of all pure Nash equilibria of mechanism M under truthful valuation profile $\mathbf{u}$. The measure of efficiency that we will use is the *pure Price of Anarchy*,

$$PoA(M) = \sup_{\mathbf{u} \in V^n} \frac{SW_{OPT}(\mathbf{u})}{\min_{\mathbf{s} \in S_{\mathbf{u}}^M} SW_M(\mathbf{u}, \mathbf{s})}$$

where $SW_M(\mathbf{u}, \mathbf{s}) = \sum_{i=1}^n \mathbb{E}[u_i(M_i(\mathbf{s}))]$ is the expected *social welfare* of mechanism M on strategy profile $\mathbf{s}$ under true valuation profile $\mathbf{u}$, and $SW_{OPT}(\mathbf{u}) = \max_{\mu \in O} \sum_{i=1}^n u_i(\mu_i)$ is the social welfare of the optimal matching. Let $OPT(\mathbf{u})$ be the optimal matching on profile $\mathbf{u}$ and let $OPT_i(\mathbf{u})$ be the restriction to the ith coordinate.

3 Price of Anarchy Guarantees

In this section, we prove the (pure) Price of Anarchy guarantees of Probabilistic Serial and Random Priority. Together with our lower bound in the next section, the results establish that both mechanisms are optimal among all mechanisms for the problem.

Probabilistic Serial. First, we consider *Probabilistic Serial*, which we abbreviate to *PS*. Informally, the mechanism is the following. Each item can be viewed as an infinitely divisible good that all agents can consume at unit speed during the unit time interval $[0, 1]$. Initially each agent consumes her most preferred item (or one of her most preferred items in case of ties) until the item is entirely consumed. Then, the agent moves on to consume the item on top of her preference list, among items that have not yet been entirely consumed. The mechanism terminates when all items have been entirely consumed. The fraction p_{ij} of item j consumed by agent i is then interpreted as the probability that agent i will be matched with item j under the mechanism.

We prove that the Price of Anarchy of PS is $O(\sqrt{n})$. Aziz et al. [5] proved that PS has pure Nash equilibria, so it makes sense to consider the pure Price of Anarchy; we will extend the result to the coarse correlated Price of Anarchy and the Bayesian Price of Anarchy in Sect. 5.

We start with the following two lemmas, which prove that in a pure Nash equilibrium of the mechanism an agent's utility cannot be much worse than what her utility would be if she were consuming the item she is matched with in the optimal allocation from the beginning of the mechanism until the item is entirely consumed. Let $t_j(\mathbf{s})$ be the time when item j is entirely consumed on profile $\mathbf{s}$ under $PS(\mathbf{s})$.

Lemma 1. *Let $\mathbf{s}$ be any strategy profile and let s_i^* be any strategy such that $j \succ_{s_i^*} \ell$ for all items $\ell \neq j$, i.e. agent i places item j on top of her preference list. Then it holds that $t_j(s_i^*, \mathbf{s_{-i}}) \geq \frac{1}{4} \cdot t_j(\mathbf{s})$.*

Proof. For ease of notation, let $\mathbf{s}^* = (s_i^*, \mathbf{s_{-i}})$. Obviously, if $j \succ_{s_i} \ell$ for all $\ell \neq j$ and since all other agents' reports are fixed, $t_j(\mathbf{s}^*) = t_j(\mathbf{s})$ and the statement of the lemma holds. Hence, we will assume that there exists some item $j' \neq j$ such that $j' \succ_{s_i} j$.

First, note that if agent i is the only one consuming item j for the duration of the mechanism, then $t_j(\mathbf{s}^*) = 1$ and we are done. Hence, assume that at least one other agent consumes item j at some point, and let τ be the time when the first agent besides agent i starts consuming item j in $\mathbf{s}^*$. Obviously, $t_j(\mathbf{s}^*) > \tau$, therefore if $\tau \geq \frac{1}{4} \cdot t_j(\mathbf{s})$ then $t_j(\mathbf{s}^*) \geq \frac{1}{4} \cdot t_j(\mathbf{s})$ and we are done. So assume that $\tau < \frac{1}{4} \cdot t_j(\mathbf{s})$. Next observe that in the interval $[\tau, t_j(\mathbf{s}^*)]$, agent i can consume at most half of what remains of item i because there exists at least one other agent consuming the item for the same duration. Overall, agent i's consumption is at most $\frac{1}{2} + \frac{1}{4}t_j(\mathbf{s})$ so at least $\frac{1}{2} - \frac{1}{4}t_j(\mathbf{s})$ of the item will be consumed by the rest of the agents.

Now consider all agents other than i in profile $\mathbf{s}$ and let α be the amount of item j that they have consumed by time $t_j(\mathbf{s})$. Notice that the total consumption speed of an item is non-decreasing in time which means in particular that for any $0 \le \beta \le 1$, agents other than i need at least $\beta t_j(\mathbf{s})$ time to consume $\alpha \cdot \beta$ in profile $\mathbf{s}$. Next, notice that since agent i starts consuming item j at time 0 in $\mathbf{s}^*$ and all other agents use the same strategies in $\mathbf{s}$ and $\mathbf{s}^*$, it holds that every agent $k \ne i$ starts consuming item j in $\mathbf{s}^*$ no sooner than she does in $\mathbf{s}$. This means that in profile $\mathbf{s}^*$, agents other than i will need more time to consume $\beta \cdot \alpha$; in particular they will need at least $\beta t_j(\mathbf{s})$ time, so $t_j(\mathbf{s}^*) \ge \beta t_j(\mathbf{s})$. However, from the previous paragraph we know that they will consume at least $\frac{1}{2} - \frac{1}{4} t_j(\mathbf{s})$, so letting $\beta = \frac{1}{\alpha} \left(\frac{1}{2} - \frac{1}{4} t_j(\mathbf{s}) \right)$ we get

$$t_j(\mathbf{s}^*) \ge \beta t_j(\mathbf{s}) \ge t_j(\mathbf{s}) \left(\frac{1}{2} - \frac{1}{4} \cdot t_j(\mathbf{s}) \right) \frac{1}{\alpha}$$

$$\ge t_j(\mathbf{s}) \left(\frac{1}{2} - \frac{1}{4} \cdot t_j(\mathbf{s}) \right) \ge \frac{1}{4} \cdot t_j(\mathbf{s}) \qquad \square$$

Now we can lower bound the utility of an agent at any pure Nash equilibrium.

Lemma 2. *Let $\mathbf{u}$ be the profile of true agent valuations and let $\mathbf{s}$ be a pure Nash equilibrium. For any agent i and any item j it holds that the utility of agent i at $\mathbf{s}$ is at least $\frac{1}{4} \cdot t_j(\mathbf{s}) \cdot u_{ij}$.*

Proof. Let $\mathbf{s}' = (s_i', \mathbf{s}_{-i})$ be the strategy profile obtained from $\mathbf{s}$ when agent i deviates to the strategy s_i' where s_i' is some strategy such that $j \succ_{s_i'} \ell$ for all items $\ell \ne j$. Since $\mathbf{s}$ is a pure Nash equilibrium, it holds that $u_i(PS_i(\mathbf{s})) \ge u_i(PS_i(\mathbf{s}')) \ge t_j(\mathbf{s}') \cdot u_{ij}$, where the last inequality holds since the utility of agent i is at least as much as the utility she obtains from the consumption of item j. By Lemma 1, it holds that $t_j(\mathbf{s}') \ge \frac{1}{4} \cdot t_j(\mathbf{s})$ and hence $u_i(PS_i(\mathbf{s})) \ge \frac{1}{4} \cdot t_j(\mathbf{s}) \cdot u_{ij}$. $\square$

We can now prove the pure Price of Anarchy guarantee of the mechanism.

Theorem 1. *The pure Price of Anarchy of Probabilistic Serial is $O(\sqrt{n})$.*

Proof. Let $\mathbf{u}$ be any profile of true agents' valuations and let $\mathbf{s}$ be any pure Nash equilibrium. First, note that by reporting truthfully, every agent i can get an allocation that is at least as good as $(1/n, \dots, 1/n)$, regardless of other agents' strategies. To see this, first consider time $t = 1/n$ and observe that during the interval $[0, 1/n]$, agent i is consuming her favorite item (say a_1) and hence $p_{ia_1} \ge 1/n$. Next, consider time $\tau = 2/n$ and observe that during the interval $[0, 2/n]$, agent i is consuming one or both of her two favorite items (a_1 and a_2) and hence $p_{ia_1} + p_{ia_2} \ge 2/n$. By a similar argument, for any k, it holds that $\sum_{j=1}^{n} p_{ia_j} \ge k/n$. This implies that regardless of other agents' strategies, agent i can achieve a utility of at least $\frac{1}{n} \sum_{j=1}^{n} u_{ij}$. Since $\mathbf{s}$ is a pure Nash equilibrium, it holds that $u_i(PS_i(\mathbf{s})) \ge (1/n) \sum_{j=1}^{n} u_{ij}$ as well. Summing over all agents, we get that $SW_{PS}(\mathbf{u}, \mathbf{s}) \geq (1/n) \sum_{i=1}^{n} \sum_{j=1}^{n} u_{ij} = 1$. If $SW_{OPT}(\mathbf{u}) \leq \sqrt{n}$ then we are done, so assume $SW_{OPT}(\mathbf{u}) > \sqrt{n}$.

Because PS is neutral we can assume $t_j(\mathbf{s}) \leq t_{j'}(\mathbf{s})$ for $j < j'$ without loss of generality. Observe that for all $j = 1, \ldots, n$, it holds that $t_j(\mathbf{s}) \geq j/n$. This is true because for any $t \in [0, 1]$, by time t, exactly tn mass of items must have been consumed by the agents. Since j is the jth item that is entirely consumed, by time $t_j(\mathbf{s})$, the mass of items that must have been consumed is at least j. By this, we get that $t_j(\mathbf{s}) \cdot n \geq j$, which implies $t_j(\mathbf{s}) \geq j/n$.

For each j let i_j be the agent that gets item j in the optimal allocation and for ease of notation, let w_{i_j} be her valuation for the item. Now by Lemma 2, it holds that

$$u_{i_j}(PS(\mathbf{s})) \geq \frac{1}{4} \frac{j}{n} w_{i_j} \quad \text{and} \quad SW_{PS}(\mathbf{u}, \mathbf{s}) \geq \frac{1}{4} \sum_{j=1}^{n} \frac{j}{n} w_{i_j}.$$

The Price of Anarchy is then at most

$$\frac{4 \sum_{j=1}^{n} w_{i_j}}{\sum_{j=1}^{n} j \cdot w_{i_j}/n}.$$

Consider the case when the above ratio is maximized and let k be an integer such that $k \leq \sum_{j=1}^{n} w_{i_j} \leq k + 1$. Then it must be that $w_{i_j} = 1$ for $j = 1, \ldots, k$ and $w_{i_j} = 0$, for $k+2 \leq i_j \leq n$. Hence the maximum ratio is $(k + w_{i_{k+1}})/(aw_{i_{k+1}} + b)$, for some $a, b > 0$, which is monotone for $w_{i_{k+1}}$ in $[0, 1]$. Therefore, the maximum value of $(k + w_{i_{k+1}})/(aw_{i_{k+1}} + b)$ is achieved when either $w_{i_{k+1}} = 0$ or $w_{i_{k+1}} = 1$. As a result, the maximum value of the ratio is obtained when $\sum_{i=1}^{n} w_{i_{k+1}} = k$ for some k. By simple calculations, the Price of Anarchy should be at most:

$$\frac{4k}{\sum_{j=1}^{k} \frac{j}{n}} \leq \frac{4k}{\frac{k(k-1)}{2n}} = \frac{8n}{k-1},$$

so the Price of Anarchy is maximized when k is minimized. By the argument earlier, $k > \sqrt{n}$ and hence the ratio is $O(\sqrt{n})$. $\qquad\square$

In Sect. 5, we extend Theorem 1 to broader solution concepts and the incomplete information setting.

Random Priority. We also consider another very well-known mechanism, Random Priority, often referred to as Random Serial Dictatorship. The mechanism first fixes an ordering of the agents uniformly at random and then according to that ordering, it sequentially matches them with their most preferred item that is still available. Filos-Ratsikas et al. [15] proved that the welfare in any truthtelling equilibrium is an $\Omega(1/\sqrt{n})$-fraction of the maximum social welfare. While Random Priority has other equilibria as well, to establish the Price of Anarchy bound, it suffices to observe that at least for distinct valuations, any strategy other than truthtelling does not affect the allocation and hence it does not affect the social welfare. Intuitively, since agents pick their most preferred items, any equilibrium strategy would place the most preferred available items on top of the preference list, while the ordering of the items that are not picked does not affect the allocation of other agents. For valuations that are not distinct, the argument can be adapted using small perturbations of the values, losing only a small fraction of welfare.

We first we prove the following lemma.

Lemma 3. *If valuations are distinct, the social welfare is the same in all mixed Nash equilibria of Random Priority.*

Proof. Let i be an agent, and let B be a subset of the items. Let **s** be a mixed Nash equilibrium with the property that with positive probability, i will be chosen to select an item at a point when B is the set of remaining items. In that case (by distinctness of i's values), i's strategy should place agent i's favourite item in B on the top of the preference list among items in B. Suppose that for items j and j', there is no set of items B that may be offered to i with positive probability, in which either j or j' is optimal. Then i may rank them either way, i.e. can announce $j \succ_i j'$ or $j' \succ_i j$. However, that choice has no effect on the other agents, in particular it cannot affect their social welfare.   □

Given the main theorem in [15], Lemma 3 implies the following.

Corollary 1. *If valuations are distinct, the Price of Anarchy of Random Priority is $\Theta(\sqrt{n})$.*

The same guarantee on the Price of Anarchy holds even when the true valuations of agents are not necessarily distinct.

Theorem 2. *The Price of Anarchy of Random Priority is $O(\sqrt{n})$.*

Proof. We know from [15] that the social welfare of Random Priority given truthful reports, is within $O(\sqrt{n})$ of the social optimum. The social welfare of a (mixed) Nash equilibrium **q** cannot be worse than the worst pure profile from **q** that occurs with positive probability, so let **s** be such a pure profile. We will say that agent i *misranks* items j and j' if $j \succ_i j'$, but $j' \succ_{s_i} j$.

If an agent misranks two items for which she has distinct values, it is because she has 0 probability in **s** to receive either item. So we can change **s** so that no items are misranked, without affecting the social welfare or the allocation. For items that the agent values equally (which are then not misranked) we can apply arbitrarily small perturbations to make them distinct. Profile **s** is thus consistent with rankings of items according to perturbed values and is truthful with respect to these values, which, being arbitrarily close to the true ones, have optimum social welfare arbitrarily close to the true optimal social welfare.   □

Theorem 2 can be extended to solution concepts more general than the mixed Nash equilibrium. Again, the details are included in Sect. 5.

4   Lower Bounds

In this section, we prove our main lower bound. Note that the result holds for any mechanism, including randomized and cardinal mechanisms. Since we are interested in mechanisms with good properties, it is natural to consider those mechanisms that have pure Nash equilibria.

Theorem 3. *The pure Price of Anarchy of any mechanism is $\Omega(\sqrt{n})$.*

Proof. Let $n = k^2$ for some $k \in \mathbb{N}$. Let M be a mechanism and consider the following valuation profile $\mathbf{u}$. There are $\sqrt{n}$ sets of agents and let G_j denote the j-th set. For every $j \in \{1, \ldots, \sqrt{n}\}$ and every agent $i \in G_j$, let $u_{ij} = 1/n + \alpha$ and $u_{ik} = 1/n - \alpha/(n-1)$, for $k \neq j$, where α is sufficiently small. Let $\mathbf{s}$ be a pure Nash equilibrium and for every set G_j, let $i_j = \arg\min_{i \in G_j} p_{ij}^{M,\mathbf{s}}$ (break ties arbitrarily). Observe that for all $j = 1, \ldots, \sqrt{n}$, it holds that $p_{i_j j}^{M,\mathbf{s}} \leq 1/\sqrt{n}$ and let $I = \{i_1, i_2, \ldots, i_{\sqrt{n}}\}$. Now consider the valuation profile $\mathbf{u}'$ where:

- For every agent $i \notin I$, $u_i' = u_i$.
- For every agent $i_j \in I$, let $u_{i_j j}' = 1$ and $u_{i_j k}' = 0$ for all $k \neq j$.

We claim that $\mathbf{s}$ is a pure Nash equilibrium under $\mathbf{u}'$ as well. For agents not in I, the valuations have not changed and hence they have no incentive to deviate. Assume now for contradiction that some agent $i \in I$ whose most preferred item is item j could deviate to some beneficial strategy s_i'. Since agent i only values item j, this would imply that $p_{ij}^{M,(s_i',\mathbf{s}_{-i})} > p_{ij}^{M,\mathbf{s}}$. However, since agent i values all items other than j equally under u_i and her most preferred item is item j, such a deviation would also be beneficial under profile $\mathbf{u}$, contradicting the fact that $\mathbf{s}$ is a pure Nash equilibrium.

Now consider the expected social welfare of M under valuation profile $\mathbf{u}'$ at the pure Nash equilibrium $\mathbf{s}$. For agents not in I and taking α to be less than $1/n^3$, the contribution to the social welfare is at most 1. For agents in I, the contribution to the welfare is then at most $(1/\sqrt{n})\sqrt{n}+1$ and hence the expected social welfare of M is at most 3. As the optimal social welfare is at least $\sqrt{n}$, the bound follows. $\qquad\square$

Interestingly, if we restrict our attention to *deterministic* mechanisms, then we can prove that only trivial pure Price of Anarchy guarantees are achievable.

Theorem 4. *The pure Price of Anarchy of any deterministic mechanism is $\Omega(n^2)$.*

Proof. Let M be a deterministic mechanism that always has a pure Nash equilibrium. Let $\mathbf{u}$ be a valuation profile such that for all agents i and i', it holds that $u_i = u_{i'}$, $u_{i1} = 1/n + 1/n^3$ and $u_{ij} > u_{ik}$ for $j < k$. Let $\mathbf{s}$ be a pure Nash equilibrium for this profile and assume without loss of generality that $M_i(\mathbf{s}) = i$.

Now fix another true valuation profile $\mathbf{u}'$ such that $u_1' = u_1$ and for agents $i = 2, \ldots, n$, $u_{i,i-1}' = 1 - \epsilon_{i,i-1}'$ and $u_{ij} = \epsilon_{ij}'$ for $j \neq i - 1$, where $0 \leq \epsilon_{ij}' \leq 1/n^3$,

$\sum_{j \neq i-1} \epsilon'_{ij} = \epsilon'_{i,i-1}$ and $\epsilon'_{ij} > \epsilon'_{ik}$ if $j < k$ when $j, k \neq i - 1$. Intuitively, in profile $\mathbf{u}'$, each agent $i \in \{2, \ldots, n\}$ has valuation close to 1 for item $i - 1$ and small valuations for all other items. Futhermore, she prefers items with smaller indices, except for item $i - 1$.

We claim that $\mathbf{s}$ is a pure Nash equilibrium under true valuation profile $\mathbf{u}$ as well. Assume for contradiction that some agent i has a benefiting deviation, which matches her with an item that she prefers more than i. But then, since the set of items that she prefers more than i in both $\mathbf{u}$ and $\mathbf{u}'$ is $\{1, \ldots, i\}$, the same deviation would match her with a more preferred item under $\mathbf{u}$ as well, contradicting the fact that $\mathbf{s}$ is a pure Nash equilibrium. It holds that $SW_{OPT}(\mathbf{u}') \geq n - 2$ whereas the social welfare of M is at most $2/n$ and the theorem follows.   □

The mechanism that naively maximizes the sum of the reported valuations with no regard to incentives, when equipped with a lexicographic tie-breaking rule has pure Nash equilibria and also achieves the above ratio in the worst-case, which means that the bounds are tight.

5   General Solution Concepts

In the previous sections, we employed the pure Nash equilibrium as the solution concept for bounding the inefficiency of mechanisms, mainly because of its simplicity. Here, we describe how to extend our results to broader well-known equilibrium concepts in the literature. Due to lack of space, we will only discuss the two most general solution concepts, the *coarse correlated equilibrium* for complete information and the *Bayes-Nash equilibrium* for incomplete information. Since other concepts (like the mixed-Nash equilibrium for instance) are special cases of those two, it suffices to use those for our extensions.

Definition 2. *Given a mechanism M, let $\mathbf{q}$ be a distribution over strategies. Also, for any distribution Δ let Δ_{-i} denote the marginal distribution without the ith index. Then a strategy profile $\mathbf{q}$ is called a*

1. coarse correlated equilibrium if

$$\mathop{\mathbb{E}}_{\mathbf{s} \sim \mathbf{q}} [u_i(M_i(\mathbf{s}))] \geq \mathop{\mathbb{E}}_{\mathbf{s} \sim \mathbf{q}} [u_i(M_i((s'_i, \mathbf{s}_{-i})))],$$

2. Bayes-Nash equilibrium for a distribution Δ_u where each $(\Delta_u)_i$ is independent, if when $\mathbf{u} \sim \Delta_u$ then $\mathbf{q}(\mathbf{u}) = \times_i q_i(u_i)$ and for all u_i in the support of $(\Delta_u)_i$,

$$\mathop{\mathbb{E}}_{\mathbf{u}_{-i}, \mathbf{s} \sim \mathbf{q}(\mathbf{u})} [u_i(M_i(\mathbf{s}))] \geq \mathop{\mathbb{E}}_{\mathbf{u}_{-i}, \mathbf{s}_{-i} \sim \mathbf{q}_{-i}(\mathbf{u}_{-i})} [u_i(M_i(s'_i, \mathbf{s}_{-i}))]$$

where the given inequalities hold for all agents i, and (pure) deviating strategies s'_i. Also notice that for randomized mechanisms definitions are with respect to an expectation over the random choices of the mechanism.

The coarse correlated and the Bayesian Price of Anarchy are defined similarly to the pure Price of Anarchy.

Again, first we mention that we can obtain the extensions to Random Priority rather straightforwardly, based on the fact that even when using probability mixtures over strategies, an agent will always (in every realization) pick her most preferred item among the set of available items when she is chosen. In other words, any pure strategy in the support of the distribution will rank the most preferred available item first, and the ordering of the remaining items does not affect the distribution.

Theorem 5. *The coarse correlated Price of Anarchy of Random Priority is $O(\sqrt{n})$. The Bayesian Price of Anarchy of Random Priority is $O(\sqrt{n})$.*

Proof. For the correlated Price of Anarchy, the argument is very similar to the one used in the proof of Theorem 2. Again, if any strategy in the support of a correlated equilibrium $\mathbf{q}$ misranks two items j and j' for any agent i, it can only be because agent i has 0 probability of receiving those items, otherwise agent i would deviate to truthtelling, violating the equilibrium condition. The remaining steps are exactly the same as in the proof of Theorem 2.

For the incomplete information case, consider any Bayes-Nash equilibrium $\mathbf{q}(\mathbf{u})$ and let $\mathbf{u}$ be a any sampled valuation profile. The expected social welfare of the Random Priority can be written as $\mathbb{E}_{\mathbf{u}}\left[\mathbb{E}_{s\sim\mathbf{q}(\mathbf{u})}\left[u_i(\mathbf{s})\right]\right]$. Using the same argument as the one in the proof of Theorem 2, we can lower bound the quantity $\mathbb{E}_{s\sim\mathbf{q}(\mathbf{u})}\left[u_i(\mathbf{s})\right]$ by $\Omega\left(\frac{SW_{OPT}(\mathbf{u})}{\sqrt{n}}\right)$ and the bound follows.   □

Next, we turn to Probabilistic Serial and prove the Price of Anarchy guarantees, with respect to coarse correlated equilibria and Bayes-Nash equilibria. Before we state our theorems however, we will briefly discuss the connection of those extensions with the *smoothness* framework of Roughgarden [25]. According to the definition in [25], a game is (λ, μ)-*smooth* if it satisfies the following condition

$$\sum_{i=1}^{n} u_i(s_i^*, \mathbf{s_{-i}}) \geq \lambda SW(\mathbf{s}^*) - \mu SW(\mathbf{s}), \tag{1}$$

where $\mathbf{s}^*$ is a pure strategy profile that corresponds to the optimal allocation and $\mathbf{s}$ is any pure strategy profile. It is not hard to see that a (λ, μ)-smooth game has a Price of Anarchy bounded by $(\mu + 1)/\lambda$.

Since establishing that a game is smooth also implies a pure Price of Anarchy bound, an alternative way of attempting to prove Theorem 1 would be to try to show smoothness of the game induced by PS, for $\mu/\lambda = \sqrt{n}$. However, this seems to be a harder task than what we actually do, since in such a proof, one would have to argue about the utilities of agents and possibly reason about the relative preferences for other items, other than the item they are matched with in the optimal allocation. Our approach only needs to consider those items, and hence it seems to be simpler.

An added benefit to the smoothness framework is the existence of the *extension theorem* in [25], which states that for a (λ, μ)-smooth game, the Price of

Anarchy guarantee extends to broader solution concepts verbatim, without any extra work. At first glance, one might think that proving smoothness for the game induced by PS might be worth the extra effort, since we would get the extensions "for free". A closer look at our proofs however shows that our approach is very similar to the proof of the extension theorem but using an alternative, simpler condition.

Specifically, the analysis in [25] uses Inequality 1 as a building block and substitutes the inequality into the expectations that naturally appear when considering randomized strategies. This can be done because the condition applies to all strategy profiles $\mathbf{s}$, when $\mathbf{s}^*$ is an optimal strategy profile. This is exactly what we do as well, but we use the inequality $t_j(s_i^*, \mathbf{s_{-i}}) \geq \frac{1}{4} \cdot t_j(\mathbf{s})$ instead, which is simpler but sufficient since it only applies to the game at hand. If $OPT_i(\mathbf{u}) = j$, which is what we use in the proof of Theorem 1, then $(s_i^*, \mathbf{s_{-i}})$ can be thought of as a profile where an agent deviates to her strategy in the optimal profile and hence the left-hand side of the inequality is analogous to the left-hand side of Inequality 1. In a sense, the inequality $t_j(s_i^*, \mathbf{s_{-i}}) \geq \frac{1}{4} \cdot t_j(\mathbf{s})$, can be viewed as a "smoothness equivalent" for the game induced by PS, which then allows us to extend the results to broader solution concepts.

First, we extend Theorem 1 to the case where the solution concept is the coarse correlated equilibrium.

Theorem 6. *The coarse correlated Price of Anarchy of Probabilistic Serial is* $O(\sqrt{n})$.

Proof. Let $\mathbf{u}$ be any valuation profile and let i be any agent. Furthermore, let $j = OPT_i(\mathbf{u})$ and let s_i' be the pure strategy that places item j on top of agent i's preference list. By Lemma 1, the inequality $t_j(s_i', \mathbf{s_{-i}}) \geq \frac{1}{4} t_j(\mathbf{s})$ holds for every strategy profile $\mathbf{s}$. In particular, it holds for any pure strategy profile $\mathbf{s}$ where s_i is in the support of the distribution of the mixed strategy q_i of agent i, for any coarse correlated equilibrium $\mathbf{q}$. This implies that

$$\underset{\mathbf{s} \sim \mathbf{q}}{\mathbb{E}} [u_i(PS_i(\mathbf{s}))] \geq \underset{\mathbf{s} \sim \mathbf{q}}{\mathbb{E}} [u_i(PS_i(s_i', \mathbf{s_{-i}}))]$$

$$\geq \underset{\mathbf{s} \sim \mathbf{q}}{\mathbb{E}} [u_{ij} t_j(s_i', \mathbf{s_{-i}}))] \geq \frac{1}{4} u_{ij} t_j(\mathbf{s}).$$

where the last inequality holds by Lemma 1. Using this, we can use very similar arguments to the arguments of the proof of Theorem 1 and obtain the bound.   □

For the incomplete information setting, when valuations are drawn from some publically known distributions, we can prove the same upper bound on the Bayesian Price of Anarchy of the mechanism.

Theorem 7. *The Bayesian Price of Anarchy of Probabilistic Serial is* $O(\sqrt{n})$.

Proof. The proof is again similar to the proof of Theorem 1. Let $\mathbf{u}$ be a valuation profile drawn from some distribution satisfying the unit-sum constraint. Let i

be any agent and let $j_u = OPT_i(\mathbf{u})$, $i \in [n]$. Note that by a similar argument as the one used in the proof of Theorem 1, the expected social welfare of PS is at least 1 and hence we can assume that $\mathbb{E}_\mathbf{u}[SW_{OPT}(\mathbf{u})] \geq 2\sqrt{2n} + 1$. Observe that in any Bayes-Nash equilibrium $\mathbf{q}(\mathbf{u})$ it holds that

$$
\begin{aligned}
\mathop{\mathbb{E}}_{\substack{\mathbf{u} \\ \mathbf{s}\sim\mathbf{q}(\mathbf{u})}} [u_i(\mathbf{s})] &= \mathop{\mathbb{E}}_{u_i}\left[\mathop{\mathbb{E}}_{\substack{\mathbf{u}_{-i} \\ \mathbf{s}\sim\mathbf{q}(\mathbf{u})}} [u_i(\mathbf{s})] \right] \\
&\geq \mathop{\mathbb{E}}_{u_i}\left[\mathop{\mathbb{E}}_{\substack{\mathbf{u}_{-i} \\ \mathbf{s}_{-i}\sim\mathbf{q}_{-i}(\mathbf{u}_{-i})}} [u_i(s_i', \mathbf{s}_{-i})] \right] \\
&\geq \mathop{\mathbb{E}}_{u_i}\left[\mathop{\mathbb{E}}_{\substack{\mathbf{u}_{-i} \\ \mathbf{s}_{-i}\sim\mathbf{q}_{-i}(\mathbf{u}_{-i})}} [u_{ij_u} t_{j_u}(s_i', \mathbf{s}_{-i})] \right] \\
&\geq \mathop{\mathbb{E}}_{u_i}\left[\mathop{\mathbb{E}}_{\substack{\mathbf{u}_{-i} \\ \mathbf{s}\sim\mathbf{q}(\mathbf{u})}} \left[\frac{1}{4} u_{ij_u} t_{j_u}(\mathbf{s}) \right] \right] \\
&= \frac{1}{4} \mathop{\mathbb{E}}_{\substack{\mathbf{u} \\ \mathbf{s}\sim\mathbf{q}(\mathbf{u})}} [u_{ij_u} t_{j_u}(\mathbf{s})]
\end{aligned}
$$

where the last inequality holds by Lemma 1 since s_i' denotes the strategy that puts item j_u on top of agent i's preference list. Note that this can be a different strategy for every different $\mathbf{u}$ that we sample. For notational convenience, we use s_i' to denote every such strategy. The expected social welfare at the Bayes-Nash equilibrium is then at least

$$
\begin{aligned}
\sum_{i=1}^{n} \mathop{\mathbb{E}}_{\mathbf{u},\mathbf{s}\sim\mathbf{q}(\mathbf{u})} [u_i(\mathbf{s})] &\geq \frac{1}{4} \sum_{i\in[n]} \mathop{\mathbb{E}}_{\substack{\mathbf{u} \\ \mathbf{s}\sim\mathbf{q}(\mathbf{u})}} [u_{ij_u} t_{j_u}(\mathbf{s})] \\
&\geq \mathop{\mathbb{E}}_{\substack{\mathbf{u} \\ \mathbf{s}\sim\mathbf{q}(\mathbf{u})}} \left[\sum_{i\in[n]} \frac{i}{4n} u_{ij_u} \right] \\
&\geq \mathop{\mathbb{E}}_{\substack{\mathbf{u} \\ \mathbf{s}\sim\mathbf{q}(\mathbf{u})}} \left[\frac{SW_{OPT}(\mathbf{u})(SW_{OPT}(\mathbf{u}) - 1)}{8n} \right] \\
&= \mathop{\mathbb{E}}_\mathbf{u} \left[\frac{SW_{OPT}(\mathbf{u})(SW_{OPT}(\mathbf{u}) - 1)}{8n} \right] \\
&\geq \frac{\mathbb{E}_\mathbf{u}\left[(SW_{OPT}(\mathbf{u}))^2\right] - \mathbb{E}_\mathbf{u}[SW_{OPT}(\mathbf{u})]}{8n} \\
&\geq \frac{\mathbb{E}_\mathbf{u}[SW_{OPT}(\mathbf{u})]}{2\sqrt{2n}},
\end{aligned}
$$

and the bound follows. $\qquad\square$

6   Extensions

6.1   Price of Stability

Theorem 3 bounds the Price of Anarchy of all mechanisms. A more optimistic (and hence stronger when proving lower bounds) measure of efficiency is the *Price of Stability*, i.e. the worst-case ratio over all valuation profiles of the optimal social welfare over the welfare attained at the *best* equilibrium.

We extend Theorem 3 to the Price of Stability of all mechanisms that satisfy a "proportionality" property.

Let $a_1 \succ_i a_2 \succ_i \cdots \succ_i a_n$ be the (possibly weak) preference ordering of agent i. A random assignment vector p_i for agent i *stochastically dominates* another random assignment vector q_i if $\sum_{j=1}^{k} p_{ia_j} \geq \sum_{j=1}^{k} q_{ia_j}$, for all $k = 1, 2, \cdots, n$. The notation that we will use for this relation is $p_i \succ_i^{sd} q_i$.

Definition 3 (Safe Strategy). *Let M be a mechanism. A strategy s_i is a safe strategy if for any strategy profile s_{-i} of the other players, it holds that $M_i(s_i, s_{-i}) \succ_i^{sd} \left(\frac{1}{n}, \frac{1}{n}, \ldots, \frac{1}{n}\right)$.*

We will say that a mechanism M has a safe strategy if every agent i has a safe strategy s_i in M. We now state our lower bound.

Theorem 8. *The pure Price of Stability of any mechanism that has a safe strategy is $\Omega(\sqrt{n})$.*

Proof. Let M be a mechanism and let $I = \{k+1, \ldots, n\}$ be a subset of agents. Let $\mathbf{u}$ be the following valuation profile.

– For all agents $i \in I$, let $u_{ij} = \frac{1}{k}$ for $j = 1, \cdots, k$ and $u_{ij} = 0$ otherwise.
– For all agents $i \notin I$, let $u_{ii} = 1$ and $u_{ij} = 0, j \neq i$.

Now let $\mathbf{s}$ be a pure Nash equilibrium on profile $\mathbf{u}$ and let s_i' be a safe strategy of agent i. The expected utility of each agent $i \in I$ in the pure Nash equilibrium $\mathbf{s}$ is

$$\mathbb{E}[u_i(\mathbf{s})] = \sum_{j \in [n]} p_{ij}(s_i, \mathbf{s_{-i}}) v_{ij} \geq \sum_{j \in [n]} p_{ij}(s_i', \mathbf{s_{-i}}) v_{ij}$$

$$\geq \frac{1}{n} \sum_{j \in [n]} v_{ij} = \frac{1}{n},$$

due to the fact that $\mathbf{s}$ is pure Nash equilibrium and s_i' is a safe strategy of agent i. On the other hand, the utility of agent $i \in I$ can be calculated by $\mathbb{E}[u_i(\mathbf{s})] = \sum_{j \in [n]} p_{ij}(s_i, s_{-i}) v_{ij} = (\sum_{j=1}^{k} p_{ij})/k$. Because $\mathbf{s}$ is a pure Nash equilibrium, it holds that $\mathbb{E}[u_i] \geq 1/n$, so we get that $\sum_{j=1}^{k} p_{ij} \geq k/n$ for all $i \in I$. As for the rest of the agents,

$$\sum_{i \in N \setminus I} \sum_{j=1}^{k} p_{ij} = k - \sum_{i \in I} \sum_{j=1}^{k} p_{ij} \leq k - (n-k)\frac{k}{n} = \frac{k^2}{n}.$$

This implies that the contribution to the social welfare from agents not in I is at most k^2/n and the expected social welfare of M will be at most $1 + (k^2/n)$. It holds that $SW_{OPT}(\mathbf{u}) \geq k$ and the bound follows by letting $k = \sqrt{n}$.   □

Due to Theorem 8, in order to obtain an $\Omega(\sqrt{n})$ bound for a mechanism M, it suffices to prove that M has a safe strategy. In fact, most reasonable mechanisms, including Random Priority and Probabilistic Serial, as well as all ordinal *envy-free* mechanisms satisfy this property.

Definition 4 (Envy-freeness). *A mechanism M is (ex-ante) envy-free if for all agents i and r and all profiles $\mathbf{s}$, it holds that $\sum_{j=1}^{n} p_{ij}s_{ij} \geq \sum_{j=1}^{n} p_{rj}s_{rj}$. Furthermore, if M is ordinal, then this implies $p_i^{M,\mathbf{s}} \succ_{s_i}^{sd} p_r^{M,\mathbf{s}}$.*

Given the interpretation of a truth-telling safe strategy as a "proportionality" property, the next lemma is not surprising.

Lemma 4. *Let M be an ordinal, envy-free mechanism. Then for any agent i, the truth-telling strategy u_i is a safe strategy.*

Proof. Let $\mathbf{s} = (u_i, \mathbf{s_{-i}})$ be the strategy profile in which agent i is truth-telling and the rest of the agents are playing some strategies $\mathbf{s_{-i}}$. Since M is envy-free and ordinal, it holds that $\sum_{j=1}^{\ell} p_{ij}^{\mathbf{s}} \geq \sum_{j=1}^{\ell} p_{rj}^{\mathbf{s}}$ for all agents $r \in \{1, \ldots, n\}$ and all $\ell \in \{1, \ldots, n\}$. Summing up these inequalities for agents $r = 1, 2, \ldots, n$ we obtain

$$n \sum_{j=1}^{\ell} p_{ij}^{\mathbf{s}} \geq \sum_{j=1}^{\ell} \sum_{r=1}^{n} p_{rj}^{\mathbf{s}} = \ell,$$

which implies that $\sum_{j=1}^{\ell} p_{ij}^{\mathbf{s}} \geq \frac{\ell}{n}$, for all $i \in \{1, \ldots, n\}$, and for all $\ell \in \{1, \ldots, n\}$.
□

Note that since Probabilistic Serial is ordinal and envy-free [9], by Lemma 4, it has a safe strategy and hence Theorem 8 applies. It is not hard to see that Random Priority has a safe strategy too.

Lemma 5. *Random Priority has a safe strategy.*

Proof. Since Random Priority first fixes an ordering of agents uniformly at random, every agent i has a probability of $1/n$ to be selected first to choose an item, a probability of $2/n$ to be selected first or second and so on. If the agent ranks her items truthfully, then for every $\ell = 1, \ldots, n$, it holds that $\sum_{i=1}^{\ell} p_{ij} \geq \ell/n$. □

In a sense, the safe strategy property is essential for the bound to hold; one can show that the *randomly dictatorial* mechanism, that matches a uniformly chosen agent with her most preferred item and the rest of the agents with items based solely on that agent's reports achieves a constant Price of Stability. On the other hand, the Price of Anarchy of the mechanism is $\Omega(n)$. It would be interesting to show whether Price of Anarchy guarantees imply Price of Stability lower bounds in general.

6.2 Unit-Range Representation

Our second extension is concerned with the other normalization that is also common in the literature [2,15,28], the unit-range representation, that is, $\max_j u_i(j) = 1$ and $\min_j u_i(j) = 0$. First, the Price of Anarchy guarantees from Sect. 3 extend directly to the unit-range case. For Random Priority, since the results in [15] hold for this normalization as well, we can apply the same techniques to prove the bounds. For Probabilistic Serial, first, observe that Lemma 2 holds independently of the representation. Secondly, in the proof of Theorem 1, it now holds that

$$SW_{PS}(\mathbf{u}, \mathbf{s}) \geq \frac{1}{n} \sum_{i=1}^{n} \sum_{j=1}^{n} u_{ij} \geq 1,$$

which is sufficient for bounding the Price of Anarchy when $SW_{OPT}(\mathbf{u}) \leq \sqrt{n}$. Finally, the arguments for the case when $SW_{OPT}(\mathbf{u}) \leq \sqrt{n}$ hold for both representations.

Next, we present a Price of Anarchy lower bound for deterministic mechanisms. First, we prove the following lemma about the structure of equilibria of deterministic mechanisms. Note that the lemma holds independently of the choice of representation.

Lemma 6. *The set of pure Nash equilibria of any deterministic mechanism is the same for all valuation profiles that induce the same preference orderings of valuations.*

Proof. Let $\mathbf{u}$ and $\mathbf{u}'$ be two different valuation profiles that induce the same preference ordering. Let $\mathbf{s}$ be a pure Nash equilibrium under true valuation profile $\mathbf{u}$ and assume for contradiction that it is not a pure Nash equilibrium under $\mathbf{u}'$. Then, there exists an agent i who by deviating from $\mathbf{s}$ is matched to a more preferred item according to u_i'. But that item would also be more preferred according to u_i and hence she would have an incentive to deviate from $\mathbf{s}$ under true valuation profile $\mathbf{u}$, contradicting the fact that $\mathbf{s}$ is a pure Nash equilibrium. □

Using Lemma 6, we can then prove the following theorem.

Theorem 9. *The Price of Anarchy of any deterministic mechanism that always has pure Nash equilibria is $\Omega(n)$ for the unit-range representation.*

Proof. Let M be a deterministic mechanism that always has a pure Nash equilibrium and let $\mathbf{u}$ be a valuation profile such that for all agents i and i', it holds that $u_i = u_{i'}$ and $u_{ij} > u_{ik}$, for all items $i < k$. Let $\mathbf{s}$ be a pure Nash equilibrium for this profile and assume without loss of generality that $M_i(\mathbf{s}) = i$. By Lemma 6, $\mathbf{s}$ is a pure Nash equilibrium for any profile $\mathbf{u}$ that induces the above ordering of valuations. In particular, it is a pure Nash equilibrium for a valuation profile satisfying

- For agents $i = 1, \ldots, \frac{n}{2}$, $u_{i1} = 1$ and $u_{ij} < \frac{1}{n^3}$, for $j > 1$.

- For agents $i = \frac{n}{2} + 1, \ldots, n$, $u_{ij} > 1 - \frac{1}{n^3}$ for $j = 1, \ldots, n/2$ and $u_{ij} < \frac{1}{n^3}$ for $j = \frac{n}{2} + 1, \ldots, n$.

It holds that $OPT(\mathbf{u}) \geq \frac{n}{2}$, whereas the social welfare of M is at most 2 and the theorem follows.   □

Again, similarly to the corresponding bound in Sect. 4, the mechanism that naively maximizes the sum of the reported valuations has pure Nash equilibria and achieves the above bound.

More importantly, it is not clear whether the general lower bound on the Price of Anarchy of all mechanisms that we proved in Theorem 3 extends to the unit-range representation as well. In fact, we do not know of any bound for the unit-range case and proving one seems to be a quite complicated task. As a first step in that direction, the following theorem obtains a lower bound for ϵ-*approximate* (pure) Nash equilibria. A strategy profile is an ϵ-approximate pure Nash equilibrium if no agent can deviate to another strategy and improve her utility by more than ϵ. While the following result applies for any positive ϵ, it is weaker than a corresponding result for exact equilibria.

Theorem 10. *Let M be a mechanism and let $\epsilon \in (0, 1)$. The ϵ-approximate Price of Anarchy of M is $\Omega(n^{1/4})$ for the unit-range representation.*

Proof. Assume $n = k^2$, where $k \in \mathbb{N}$ will be the size of a subset I of "important" agents. We consider valuation profiles where, for some parameter $\delta \in (0, 1)$,

- all agents have value 1 for item 1,
- there is a subset I of agents with $|I| = k$ for which any agent $i \in I$ has value δ^2 for any item $j \in \{2, \ldots, k+1\}$ and 0 for all other items,
- for agent $i \notin I$, i has value δ^3 for items $j \in \{2, \ldots, k+1\}$ and 0 for all other items.

Let $\mathbf{u}$ be such a valuation profile and let $\mathbf{s}$ be a Nash equilibrium. In the optimal allocation members of I receive items $\{2, \ldots, k+1\}$ and such an allocation has social welfare $k\delta^2 + 1$.

First, we claim that there are $k(1 - 2\delta)$ members of I whose payoffs in $\mathbf{s}$ are at most δ; call this set X. If that were false, then there would be more than $2k\delta$ members of I whose payoffs in $\mathbf{s}$ were more than δ. That would imply that the social welfare of $\mathbf{s}$ was more than $2k\delta^2$, which would contradict the optimal social welfare attainable, for large enough n (specifically, $n > 1/\delta^4$).

Next, we claim that there are at least $k(1 - 2\delta)$ non-members of I whose probability (in $\mathbf{s}$) to receive any item in $\{1, \ldots, k+1\}$ is at most $4(k+1)/n$; call this set Y. To see this, observe that there are at least $\frac{3}{4}n$ agents who all have probability $\leq 4/n$ to receive item 1. Furthermore, there are at least $3n/4$ agents who all have probability $\leq 4k/n$ to receive an item from the set $2, \ldots, k+1$. Hence there are at least $n/2$ agents whose probabilities to obtain these items satisfy both properties.

We now consider the operation of swapping the valuations of the agents in sets X and Y so that the members of I from X become non-members, and vice versa. We will argue that given that they were best-responding beforehand, they are δ-best-responding afterwards. Consequently $\mathbf{s}$ is an δ-NE of the modified set of agents. The optimum social welfare is unchanged by this operation since it only involves exchanging the payoff functions of pairs of agents. We show that the social welfare of $\mathbf{s}$ is some fraction of the optimal social welfare, that goes to 0 as n increases and δ decreases.

Let I' be the set of agents who, after the swap, have the higher utility of δ^2 for getting items from $\{2, \ldots, k+1\}$. That is, I' is the set of agents in Y, together with I minus the agents in X.

Following the above valuation swap, the agents in X are δ-best responding. To see this, note that these agents have had a reduction to their utilities for the outcome of receiving items from $\{2, \ldots, k+1\}$. This means that a profitable deviation for such agents should result in them being more likely to obtain item 1, in return for them being less likely to obtain an item from $\{2, \ldots, k+1\}$. However they cannot have probability more than δ to receive item 1, since that would contradict the property that their expected payoff was at most δ.

After the swap, the agents in Y are also δ-best responding. Again, these agents have had their utilities increased from δ^3 to δ^2 for the outcome of receiving an item from $\{2, \ldots, k+1\}$. Hence any profitable deviation for such an agent would involve a reduction in the probability to get item 1 in return for an increased probability to get an item from $\{2, \ldots, k+1\}$. However, since the payoff for any item from $\{2, \ldots, k+1\}$ is only δ^2, such a deviation pays less than δ.

Finally, observe that the social welfare of $\mathbf{s}$ under the new profile (after the swap) is at most $1 + 3k\delta^3$. To see this, note that (by an earlier argument and the definition of I') $k(1 - 2\delta)$ members of I' have probability at most $4(k+1)/n$ to receive any item from $\{1, \ldots, k+1\}$. To upper bound the expected social welfare, note that item 1 contributes 1 to the social welfare. Items in $\{2, \ldots, k+1\}$ contribute in total, δ^2 times the expected number of members of I' who get them, plus δ^3 times the expected number of non-members of I' who get them, which is at most $\delta^2 k 2\delta + \delta^3 k(1 - 2\delta)$ which is less than $3k\delta^3$.

Overall, the price of anarchy is at least $(k\delta^2 + 1)/3k\delta^3$, which is more than $1/\delta$. The statement of the theorem is obtained by choosing δ to be less than ϵ, n large enough for the arguments to hold for the chosen δ, i.e. $n > 1/\delta^4$.   □

7   Conclusion and Future Work

Our results are rather negative: we identify a non-constant lower bound on the Price of Anarchy for one-sided matching, and find a matching upper bound achieved by well-known ordinal mechanisms. However, such negative results are important to understand the challenge faced by a social-welfare maximizer: for example, we establish that it is not enough to elicit cardinal valuations, in order to obtain good social welfare. It may be that better welfare guarantees should use some assumption of truth-bias, or some assumption of additional structure in agents' preferences.

An interesting direction of research would be to identify conditions on the valuation space that allow for constant values of the Price of Anarchy or impose some distributional assumption on the inputs and quantify the average loss in welfare due to selfish behavior. For the general, worst-case setting, one question raised is whether one can obtain Price of Anarchy or Price of Stability bounds that match our upper bounds for the unit-range representation as well.

Acknowledgements. The authors would like to thank Piotr Krysta for useful discussion.

References

1. Abdulkadiroğlu, A., Sönmez, T., Markets, M.: Theory and practice. In: Advances in Economics and Econometrics (Tenth World Congress), pp. 3–47 (2013)
2. Adamczyk, M., Sankowski, P., Zhang, Q.: Efficiency of truthful and symmetric mechanisms in one-sided matching. In: Lavi, R. (ed.) SAGT 2014. LNCS, vol. 8768, pp. 13–24. Springer, Heidelberg (2014). doi:10.1007/978-3-662-44803-8_2
3. Anshelevich, E., Dasgupta, A., Kleinberg, J., Tardos, E., Wexler, T., Roughgarden, T.: The price of stability for network design with fair cost allocation. SIAM J. Comput. **38**(4), 1602–1623 (2008)
4. Aziz, H., Brandt, F., Brill, M.: The computational complexity of random serial dictatorship. Econ. Lett. **121**(3), 341–345 (2013)
5. Aziz, H., Gaspers, S., Mackenzie, S., Mattei, N., Narodytska, N., Walsh, T.: Equilibria under the probabilistic serial rule. arXiv preprint arXiv:1502.04888 (2015)
6. Aziz, H., Gaspers, S., Mackenzie, S., Mattei, N., Narodytska, N., Walsh, T.: Manipulating the probabilistic serial rule. In: Proceedings of the 2015 International Conference on Autonomous Agents and Multiagent Systems, pp. 1451–1459. International Foundation for Autonomous Agents and Multiagent Systems (2015)
7. Aziz, H., Gaspers, S., Mattei, N., Narodytska, N., Walsh, T.: Strategic aspects of the probabilistic serial rule for the allocation of goods. arXiv preprint arXiv: 1401.6523 (2014)
8. Bhalgat, A., Chakrabarty, D., Khanna, S.: Social welfare in one-sided matching markets without money. In: Goldberg, L.A., Jansen, K., Ravi, R., Rolim, J.D.P. (eds.) APPROX/RANDOM 2011. LNCS, vol. 6845, pp. 87–98. Springer, Heidelberg (2011). doi:10.1007/978-3-642-22935-0_8
9. Bogomolnaia, A., Moulin, H.: A new solution to the random assignment problem. J. Econ. Theory **100**, 295–328 (2001)
10. Brams, S.J., Feldman, M., Lai, J.K., Morgenstern, J., Procaccia, A.D.: On maxsum fair cake divisions. In: AAAI (2012)
11. Caragiannis, I., Kaklamanis, C., Kanellopoulos, P., Kyropoulou, M.: The efficiency of fair division. Theory Comput. Syst. **50**(4), 589–610 (2012)
12. Chakrabarty, D., Swamy, C.: Welfare maximization and truthfulness in mechanism design with ordinal preferences. In: Proceedings of the 5th Conference on Innovations in Theoretical Computer Science, pp. 105–120 (2014)
13. Christodoulou, G., Kovács, A., Schapira, M.: Bayesian combinatorial auctions. In: Aceto, L., Damgård, I., Goldberg, L.A., Halldórsson, M.M., Ingólfsdóttir, A., Walukiewicz, I. (eds.) ICALP 2008. LNCS, vol. 5125, pp. 820–832. Springer, Heidelberg (2008). doi:10.1007/978-3-540-70575-8_67

14. Ekici, O., Kesten, O.: On the ordinal nash equilibria of the probabilistic serial mechanism. Technical report, working paper, Tepper School of Business, Carnegie Mellon University (2010)
15. Filos-Ratsikas, A., Frederiksen, S.K.S., Zhang, J.: Social welfare in one-sided matchings: random priority and beyond. In: Lavi, R. (ed.) SAGT 2014. LNCS, vol. 8768, pp. 1–12. Springer, Heidelberg (2014). doi:10.1007/978-3-662-44803-8_1
16. Guo, M., Conitzer, V.: Strategy-proof allocation of multiple items between two agents without payments or priors. In: Proceedings of the 9th International Conference on Autonomous Agents and Multiagent Systems, vol. 1, pp. 881–888 (2010)
17. Hashimoto, T., Hirata, D., Kesten, O., Kurino, M., Utku Ünver, M.: Two axiomatic approaches to the probabilistic serial mechanism. Theor. Econ. **9**(1), 253–277 (2014)
18. Hylland, A., Zeckhauser, R.: The efficient allocation of individuals to positions. J. Polit. Econ. **87**(2), 293–314 (1979)
19. Katta, A.-K., Sethuraman, J.: A solution to the random assignment problem on the full preference domain. J. Econ. Theory **131**(1), 231–250 (2006)
20. Kesten, O: Probabilistic serial and top trading cycles from equal division for the random assignment problem. Technical report, mimeo (2006)
21. Kojima, F., Manea, M.: Incentives in the probabilistic serial mechanism. J. Econ. Theory **145**(1), 106–123 (2010)
22. Koutsoupias, E., Papadimitriou, C.: Worst-case equilibria. In: Meinel, C., Tison, S. (eds.) STACS 1999. LNCS, vol. 1563, pp. 404–413. Springer, Heidelberg (1999). doi:10.1007/3-540-49116-3_38
23. Krysta, P., Manlove, D., Rastegari, B., Zhang, J.: Size versus truthfulness in the house allocation problem. In: Proceedings of the 15th ACM Conference on Economics and Computation, pp. 453–470. ACM (2014)
24. Procaccia, A.D., Tennenholtz, M.: Approximate mechanism design without money. In: Proceedings of the 10th ACM Conference on Electronic Commerce, pp. 177–186. ACM (2009)
25. Roughgarden, T.: Intrinsic robustness of the price of anarchy. In: Proceedings of the Forty-First Annual ACM Symposium on Theory of Computing, pp. 513–522. ACM (2009)
26. Syrgkanis, V., Tardos, E.: Composable and efficient mechanisms. In: STOC 2013: Proceedings of the 45th Symposium on Theory of Computing, November 2013
27. Von Neumann, J., Morgenstern, O.: Theory of games and economic behavior (60th Anniversary Commemorative Edition). Princeton University Press, Princeton (2007)
28. Zhou, L.: On a conjecture by gale about one-sided matching problems. J. Econ. Theory **52**, 123–135 (1990)

Using Multiagent Negotiation to Model Water Resources Systems Operations

Francesco Amigoni[✉], Andrea Castelletti, Paolo Gazzotti, Matteo Giuliani, and Emanuele Mason

Politecnico di Milano, Piazza Leonardo da Vinci 32, 20133 Milano, Italy
{francesco.amigoni,andrea.castelletti,matteo.giuliani,
emanuele.mason}@polimi.it, paolo.gazzotti@mail.polimi.it

Abstract. The operations of water resources infrastructures, such as dams and diversions, often involve multiple conflicting interests and stakeholders. Among the approaches that have been proposed to design optimal operating policies for these systems, those based on agents have recently attracted an increasing attention. The different stakeholders are represented as different agents and their interactions are usually modeled as distributed constraint optimization problems. Those few works that have attempted to model the interactions between stakeholders as negotiations present some significant limitations, like the necessity for each agent to know the preferences of all other agents. To overcome this drawback, in this paper we contribute a general monotonic concession protocol that allows the stakeholders-agents of a regulated lake to periodically reach agreements on the amount of water to release daily, trying to control lake floods and to supply water to agricultural districts downstream. In particular, we study two specific instances of the general protocol according to their ability to converge, reach Pareto optimal agreements, limit complexity, and show good experimental performance.

1 Introduction

The operations of water resources infrastructures, such as dams and diversions, often involve multiple stakeholders with conflicting interests. However, the traditional approach assumes a centralized perspective, studying large and disputed transnational river basins with the aim of exploring efficient water management policies at a systemwide scale [26]. Recently, agent-based approaches have been proposed to better represent the variety of stakeholders and decision makers [16,27]. To better capture the conflicting nature of the stakeholders' interactions, few works have attempted to model such interactions as negotiations [1,24]. Yet, they introduce strong and somehow unrealistic assumptions, like the necessity for each agent to know the preferences of all other agents.

In this paper, we propose a model based on a general *monotonic concession negotiation* framework that allows the stakeholders-agents of a regulated lake

A summary of this work appears, as extended abstract, in the Proceedings of the Autonomous Agents and Multiagent Systems Conference (AAMAS) 2016.

© Springer International Publishing AG 2016
N. Osman and C. Sierra (Eds.): AAMAS 2016 Ws Best Papers, LNAI 10002, pp. 51–72, 2016.
DOI: 10.1007/978-3-319-46882-2_4

to periodically reach agreements on the lake operating policy that determines the amount of water to release daily, trying to control lake floods and to reliably supply water to agricultural districts downstream. The agreement reached by the negotiation process mimics the outcome of the decision-making process of the lake regulator, who has to balance different goals. In our framework, a mediator coordinates the negotiation process, without the need for agents (including the mediator) to know all their preferences. This aspect is important, for example, for transboundary basins, in which information sharing is rarely documented in the literature [15]. Little willingness to share information can also be found at smaller scales, in river basins that we consider in our work. In particular, we define two specific protocols as instances of the general framework, which are inspired to those introduced in [4,6], respectively. We evaluate these two protocols both theoretically and empirically (using synthetic but realistic data), according to their convergence, Pareto optimality, complexity, and experimental performance.

The main original contributions of this paper are the application of a negotiation framework that does not require agents to know each other's preferences to the operations of water resources systems, the study of the Pareto optimality of the agreements found by the protocols introduced in [4,6], and the demonstration of the flexibility of the proposed model to account for behaviors observed in actual regulators of lake basins.

2   Related Work

Most of the world's largest and disputed transnational river basins, such as the Nile [8], the Zambezi [25], or the Euphrates-Tigris [2], have been studied from a centralized perspective, exploring the potential for more efficient water management policies at a systemwide scale. However, there is growing consensus that the solutions found by centralized approaches, often assuming both full knowledge and perfect application of the generated policy by all actors, are not adequate for real world situations characterized by private knowledge and individual decision-making [28].

To overcome these limitations, the use of agent-based modeling is recently expanding in the water resources planning and management literature (for a review, see [7] and references therein), particularly to study the value of coordination in large-scale systems [15,19]. Usually, agent-based approaches provide sub-optimal solutions that are nevertheless more acceptable to the stakeholders than the optimal solutions provided by the centralized approaches [16].

In [27], each agent represents a stakeholder of a shared water resources system. A decentralized optimization process is proposed in which each agent optimizes a local cost function that balances the local goals of the agent and the global goals of the system, according to a behavioral parameter determining the more individualistic or the more cooperative nature of the agent. The approach is extended in [16] by casting the problem in the well-known frameworks of Distributed Constraint Satisfaction Problems (DCSPs) and Distributed Constraint

Optimization Problems (DCOPs). The results of [16] show that the quality of the solutions obtained with DCSP/DCOP is between that of the solutions found with a centralized approach and that of the solutions returned by a completely unco-ordinated approach in which agents are fully selfish. A further multi-objective extension that looks for Pareto optimal solutions is presented in [3].

Distributed constraint reasoning, however, does not fully capture the com-petitive nature of most interactions between stakeholders of water resources systems. In this sense, modeling these interactions as negotiations appears as an interesting approach. To the best of our knowledge, [1,24] are the only works that use negotiation to find optimal policies for shared water resources systems. In both works, the negotiation protocol employed is that defined in [21], in which each agent has an individual preference about the policy to be adopted and full knowledge about the preferences of the other agents. The negotiation proceeds in rounds, with a fixed maximum number of rounds T known by the agents. At each round, an agent i is selected with probability β_i, calculates a policy p_i using backward induction, and proposes it to the other agents in order to reach an agreement as soon as possible.

In this paper, we adopt the idea of using negotiation to model the trade-off between different interests in the decision-making process relative to a lake basin, by proposing a monotonic concession negotiation approach that, differ-ently from [1,24], does not require agents to know the preferences of each other to converge to an agreement.

3 The Case Study

We consider a realistic test case inspired by a real world context, the Lake Como system, in Northern Italy. Lake Como is a regulated lake, i.e., a formerly natural lake dammed on the outlet. The lake dam is operated to supply water downstream mostly for irrigation and to control floods on the lake shores. In our simplified case study, we consider the same operating objectives of the Lake Como operator, i.e., flood control and water supply, but a simplified model of the reservoir (linear shape and outlet) and of the feeding watershed (stationary) to derive a more tractable model [20].

The lake storage dynamics is described through a mass balance equation on a daily time step τ:

$$s_{\tau+1} = s_\tau + q_{\tau+1} - r_{\tau+1}$$

where s_τ and $s_{\tau+1}$ are the volumes of water stored in the reservoir at days τ and $\tau + 1$, respectively (both expressed in m^3); $q_{\tau+1}$ is the net inflow (i.e., including evaporation and direct precipitation, and expressed in m^3/day) flowing into the lake between τ and $\tau + 1$; and $r_{\tau+1}$ is the release between τ and $\tau + 1$ (expressed in m^3/day), which is to be controlled.

Assuming the lake as a perfect cylinder (i.e., the lake surface is perfectly horizontal and the shape is invariant wrt the level), the storage s_τ can be related to the area of the lake S and to the level h_τ of the water measured at day τ: $s_\tau = S \cdot h_\tau$. We call $\bar{h}$ the flooding threshold above which the shores are inundated.

In our numerical experiments, we assume conventional values $S = 1 \times 10^8$ m^2 and $\bar{h} = 50$ m.

The inflow $q_{\tau+1}$ is stochastically generated from a normal distribution $q_\tau \sim N(\mu_q, \sigma_q)$ with $\mu_q = 40$ m^3/day and $\sigma_q = 10$ m^3/day. These data do not show the periodicity of real inflow data (e.g., due to seasons) in order to consider the water requested for irrigation $\bar{\omega}$ (see below) constant at every day. However, our data realistically trigger the conflicts between floods and water demand that are observed in real systems and are thus adequate for testing our negotiation approach. We generate time series of 5,000 samples (one sample per day) and divide them in blocks $B_1, B_2, \ldots, B_j, \ldots$ of $b = 90$ days each.

The release $r_{\tau+1}$ depends on the release decision u_τ and on the physical constraints over the actuation (see Fig. 1). The maximum water volume that can be released, V_{max}, depends on the lake storage, i.e., $V_{max} = s_\tau$. The minimum release is equal to zero if the lake level is below 100 m. When the lake level reaches the critical threshold of 100 m, the dam's spillways are activated so that the water does not overtop the dam, which may produce structural damages or even destroy the dam. The minimum release v_{min} is hence defined as $v_{min} = \max(s_\tau/S - 100, 0)$. The dam is operated with a feedback control law $\pi()$ mapping the lake storage s_τ into the release decision u_τ, i.e., $u_\tau = \pi(s_\tau)$. When actuated, u_τ produces $r_{\tau+1}$ according to the above constraints (green region of Fig. 1). As a control law $\pi()$, we consider the piecewise linear function reported in Fig. 1, known in the water science literature as the Standard Operating Policy [10], which depends on three parameters: x_1, x_2, and x_3, from which the coordinates of the relevant points can be calculated:

$$A = \left(0, 0\right) \qquad C = \left(\frac{\bar{\omega}}{\tan(x_1)} + x_2, \bar{\omega}\right)$$
$$B = \left(\frac{\bar{\omega}}{\tan(x_1)}, \bar{\omega}\right) \quad D = \left(S_{max}, \tan(x_3) \cdot (S_{max} - x_2) + \bar{\omega}\right)$$

where $\bar{\omega}$ is the (constant) water request for irrigation and S_{max} is the maximum possible level the lake can reach in our synthetic case study, given the linear discharge function and the other constraints.

Parameters x_1, x_2, and x_3 determine the shape of the release policy and are traded-off among the conflicting agents via negotiations, which occur every b days.

We consider the conflicting interests of the lake regulator who operates the dam as two agents. The *city agent* represents the communities living on the lake shores, who are worried about floods that happen when the water level is above the threshold $\bar{h}$. The *irr agent* represents the farmers in the downstream irrigation districts that need water supply to grow their crops. According to previous studies [5,9], the cost functions of the city agent $\mathcal{J}_{B_j}^{city}$ and of the irr agent $\mathcal{J}_{B_j}^{irr}$ over a block B_j of b days are formulated as follows:

$$\mathcal{J}_{B_j}^{city} = \frac{1}{b} \sum_{\tau \in B_j} (max(h_\tau - \bar{h}, 0)), \tag{1}$$

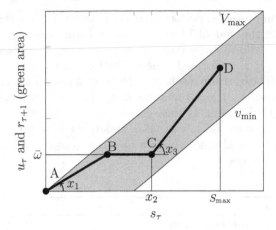

Fig. 1. The control law rule used for the lake operations within the feasible regulation region (in green). (Color figure online)

$$\mathcal{J}_{B_j}^{\text{irr}} = \frac{1}{b} \sum_{\tau \in B_j} (max(\bar{\omega} - r_{\tau+1}, 0))^2. \tag{2}$$

The quadratic formulation of (2) aims to penalize severe deficits in a single day, which are extremely dangerous for crops, while allowing for more frequent, small shortages [17]. The cost functions have been identified interacting with the stakeholders [23].

Different agents have different preferences on the values of the parameters x_1, x_2, and x_3 of the release policy. While the city agent prefers to maximize the release at every water level, the irr agent wants the release to satisfy the fixed demand and to not waste water that can be used in the future. Hence, values of x_1, x_2, and x_3 are the issues that are negotiated with the protocols illustrated in the next section. Note that the negotiated issue is the operating policy, not the water resource.

4   The Negotiation Protocols

In this paper, we consider two negotiation protocols that belong to the family of monotonic concession protocols [22]. In particular, according to the taxonomy of [12], they belong to *egocentric concession* protocols in which each agent makes new proposals that are worse for itself.

We assume, in general, the presence of n agents that are negotiating over m variables that can take real values belonging to some domain (in our application, $n = 2$ and $m = 3$). As in [4,6], we suppose the presence of a mediator to reduce the number of messages that agents exchange and to facilitate coordination. The negotiation process evolves in steps (rounds). At each step, first, the agents send their proposals to the mediator and, then, the mediator sends its counter-proposal (current agreement) to the agents.

The negotiation process is performed every b days to decide the release policy. More precisely, at the end of block B_j, the release policy for block B_{j+1} is negotiated. In the following, we consider a generic negotiation, so we omit the block B_j at which it is performed. The algorithm for an agent i is reported as Algorithm 1. In the algorithm, $\mathcal{U}_i$ is the utility function of agent i[1]; p_i^0, p_i^t, and p_i^{t+1} are the *proposals* of agent i at steps 0, t, and $t+1$, respectively; a^t is the counter-proposal of mediator at time t; and $\mathcal{F}_i(p_i^t, a^t)$ is the *strategy function* of agent i. The rationale is that agent i makes its best proposal at the first negotiation step $t = 0$ and then revises it at later steps to take into account the proposals of other agents.

Algorithm 1. Agent i

1: $\mathcal{U}_i \leftarrow$ CalculateMyUtilityFunction()
2: $p_i^0 \leftarrow$ Maximize($\mathcal{U}_i$)
3: SendToMediator(p_i^0)
4: **loop**
5:    $a^t \leftarrow$ WaitForMediatorAnswer()
6:    **if** a^t.status = *agreement_found* **then return** a^t.values
7:    **else**
8:       $p_i^{t+1} \leftarrow \mathcal{F}_i(p_i^t, a^t)$
9:       SendToMediator(p_i^{t+1})
10:       $t \leftarrow t + 1$
11:    **end if**
12: **end loop**

The algorithm for the mediator is shown as Algorithm 2, where $\mathcal{A}(\{p_1^t, p_2^t, \ldots, p_n^t\})$ is the *agreement function* calculating the current agreement between agents proposals.

Algorithm 2. Mediator

1: **repeat**
2:    $\{p_1^t, p_2^t, \ldots, p_n^t\} \leftarrow$ CollectAllProposalsFromAgents()
3:    $a^t \leftarrow \mathcal{A}(\{p_1^t, p_2^t, \ldots, p_n^t\})$
4:    SendToAgents(a^t)
5: **until** a^t.status = *agreement_found*

The negotiation process can terminate with an agreement over the values of the m variables or with a *conflict deal*, which means that no agreement has been found. In the following, this general monotonic concession protocol is instantiated in two specific protocols by specifying how p_i^t, a^t, $\mathcal{F}_i()$, and $\mathcal{A}()$ are implemented.

---

[1] Note that the negotiation protocols are presented referring to utility functions $\mathcal{U}_i$ for uniformity with relevant literature, but in our application we consider cost functions $\mathcal{J}_{B_j}^i$. The two representations are related by: $\mathcal{U}_i = 1/\mathcal{J}_{B_j}^i$.

We call *set of interest* for agent i the set $I_i = \{x \in \Re^m \mid \mathcal{U}_i(x) \geq 0\}$ of individually rational options. Namely, I_i represents the portion of the space of the m variables in which agent i is interested in negotiating (i.e., it does not receive a negative utility). We call *negotiation space* the set $\mathcal{I}_a = \bigcap_{i=1}^n I_i$, which is the portion of the space of the m variables in which *all* agents are interested to negotiate. Any final agreement must belong to $\mathcal{I}_a$. If $\mathcal{I}_a = \emptyset$, then no agreement can be found. However, unless agents explicitly communicate their sets of interests I_i, there is in general no way for the mediator to discover *a priori* that a negotiation will end with the conflict deal. In general, we assume that the agents are self-interested, but have a cooperative and truthful attitude in order to reach an agreement. Agents can thus implement their private strategy functions $\mathcal{F}_i()$. The protocol would still work without the mediator: all agents broadcast proposals and calculate the current agreement and the new proposals.

4.1 Point-Based Protocol

The first protocol is called *point-based* and has been originally presented in [4]. A variant of the protocol that is able to find *approximate* Pareto optimal agreements has been proposed in [14]. The point-based protocol is obtained from the general monotonic concession protocol described above by considering proposals as vectors of m elements:

$$p_i^t = [x_1, x_2, \ldots, x_m] \in \Re^m$$

with the meaning that p_i^t contains the values that agent i would like to assign to the m variables at step t (in our application, a proposal is the release policy that agent i would like to adopt for the next block).

The strategy function of agent i is:

$$p_i^{t+1} = \mathcal{F}_i(p_i^t, a^t) = p_i^t + \alpha_i \cdot (a^t - p_i^t) \tag{3}$$

where $\alpha_i \in (0, 1]$ is called *concession coefficient* and represents the rigidity of agent i to move toward the counter-proposal received from the mediator ($\alpha_i \to 0$ means that agent i is rigid, $\alpha_i \to 1$ means that it is concessive).

The agreement function $\mathcal{A}(\{p_1^t, p_2^t, \ldots, p_n^t\})$ averages the proposals p_i^t of the n agents:

$$a^t.\text{values} = \frac{\sum_{i=1}^n p_i^t}{n} \tag{4}$$

and, in a way, expresses the aggregated preferences of all agents. When, at some t, all p_i^t are equal to the same value $\bar{p}$, then the final agreement is reached, and the negotiation process ends. In this case, $a^t.\text{status} = agreement\_found$ and $a^t.\text{values} = \bar{p}$.

Under conditions satisfied by (3) and basically related to the fact that all $\alpha_i \neq 0$, the point-based protocol is guaranteed to eventually converge to an agreement by Theorem 5.9 of [4].

About optimality, namely the ability of the point-based protocol to always end with a Pareto-optimal agreement[2], no general guarantee is provided in [4,14]. However, in our application, to guarantee their efficiency at the systemwide scale, it is important to ensure that the final agreements are Pareto optimal. We thus study this issue in more detail. We first note that the strategy function (3) of an agent i returns incremental variations of the initial optimal proposal p_i^0 and that the entity of these variations depends on the sequence of agreements a^t and, in a intertwined way, on the sequence of proposals of the other agents. As a consequence, an agent i has no "control" on the value of its utility function $\mathcal{U}_i$ at the final agreement. If we consider the single variable case, $m = 1$, it is possible to find examples in which a Pareto optimal agreement is not reached. For instance, consider the case of $n = 2$ agents with the utility functions[3] reported in Fig. 2, with $I_1 = I_2 = [0, 3]$. The final agreement $\bar{p}$ to which the protocol converges is not Pareto optimal, because there are other solutions more convenient for both agents (e.g., $x = 0.5$). A sufficient condition for having a Pareto optimal agreement in the single variable case follows (proof is trivial and not reported).

Proposition 1. *A point-based negotiation with $m = 1$ is guaranteed to converge to a Pareto optimal agreement if $\mathcal{I}_a$ is limited and, for each agent i, $\mathcal{U}_i$ has at most one local maximum.*

Utility functions of Fig. 2 clearly do not satisfy the above condition and so Pareto optimality of the final agreement is not guaranteed (and, as we have seen, the final agreement is actually not Pareto optimal). This is related to the fact that, in the point-based protocol, the concession is actually on issues values and it is a monotonic egocentric concession [12] on utility values if the conditions of Proposition 1 hold.

When considering the general case of more variables, conditions of Proposition 1 are not enough to guarantee that a Pareto optimal agreement will be reached. For example, consider Fig. 3 that refers to $m = 2$ and $n = 2$ and in which, although the utility functions of the agents are monotonic in both variables, the final agreement $\bar{p}$ is not Pareto optimal, since the point D (for example) dominates it. The reason is that agents negotiate not over the entire $\mathcal{I}_a$, but only along the line connecting their initial offers p_1^0 and p_2^0 (because of the linearity of (3) and of (4)). More in general, with $m > 2$ variables, the proposals of the agents are confined in a sub-region κ of $\mathcal{I}_a$, that is defined by the initial proposals p_i^0 of the agents. When, as in the case of Fig. 3, Pareto optimal agreements are outside κ, then the point-based protocol cannot reach them.

Let now analyze the complexity of the point-based protocol. In our application, utility functions of the agents are not calculated analytically, but are stored in tabular form (because values are obtained via simulation, see Sect. 5).

---

[2] An agreement $x \in \Re^m$ is Pareto optimal if it is not dominated by any other $x' \in \Re^m$; where x' dominates x when, for all i, $\mathcal{U}_i(x') \geq \mathcal{U}_i(x)$ and, for at least a $\bar{i}$, $\mathcal{U}_{\bar{i}}(x') > \mathcal{U}_{\bar{i}}(x)$.

[3] All the utilities functions reported in this section are not related to our application, but have been built manually for illustration purposes.

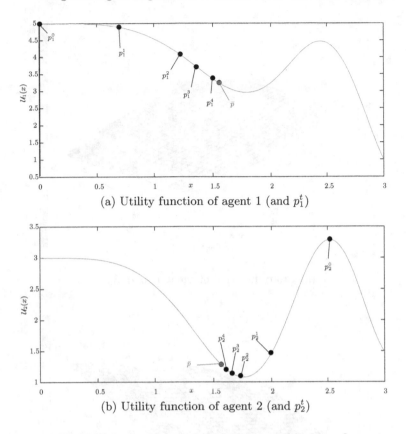

(a) Utility function of agent 1 (and p_1^t)

(b) Utility function of agent 2 (and p_2^t)

Fig. 2. Point-based negotiation with $m = 1$ and $n = 2$.

Continuous domains of the variables are thus discretized in finite domains. Since different domains are discretized with different granularities, let call G the number of elements in the largest discrete domain. Then, the space complexity of the point-based protocol is $O(G^m)$ for a generic agent i (to store its utility function) and $O(n \times m)$ for the mediator (to store all the proposals received at a step). The temporal complexity of the point-based protocol for a generic agent i is $O(Z_i + T)$, due to the optimization of the utility function (performed only once, in $O(Z_i)$, Maximize($\mathcal{U}_i$) of Algorithm 1) and, for each one of the T iterations of the negotiation, to the constant-time update of the proposal (3). The mediator has only to calculate the current agreement (4), that can be done in $O(n)$.

4.2   Set-Based Protocol

The second protocol is called *set-based* and has been originally introduced in [6] (but, to the best of our knowledge, never applied to any practical setting). Let call $\mathcal{P}_i(\Gamma_i^t) = \{x \in I_i \mid \mathcal{U}_i(x) \geq \Gamma_i^t\}$ the set of proposals that agent i accepts given an *acceptability threshold* Γ_i^t. Namely, $\mathcal{P}_i(\Gamma_i^t)$ contains all the combinations

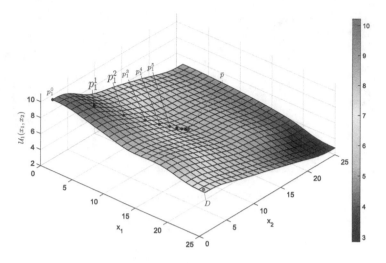

(a) Utility function of agent 1 (and p_1^t)

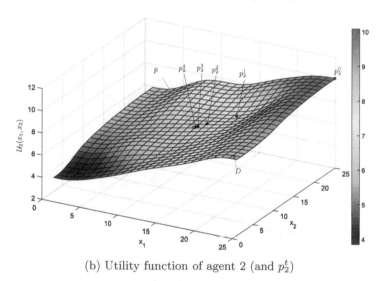

(b) Utility function of agent 2 (and p_2^t)

Fig. 3. Point-based negotiation with $m = 2$ and $n = 2$.

of values for the m variables that give agent i an utility that is at least Γ_i^t. The set-based protocol is an instance of the general monotonic concession protocol illustrated above in which the proposals are:

$$p_i^t = \mathcal{P}_i(\Gamma_i^t)$$

namely agent i, at each step t of the negotiation, proposes the set of *all* the combinations of values for the m variables that it can accept (in our application, a proposal is the set of release policies that agent i can adopt for the next block).

The strategy function of agent i is based on updating the acceptability threshold Γ_i^t in order to concede, namely in order to have $\Gamma_i^{t+1} < \Gamma_i^t$. A possible update rule is:

$$\Gamma_i^{t+1} = \Gamma_i^t - c_i \tag{5}$$

where $c_i > 0$ is called *concession step*. For values of c_i close to 0, agent i is rigid in conceding, while, for larger values of c_i, agent i is more cooperative and willing to concede.

The agreement function $\mathcal{A}(\{p_1^t, p_2^t, \ldots, p_n^t\})$ used by the mediator is:

$$a^t.\text{values} = \bigcap_{i=1}^n p_i^t = \bigcap_{i=1}^n \mathcal{P}_i(\Gamma_i^t) = \mathcal{A}^t$$

If, at some step t, $\mathcal{A}^t \neq \emptyset$, then an agreement is found. Namely, at least a combination of values for the m variables that is currently acceptable by all agents is found. In this case, the agreement a^t sent to the agents has $a^t.\text{status} = agreement\_found$ and $a^t.\text{values} = $ an element of $\mathcal{A}^t$.

Figure 4 shows an example of a negotiation with the set-based protocol between two agents on a single variable. The graphs show the evolution of the acceptability thresholds and the corresponding evolution of the proposals of the agents, represented as intervals. The black interval at the bottom is the non-empty set $\mathcal{A}^{t=4}$.

Considering the strategy functions of the agents, it is easy to show the following property.

Proposition 2. *Given a set-based negotiation, an agent i, and two steps t and t' such that $t' > t$, then $\Gamma_i^{t'} < \Gamma_i^t$ and $\mathcal{P}_i(\Gamma_i^{t'}) \supseteq \mathcal{P}_i(\Gamma_i^t)$.*

The above property highlights the egocentric concessions made by agent i over steps. The rate at which the set $\mathcal{P}_i(\Gamma_i^t)$ grows depends on the concession step c_i. The convergence of a set-based negotiation defined as above to a final agreement is thus guaranteed, provided that I_i are limited for all agents i and $\mathcal{I}_a \neq \emptyset$ (as also stated in Proposition 1 of [6]). Note that the termination without an agreement can be detected by the mediator if we allow agents to communicate when their proposals $\mathcal{P}_i(\Gamma_i^t)$ are equal to I_i (i.e., when they cannot offer any more). If, at some step t, the mediator discovers that $\mathcal{A}^t = \emptyset$ and that, for at least two agents, $\mathcal{P}_i(\Gamma_i^t) = I_i$, then there is no solution and the negotiation ends with the conflict deal.

To investigate the Pareto optimality of the set-based protocol (which is not studied in [6]), it is convenient to consider first the case in which all c_i are infinitesimal positive quantities. Assuming no degenerate cases in which the utility functions have horizontal portions, at the first step t at which it is non-empty, $\mathcal{A}^t$ contains a single agreement that is Pareto optimal. Indeed, if an agreement dominating that in $\mathcal{A}^t$ existed, it would have been found in a previous step. In the general case of finite $c_i > 0$, we can guarantee that at least an agreement in $\mathcal{A}^t \neq \emptyset$ is Pareto optimal and state a related bound.

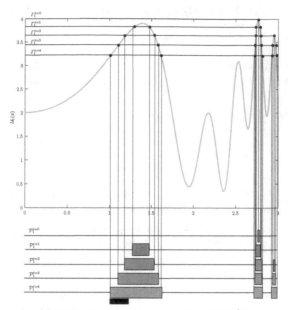

(a) Utility function of agent 1 (and $\mathcal{P}_1(\Gamma_1^t)$)

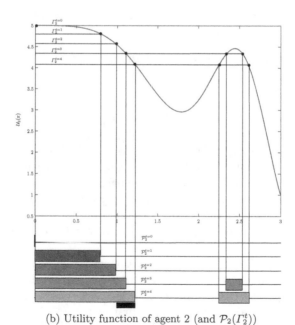

(b) Utility function of agent 2 (and $\mathcal{P}_2(\Gamma_2^t)$)

Fig. 4. Set-based negotiation with $m = 1$ and $n = 2$.

Proposition 3. *Given a set-based negotiation, if, at some step t, $A^t \neq \emptyset$, then A^t contains at least a Pareto optimal agreement.*

Proposition 4. *Given a set-based negotiation and the first step t at which $A^t \neq \emptyset$, call x^* a Pareto optimal agreement in A^t, then, considering any agreement $x \in A^t$, $|\mathcal{U}_i(x^*) - \mathcal{U}_i(x)| \leq c_i$, for all agents i.*

(Proofs are not reported, but are straightforward.) Thus, differently from the point-based protocol, the set-based protocol is always able to find a set of agreements A^t containing at least a Pareto optimal agreement, with the guarantee that any agreement in A^t differs from a Pareto optimal agreement for no more than c_i.

Given that A^t can contain multiple agreements, there is the problem to select one of them. We resort to selecting the Nash bargaining solution that maximizes the product of agents' utilities: $\bar{x} = \mathrm{argmax}_{x \in A^t} \left(\prod_i \mathcal{U}_i(x) \right)$. In this case, the selected agreement is guaranteed to be Pareto optimal [13].

The space complexity of the set-based protocol is $O(G^m)$ for an agent i, as in the case of the point-based protocol. For the mediator, instead, the space complexity now becomes $O(n \times G^m)$ since, in the worst case, it has to store the entire utility functions of all the agents. According to Proposition 2, the amount of memory the mediator requires to store the proposals of the agents is not decreasing over the negotiation steps. The temporal complexity for agent i is $O(Z_i + T \times G^m)$ and involves the initial optimization ($O(Z_i)$) and the determination of the new proposal, which is performed in $O(G^m)$ with a naive algorithm. The duration T of the negotiation depends on the concession steps c_i. The time complexity for the mediator is related to finding common elements in the proposals p_i^t, namely $O(n \times G^2)$ (using a naive algorithm). Thus, the set-based protocol has higher space and time (worst case) complexity than the point-based protocol.

5   Simulations

We have implemented the two protocols described in the previous section in MATLAB. Values for q_τ generated as illustrated in Sect. 3 are called the basic inflow data.

For the negotiation relative to block B_{j+1}, the cost function $\mathcal{J}_{B_j}^i(x_1, x_2, x_3)$ of each agent $i \in \{city, irr\}$ is calculated (see CalculateMyUtilityFunction() of Algorithm 1) by considering all the combinations of values of x_1, x_2, and x_3 (whose domains and discretization steps are reported in Table 1) and, for each combination, by evaluating (1) and (2) over block B_j. This approach is appropriate with our stochastically generated data because they are stationary. (Removing the stationarity assumption, in principle, there could be a different operating policy (with a different shape) per each day, dramatically increasing the number of variables over which the agents negotiate, but without changing the nature of the negotiation problem.) If real inflow data are considered, then periodic patterns (like seasons) should be taken into account too. For example, if

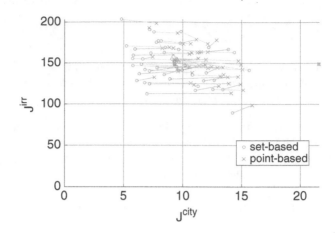

Fig. 5. Actual costs incurred by the agents. (Color figure online)

blocks correspond to seasons and block B_{j+1} spans over summer days, functions $\mathcal{J}^i_{B_{j+1}}$ for block B_{j+1} should be calculated considering last summer block B_{j-3} and not B_j.

Table 1. Domains, discretization steps, and initial values for the three variables.

	x_1	x_2	x_3
Domain	$[0, \pi/4]$	$[0, 100]$	$[0, \pi/2]$
Discretization steps	0.05	5	0.07
Initial value	0.6	5	0.6

Experiments confirm that a Pareto optimal agreement is not reached in many cases when using the point-based protocol. This does not happen when using the set-based protocol, in accordance with the theoretical analysis of the previous section. Figure 5 shows the *actual* costs (1) and (2), incurred by the two agents for the policies corresponding to the agreements found over all the blocks with the point-based (green) and the set-based (orange) protocols. Agreements relative to the same block are connected with a line segment that is orange if the policy found by the set-based protocol dominates that found by the point-based protocol, green if the opposite happens, and grey if the two policies are not dominated. Beyond the theoretical result for which the policies for block B_{j+1} found by the set-based protocol are Pareto optimal when applied to block B_j (remember that cost functions $\mathcal{J}^i_{B_{j+1}}$ are calculated on B_j), the figure shows also that these policies almost always dominate those found by the point-based protocol when actually applied to (unseen data of) block B_{j+1}.

Given its ability to find Pareto optimal agreements, in the following we focus only on the set-based protocol. In particular, we use it for investigating how the

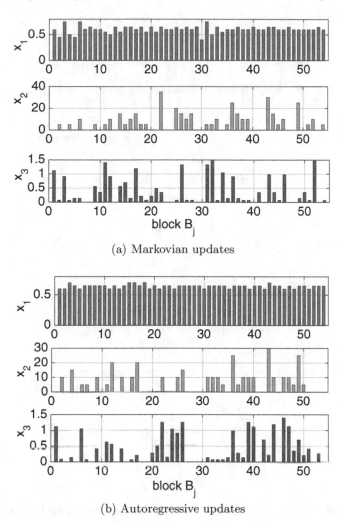

(a) Markovian updates

(b) Autoregressive updates

Fig. 6. Values of the variables at the final agreements reached by the set-based negotiation.

results of the negotiation, and the corresponding release policy, can be altered in response to dynamic changes in asset thresholds [18]. It has been observed that, after having experienced a flood, a regulator tends to favor the city agent over the irr agent and that, after a shortage of water for irrigation, the regulator tends to do the opposite. This behavior can be naturally captured in our model by considering the values of concession steps c_{city} and c_{irr} connected to the previous performance of city and irr agents, respectively (namely by looking at the history for deciding the degree of concession). We calculate the concession step as: $c_i = \alpha_i \cdot \mathbf{P}_{\text{base}}^i$, where $\alpha_i \in (0, 1]$ is the concession coefficient of (3) and $\mathbf{P}_{\text{base}}^i$ is:

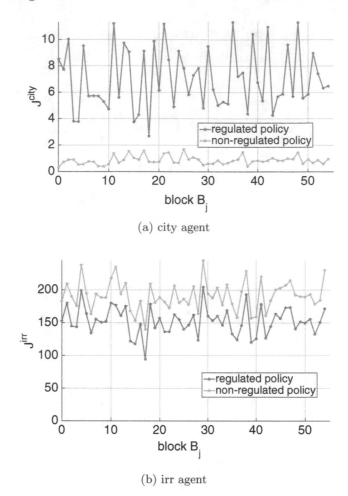

(a) city agent

(b) irr agent

Fig. 7. Actual costs of the agents with set-based negotiation for the basic inflow.

$$\mathbf{P}_{\text{base}}^{i} = \frac{\max(\mathcal{J}_{B_j}^{i}) - \min(\mathcal{J}_{B_j}^{i})}{C}$$

where C is fixed and represents the maximum number of updates (5) (consequently, C influences the maximum number of proposals and the maximum number of steps of the negotiation). $\mathbf{P}_{\text{base}}^{i}$ normalizes the concessions to the ranges of the cost functions of the agents, which are in general different. We call *satisfaction* of agent i in block B_j the value:

$$\gamma_{B_j}^{i} = \begin{cases} \dfrac{\mathcal{J}_{rif}^{i} - \mathcal{J}_{B_j}^{i}{}^{*}}{\mathcal{J}_{rif}^{i} - \min(\mathcal{J}_{B_j}^{i})} & \text{if } \mathcal{J}_{B_j}^{i}{}^{*} < \mathcal{J}_{rif}^{i} \\ 0 & \text{otherwise} \end{cases}$$

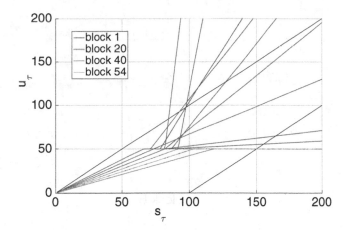

Fig. 8. Release policies obtained by the set-based negotiation for a decreasing average inflow. (Color figure online)

that measures how far is the cost $\mathcal{J}_{B_j}^{i}{}^{*}$ actually experienced by agent i in block B_j (using the negotiated policy) from the worst cost $\mathcal{J}_{rif}^{i}$ experienced by agent i over blocks $B_0, B_1, \ldots, B_j$. This difference is normalized over the best possible cost $\min(\mathcal{J}_{B_j}^{i})$ obtainable with the optimal policy on block B_j (that corresponds to the first proposal of agent i in the negotiation for deciding the policy of block B_{j+1}). Values of $\gamma_{B_j}^{i}$ close to 0 mean that agent i is unsatisfied, while values close to 1 mean that agent i is satisfied.

To relate α_i to $\gamma_{B_j}^{i}$, we consider two approaches.

- **Markovian.** The value of α_i in negotiating the policy for block B_{j+1} depends only on the satisfaction of agent i in the last block: $\alpha^i = \gamma_{B_j}^{i} + \epsilon$ (the small positive quantity ϵ is added to avoid to have $\alpha_i = 0$, which can prevent convergence).
- **Autoregressive.** The value of α_i in negotiating the policy for block B_{j+1} depends on the satisfaction of agent i in the last z blocks:

$$\alpha^i = \frac{w_1\gamma_{B_j}^{i} + w_2\gamma_{B_{j-1}}^{i} + \cdots + w_z\gamma_{B_{j-(z-1)}}^{i}}{\sum_{k=1}^{z} w_k} + \epsilon$$

with $w_1 > w_2 > \ldots > w_z$. In our experiments, $z = 4$ and $w_1 = 1$, $w_2 = 0.6$, $w_3 = 0.4$, and $w_4 = 0.2$.

Figure 6 shows the values for x_1, x_2, and x_3, as resulting from the set-based negotiations with the basic inflow data, using the Markovian and the autoregressive updates. The autoregressive approach is more "stable" in assigning values, especially for x_1 and, partially, for x_3, leading to more "stable" release policies that are clearly preferred from an applicative point of view. For the above reason, in the following we consider only the autoregressive approach to calculate

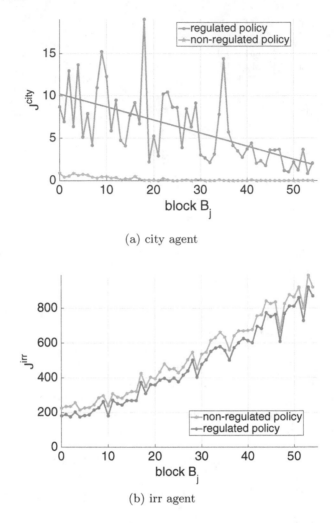

Fig. 9. Actual costs of the agents with set-based negotiation for a decreasing average inflow.

c_i. Figure 7 reports the cost functions of the city and irr agents compared with those relative to a non-regulated policy (in which the water is free to flow out of the lake, line $V_{\max}$ of Fig. 1). As expected, with respect to the non-regulated policy, costs are smaller for the irrigation district with an increase in the costs for the inhabitants of the city. This is the result of the trade-off between conflicting objectives reached via negotiation.

We now study how our model behaves under different inflow data streams. We consider the case of a decreasing average inflow data stream, which represents a frequent situation due to climate change. Values for q_τ are generated as in Sect. 3, but with $\mu_q = 40 - (\tau/250)$ m^3/day, where $\tau = 0$ is the first

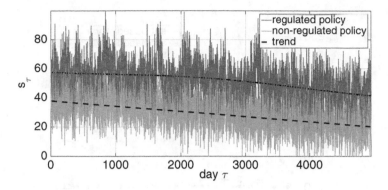

Fig. 10. Evolution of the volume of water stored in the lake s_τ with set-based negotiation for a decreasing average inflow.

day of the simulation. In this case, the regulator should prevent water shortages that become more and more severe as the simulation goes on. Figure 8 shows the release functions (policies) that are found by negotiation. It is evident how, after the first 10 blocks, the regulator tends to adopt protectionist policies and to limit the release (curves are moving down as they change from blue, corresponding to B_1, to green, corresponding to B_{54}) in the attempt to save the water resource. Figure 9 shows that the costs for the city agent decrease and, correspondingly, its satisfaction and concession coefficients increase, while for the irr agent the opposite trends are observed. However, the cost for the irr agent is less than that relative to the non-regulated policy. Figure 10 reports the evolution of the volume of water in the lake s_τ over the 5,000 days of the simulation with decreasing average inflow data, showing that the regulation policy provided by our negotiation better exploits the possibility of storing water in the reservoir to ensure availability to irrigation districts when compared to the non-regulated policy. Similar qualitatively sound results have been obtained also for increasing and sinusoidal average μ_q and for decreasing, increasing, and sinusoidal standard deviation σ_q of the inflow data (results are not reported here due to space constraints).

Finally, we present some results on the computing effort of the negotiation protocols. Figure 11 displays the time required by negotiations (including the initial optimization of cost functions) for different precisions (precision 3× corresponds to the discretization steps reported in Table 1 and, for example, precision 6× corresponds to the same discretization steps divided by 2). The number of variables m has a larger impact than the precision on the time complexity of the negotiations, confirming that the time complexity is related to $O(G^m)$ (see Sect. 4). As expected, the point-based protocol is less demanding than the set-based protocol.

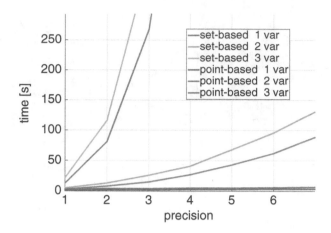

Fig. 11. Time required by negotiations.

6   Conclusions

In this paper, we have proposed to use a monotonic concession negotiation approach to model the interaction between agents representing different stakeholders of water resources systems. Differently from previous negotiation approaches to water resources systems operations, our mediator-based proposal does not require that agents know each other's preferences. We have defined two specific protocols as instances of the general negotiation framework, in which proposals are single policies and sets of policies, respectively. We have assessed the convergence and Pareto optimality properties of the two protocols and we have tested them experimentally with simulated realistic data and shown that they are able to capture some behaviors observed in the actual regulation of lake basins. In particular, the application of the set-based protocol to a real case study has been found to be promising.

Future work includes the application of our approach to real data relative to Lake Como. Moreover, compact ways to represent cost functions and to express proposals for the set-based protocol (for example inspired to those used in coalitional games [11]) could be investigated. Also other properties of the two protocols could be studied, like the distance between agreements and the initial proposals of the agents. More generally, use of agent-based approaches for water resources systems will be further explored.

References

1. Adams, G., Rausser, G., Simon, L.: Modelling multilateral negotiations: an application to California water policy. J. Econ. Behav. Organ. **30**(1), 97–111 (1996)
2. Altinbilek, D.: Development and management of the Euphrates-Tigris basin. Int. J. Water Resour. Dev. **20**(1), 15–33 (2004)

3. Amigoni, F., Castelletti, A., Giuliani, M.: Modeling the management of water resources systems using multi-objective DCOPs. In: Proceedings of the International Conference on Autonomous Agents and Multiagent Systems (AAMAS), pp. 821–829 (2015)
4. Amigoni, F., Gatti, N.: A formal framework for connective stability of highly decentralized cooperative negotiations. Auton. Agent. Multi-Agent Syst. **15**(3), 253–279 (2007)
5. Anghileri, D., Castelletti, A., Pianosi, F., Soncini-Sessa, R., Weber, E.: Optimizing watershed management by coordinated operation of storing facilities. J. Water Resour. Plann. Manage. **139**(5), 492–500 (2013)
6. Badica, C., Badica, A.: A set-based approach to negotiation with concessions. In: Proceedings of the Balkan Conference in Informatics (BCI), pp. 239–242 (2012)
7. Berglund, E.: Using agent-based modeling for water resources planning and management. J. Water Resour. Plann. Manage. **141**(11), 04015025 (2015)
8. Block, P., Strzepek, K.: Economic analysis of large-scale upstream river basin development on the Blue Nile in Ethiopia considering transient conditions, climate variability, and climate change. J. Water Resour. Plann. Manage. **136**(2), 156–166 (2010)
9. Castelletti, A., Galelli, S., Restelli, M., Soncini-Sessa, R.: Tree-based reinforcement learning for optimal water reservoir operation. Water Resour. Res. **46**(9), W09507 (2010)
10. Draper, A., Lund, J.: Optimal hedging and carryover storage value. J. Water Resour. Plann. Manage. **130**(1), 83–87 (2004)
11. Elkind, E., Rahwan, T., Jennings, N.: Computational coalition formation. In: Weiss, G. (ed.) Multiagent Systems, pp. 329–380. MIT Press, Cambridge (2013)
12. Endriss, U.: Monotonic concession protocols for multilateral negotiation. In: Proceedings of the International Conference on Autonomous Agents and Multiagent Systems (AAMAS), pp. 392–399 (2006)
13. Fatima, S., Rahwan, I.: Negotiation and bargaining. In: Weiss, G. (ed.) Multiagent Systems, pp. 143–176. MIT Press, Cambridge (2013)
14. Gatti, N., Amigoni, F.: An approximate Pareto optimal cooperative negotiation model for multiple continuous dependent issues. In: Proceedings of the IEEE/WIC/ACM International Conference on Intelligent Agent Technology, pp. 565–571 (2005)
15. Giuliani, M., Castelletti, A.: Assessing the value of cooperation and information exchange in large water resources systems by agent-based optimization. Water Resour. Res. **49**(7), 3912–3926 (2013)
16. Giuliani, M., Castelletti, A., Amigoni, F., Cai, X.: Multiagent systems and distributed constraint reasoning for regulatory mechanism design in water management. J. Water Resour. Plann. Manage. **141**(4), 04014068 (2015)
17. Hashimoto, T., Stedinger, J., Loucks, D.: Reliability, resiliency, and vulnerability criteria for water resource system performance evaluation. Water Resour. Res. **18**(1), 14–20 (1982)
18. Lybbert, T., Barrett, C.: Risk responses to dynamic asset thresholds. Appl. Econ. Perspect. Policy **29**(3), 412–418 (2007)
19. Marques, G., Tilmant, A.: The economic value of coordination in large-scale multireservoir systems: the Parana River case. Water Resour. Res. **49**(11), 7546–7557 (2013)
20. Pianosi, F., Castelletti, A., Restelli, M.: Tree-based fitted Q-iteration for multiobjective Markov decision processes in water resource management. J. Hydroinformatics **15**(2), 258–270 (2013)

21. Rausser, G., Simon, L.: A noncooperative model of collective decision making: a multilateral bargaining approach. Technical report, UC Berkeley, Department of Agricultural and Resource Economics (1992). http://escholarship.org/uc/item/1p. 67k0dp

22. Rosenschein, J., Zlotkin, G.: Rules of Encounter: Designing Conventions for Automated Negotiation among Computers. MIT Press, Cambridge (1994)

23. Soncini Sessa, R., Castelletti, A., Weber, E.: Integrated and Participatory Water Resources Management: Theory. Elsevier, Amsterdam (2007)

24. Thoyer, S., Morardet, S., Rio, P., Simon, L., Goodhue, R., Rausser, G.: A bargaining model to simulate negotiations between water users. J. Artif. Soc. Soc. Simul. **4**(2) (2001)

25. Tilmant, A., Beevers, L., Muyunda, B.: Restoring a flow regime through the coordinated operation of a multireservoir system: the case of the Zambezi River basin. Water Resour. Res. **46**(7), 1–11 (2010)

26. Wallace, J., Acreman, M., Sullivan, C.: The sharing of water between society and ecosystems: from conflict to catchment-based co-management. Philos. Trans. R. Soc. Lond. Ser. B Biol. Sci. **358**(1440), 2011–2026 (2003)

27. Yang, Y., Cai, X., Stipanovič, D.: A decentralized optimization algorithm for multi-agent system-based watershed management. Water Resour. Res. **45**(8), 1–18 (2009)

28. Zeitoun, M., Warner, J.: Hydro-hegemony - a framework for analysis of transboundary water conflicts. Water Policy **8**(5), 435–460 (2006)

To Big Wing, or Not to Big Wing, Now an Answer

Matthew Oldham[✉]

Computational Social Science Program,
Department of Computational and Data Sciences,
George Mason University, 4400 University Drive, Fairfax, VA 22030, USA
moldham@gmu.edu

Abstract. The Churchillian quote "Never, in the field of human conflict, was so much owed by so many to so few" [3], encapsulates perfectly the heroics of Royal Air Force (RAF) Fighter Command (FC) during the Battle of Britain. Despite the undoubted heroics, questions remain about how FC employed the 'so few'. In particular, the question as to whether FC should have employed the 'Big Wing' tactics, as per 12 Group, or implement the smaller wings as per 11 Group, remains a source of much debate. In this paper, I create an agent based model (ABM) simulation of the Battle of Britain, which provides valuable insight into the key components that influenced the loss rates of both sides. It provides mixed support for the tactics employed by 11 Group, as the model identified numerous variables that impacted the success or otherwise of the British.

1 Introduction

1.1 The Battle of Britain

The air war that raged over Britain between the 10th of July and 31st of October 1940 is colloquially known as the Battle of Britain. The battle's significance comes from the fact that not only did the Germans fail to achieve either of their objectives, but it is seen as the first major campaign to be fought entirely by air forces [2]. The initial phase of the battle revolved around the German's attempt to gain air superiority prior to their planned invasion of England – Operation Sea Lion. After September 6th, the Germans shifted to bombing civilian targets, a period that has become known as the 'Blitz', as they attempted to force Britain into surrender.

At the commencement of the battle, the RAF was at a numerical disadvantage having only 754 front line fighters spread across the entire country to combat the combined Luftwaffe force of 2,288 (1,029 fighters and 1,259 bombers) [2]. Despite this numerical disadvantage, the RAF managed to match or exceed the daily sortie rate of the Luftwaffe [5], achieved with some pilots flying up to four sorties a day. The cost of the battle was high for both sides, with FC losing over 1,000 aircraft and 544 of the approximate 3,000 aircrew that participated. Luftwaffe losses totaled nearly 1,900 aircraft and more than 2,600 of their airmen killed [2].

© Springer International Publishing AG 2016
N. Osman and C. Sierra (Eds.): AAMAS 2016 Ws Best Papers, LNAI 10002, pp. 73–89, 2016.
DOI: 10.1007/978-3-319-46882-2_5

Prior to World War II (WWII) the RAF developed its fighter defense strategy in line with the principles of concentration [7], which stemmed from the Lanchester equation [6] of aimed fire. When it came time to defend Britain, there were two implementations of the FC doctrine. Air Vice Marshall Keith Park, who controlled 11 Group, the Group which bore the brunt of the action in the Battle of Britain, tended to send single or pairs of squadrons (12 aircraft per squadron) to intercept the enemy. This allowed Park to confront the enemy while denying the Luftwaffe a major engagement. Air Vice Marshall Leigh-Mallory who controlled 12 Group, which was typically held in reserve, preferred to form a 'Big Wing' of 5 or more squadrons before engaging [7]. The main issue with this tactic was the time it took to arrange the 'Big Wing', which in turn limited the time the wing had to search for the enemy, and ultimately engage it. Another negative of the tactic for the RAF was that a larger formation was what the Luftwaffe was seeking, as it improved its chances of inflicting greater losses [5].

1.2 The Lanchester Model

The advent of air warfare during the First World War (WWI) necessitated a rethink of existing military doctrine. One such attempt was provided in [6], where Lanchester developed a mathematical model addressing the implications of various combat scenarios, including directed fire. Equation 1 illustrates the general form of the model, where a force's loss rate $\left(\frac{dB}{dt} \ or \ \frac{dG}{dt}\right)$ is dependent on $g(b)$, the kill rate/effectiveness of the opposition, the strengthen of the opposition as given by $G(B)$, raised to a particular power $g1(b2)$, and the strengthen of your force $B(G)$, raised to a particular power $b1(g2)$[1].

$$\frac{dB}{dt} = -gG^{g1}B^{b1}, \qquad \frac{dG}{dt} = -bB^{b2}G^{g2}. \qquad (1)$$

One particular form of the model is the aimed fire model, where $g1 = b2 = 1$ and $b1 = g2 = 0$. These values allow Eq. 1 to be simplified and after setting the conditions by which both forces suffer the same proportional losses $\left(\frac{dB}{dt}\right)/B = \left(\frac{dG}{dt}\right)/G$, the following equation is derived:

$$gG^2 = bB^2. \qquad (2)$$

The importance of Eq. 2 is that when forces are using aimed fire; their fighting strength becomes proportional to a weapon's effectiveness multiplied by the square of the number of weapons employed. The implication being, the concentration of force becomes a vital consideration in military strategy [5].

An analysis of the Battle of Britain utilizing the Lanchester model was undertaken by [5] in an attempt to understand whether the 'Big Wing' approach was the correct approach. The conclusion of [5] was that the model was right about British losses, a large German force meant greater losses, but not about German losses. Therefore, the 'Big Wing' appeared to fail as massed battles weakly favored the Germans [5].

---

[1] [5] make the point that the $g1$, $b1$, $g2$ and $b2$ have no justification and are used solely to facilitate modeling.

1.3 Agent Based Models

The evidence provided by [5] in support of the strategy employed by Park and 11 Group came from fitting the actual daily data from the Battle of Britain to the Lanchester model via regression analysis. While this provided insight in terms of the relevance of the Lanchester model, the results do not provide insight into the dynamics that produced the result. In particular, there is no insight into how Park achieved the 'defender's advantage'. A source of this problem, as [5] points out, is that "the Lanchester models are spatially and temporally homogenous, allowing for no variation in unit type, terrain or tactics, command or control, skill or doctrine". These assumptions appear inconsistent with modern warfare, which is ultimately dynamic and heterogeneous.

The approach utilized by [5] saw the force size estimated by the number of sorties flown by each side on a particular day. [5] indicates that ideally the data would be per raid. However, this was not possible due to the lack of records[2]. While the data shows the proportional loss rate of both sides, importantly it does not convene the loss rate per battle contact, as many sorties did not engage the enemy for a variety of reasons. Therefore, the true performance of the RAF against the Luftwaffe is lost.

An alternate approach is to implement an ABM that is capable of creating a virtual Battle of Britain. The model can be designed to explore the various tactics, and in particular whether the tactics of Park were indeed more effective than those of Leigh-Mallory. Agent-based models (ABMs) allow for the interaction of individual agents (aircraft/pilots in the proposed model), who undertake actions based on the context of their environment using basic rules. [4] successfully demonstrated the ability of an ABM to analyze air combat by creating a model of the Falklands War air battle. The model produced results consistent with what was observed in the conflict and tested various scenarios by varying the capabilities of both the U.K. and Argentinean forces.

For this paper certain abstractions were made to ensure that the research questions could be addressed in a timely manner. To achieve this, agents perform simplified actions that are supportable by fact or theory. The justification for the abstractions is that the aim of the model was to better understand the consequences of changing the number of squadrons per wing while removing noise from other factors. While this approach may not be fully authentic, it is more realistic than the Lanchester model and further iterations of the model can enhance the level of authenticity.

The level of abstraction means the model is not a one for one simulation, with a tick accounting for approximately 30 s. Determining the actions of each plane within a 30 s window is all but impossible, hence the simplifications and assumptions. Other abstractions include the weather having no impact, there

---

[2] While [5] were able to provide supporting evidence that binning data by day rather than raid did not invalidate the approach, this author feels an alternative approach is warranted.

being a 100 % chance of the RAF making contact with an incoming raid[3], and the dogfight algorithm being simplified with concepts such as the role of a wingman removed.

The level of abstraction and available data did present a problem in terms of calibrating the model. Using the data from [5], the Luftwaffe and RAF losses and the number of sorties for each day are known. However, the actual loss rates per combat interactions are not known, which is what the model is actually simulating. An alternate approach was to review the diaries of the individual RAF squadrons. However, these tended to overstate the success rate of the pilots.

2   Model Design

2.1   RAF Forces

The objective of the implemented model was to have two forces; the RAF and the Luftwaffe, engage in an aerial battle over the English Channel, with the RAF fighters defending and trying to disrupt the incoming Luftwaffe attack. The various variables and agents associated with the RAF are summarized in Table 1. To allow altitude to be a consideration, the model was implemented in the 3D version of Netlogo [11].

2.2   German Forces

Table 2 summarizes the variables and agents associated with the Luftwaffe.

2.3   Model Functionality

The model's objective, and therefore its functionality, is centered around being able to answer the question of how the RAF could best arrange their forces to maximize the damage to the Luftwaffe, while minimizing their own damage. Therefore, at a high level the model must account for a defending force finding and then engaging the enemy, plus an offensive force that moves towards their assigned targets, that also has the ability to defend itself. In addition, the output of the model needs to provide key insights into the dynamics involved in producing the results in a more meaningful manner than the Lanchester model.

The RAF fighters' role was to intercept the incoming Luftwaffe wave(s) and destroy as many aircraft as possible, while avoiding being shot down, before returning to base. Figure 1 provides a flow chart of how the behavior of the RAF fighters was designed to meet this requirement along with other considerations of air combat.

---

[3] In reality, this was not the case, as some RAF sorties were patrols that did not make contact with the enemy or were scrambled to meet a raid but failed to make contact. However, given the intent was to analyze actual combat performance the decision was made to ensure contact was made between the two forces.

Table 1. RAF variables and agents.

Variable	Purpose
Variables	
`number_of_wings` (wings)	The user selects the number of wings, between 1 and 5, that the FC scrambles. Each wing is assigned to a rally point and then has the fighters of a squadron(s) deployed to it. As per RAF standards, a squadron consists of 12 aircraft.
`squadrons_per_` wing (sPW)	The user decides how many squadrons are assigned to each wing, as determined above. The option is again between 1 and 5. Therefore, the user can test Leigh-Mallory's single 'Big Wing' (5 squadrons per wing, which means scrambling 60 fighters) compared to Park's smaller multiple wings (1–2 squadrons per wing or 12–24 fighters per wing).
`number_of_home_` bases	The user sets the number of home bases that the FC forces are spread across. This allows the model to test for the implications of forming a large wing with fighters from multiple bases. This was a key consideration of the 'Big Wing' approach [10]. In the actual battle, 11 Group had 27 squadrons who had access to 25 airfields, while 12 Group had 15 squadrons spread across 12 bases [2].
Agents	
Rally points	When initializing the RAF force, rally points are created first being spread evenly across the y axis (longitude) while having the same x (latitude) and z coordinates (altitude). These settings are independent from the coordinates of the incoming raid. As part of their initialization, RAF fighters are "hatched" by their rally point and allocated to a home base. Fighters form up at their rally point coordinates via the scramble routine. Rally points act as radar stations and direct their aircraft towards the enemy via the search routine, which covers 40 patches in a 360-degree arc.
Home bases	Home bases are spread evenly across the y axis within the British mainland. RAF fighters are assigned to a home base(s) nearest to their rally point. All fighters start a simulation at their home base.
Hurricanes	The RAF has two classes of fighters. Hurricanes attack incoming bombers while Spitfires attack enemy fighters. This is consistent with the tactics of 11 Group [5]. Two key variables the fighters own are **status** and **evading?** The combination of these two determines the actions of a fighter. **evading?** has the value of **true** or **false**, while status can take the following values: **scramble, formation, engaged, searching, homebound** or **shot down**.
Spitfires	Spitfires pursue enemy fighters. Note in this version of the model the different performance characteristics of the two fighters was not included

Table 2. Luftwaffe variables and agents.

Variable	Purpose
Variables	
ratio_to_RAF (r2RAF)	The size of the Luftwaffe force is set as a ratio to the RAF force that has been scrambled to meet the incoming raid. In reality, the reverse would be true, but it ultimately makes no difference to the model. The ratio varied greatly throughout the battle as both sides altered tactics [1].
ration_fighters_bombers (rationGFGB)	The composition of a raid can be varied by the ratio of enemy fighters to enemy bombers. During the battle this ratio ranged from 3 fighters per bomber up to 5 [1].
number_of_waves (waves)	Sets the number of waves that the Luftwaffe is sending during a particular raid. [2] provides support for this value ranging between 1 and 3.
number_of_targets (targets)	This sets the number of targets that the Luftwaffe pursue. The combination of targets and waves influences how compact or otherwise the raid is.
Agents	
Targets	Targets are initialized with randomly created x and y coordinates within Britain. The coordinates are then assigned to the Luftwaffe force who track towards their allocated target.
Waves	The initial class created for the Luftwaffe is a wave. Based on waves, their coordinates are set evenly along the y axis. Next aircraft are created for each of the waves. The number per wave is based firstly on the ratio of the Luftwaffe forces to the RAF (r2RAF), and then the number of waves. The aircraft's x and y coordinates are spread out in a formation around their wave's coordinates, while the fighters have a higher altitude (z coordinate) than the bombers.
Bombers	The bomber class has the role of tracking to their target and once they reach it, dropping their bombs before returning home. The number of bomb hits is recorded in an attempt to judge the success of a raid. Bombers are also capable of defending themselves against the fighters. Bombers do not own the **evading?** variable and have formation, homebound or **shotdown** as their possible **status** settings.
Fighters	The fighter's role is to defend the bombers. Each fighter has a tolerance variable and when the number of RAF fighters within a 3-patch radius exceeds their tolerance, they will break off and attack the RAF. The Luftwaffe fighters have the **evading?** variable. Their **status** includes **formation**, **engaged**, **shotdown** and **homebound**

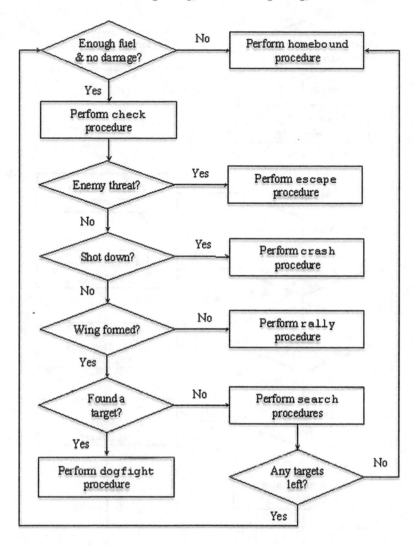

Fig. 1. Flow chart for the RAF fighters.

The Luftwaffe fighters' primary role was to escort and defend their bombers. As mentioned above, the fighters would remain in formation until the number of RAF fighters around them exceeded their tolerance, at which point they would break off and attack the RAF. The Luftwaffe bombers' key objective was to find their target, drop their bombs and then return home. An abbreviated illustration of how the Luftwaffe fighters' operated is provided in Fig. 2.[4]

The behavior of the agents is controlled by a combination of their **status** and **evading?** Variables. With the two forces having different objectives and

---

[4] Given the simplicity of the bombers role, it was felt a flow chart was unnecessary.

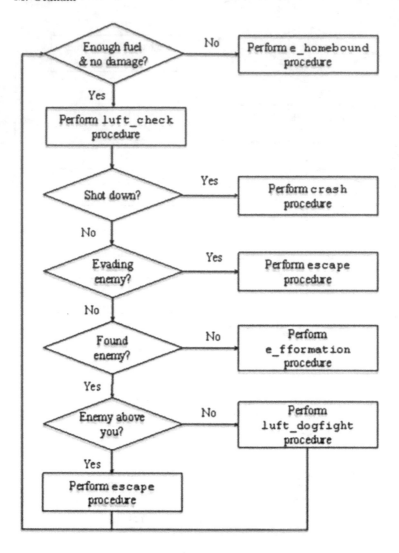

Fig. 2. Flow chart for the Luftwaffe fighters.

procedures they require different set of statuses. The RAF fighters maintain more possibilities because they are required to scramble, form their wing, find the enemy and engage. In contrast, the Luftwaffe fighters are already airborne and only need to find the enemy, before engaging. The requirements for the bombers are simpler again; as they head towards their target and defend themselves when attacked but do not change course. The agent sets do have some similar statuses, such as; shotdown and homebound. They also have some similar procedures, such as; checking whether they are being attacked and whether they have enough fuel to return home.

A high level flow of the model and therefore a description of Figs. 1 and 2 is;

- Both sides are initialized as per the user settings (see Sects. 2.2 and 2.3),
- At each step each plane will check their fuel and damage. Their **status** is updated to **homebound** and they will head home if their fuel levels are just sufficient to get them home or their damage level is over 0.5. The model reduces the fuel for the agents by 1 unit at each tick. The agents also check that their status is not **shotdown**. If they are shot down they perform the **crash** procedure,
- At each tick fighters also check they do not have an enemy plane on their tail via their **check** procedure. If they do, the **evading?** variable is set to **true** and their opponent is set to 'nobody'. If a plane is required to evade it will implement one of 5 strategies to move away from their threat. A plane cannot attack while they are evading the enemy. This procedure is consistent with the standard air battle tactic of breaking off an attack if you are in immediate danger of being shot down,
- Through the **rally** procedure the RAF scrambles their forces with the fighters climbing towards their assigned wing's rally point. All fighters have the **status** of **scramble** at this point and cannot engage the enemy,
- Once all the RAF fighters have reached their assigned rally point, the fighters have their **status** updated to **formation** and the wing is directed towards the incoming enemy wave(s) by their rally point and they are now able to attack. Rally points become aware of the exact coordinates of the incoming wave via their **search** routine which covers an area of 40 patches in a 360-degree arc,
- Once the rally point confirms the raid, through its **search** procedure, it will assign an enemy opponent to each of their fighters. The **status** of the fighters is updated to **engaged**.
- Meanwhile the Luftwaffe fighters have the **status formation**. At this point their **e_fformation** procedure has them moving towards the allocated targets of their bombers, while also being on the "look out" for the RAF. If they spot the RAF and the number of RAF fighters within a 3-patch radius is greater than their tolerance, their **status** is updated to **engaged**. However, if the RAF is above them they will take evasive action, through the **escape** procedure, before pressing an attack on the enemy. This is true of all offensive actions for both fighter forces and is an example of how the model utilizes basic air combat procedure,
- Once a fighter's **status** is updated to **engaged** their **dogfight** procedure is called with the sequence of an attack being; the attacking plane will set their heading and pitch to intercept their assigned opponent. This will either be a head on attack or the fighter will chase down their opponent from behind. When the attacker is close enough, within a 1 patch radius and within a 10-degree cone of sight, they will fire upon their opponent. The damage inflicted upon the opponent in the attack is a random float up to the value of 0.9. If a plane sustains damage above their survival level (.9) their **status** is updated to **shotdown**. The amount of damage inflicted per attack was determined by calibrating the model such that a representative battle of 24 RAF aircraft

against 36 Luftwaffe aircraft recorded a similar loss ratio as an actual battle, which was around 5–10 %,
- After an attack, the attacking fighter's status is changed. The RAF fighters are changed to **searching** while the Luftwaffe fighters change to **formation**, a status that ensures that the Luftwaffe is searching for the RAF. There are some minor differences in the search routines for the two fighter forces. While the RAF fighters check themselves for enemy fighters within 4 patches, if they cannot find any, they ask their rally point whether they are tracking any enemy planes, remembering the rally point has a broader search arc. If the rally point is tracking enemy targets, then it provides the coordinates of an enemy aircraft to their fighter, otherwise the battle is considered over and the RAF returns home via the **homebound** procedure. This process is consistent with the RAF having the advantage of radar to assist in finding the enemy. In contrast, the Luftwaffe fighters are solely responsible for finding their own target and will return home after reaching the target, unless have sustained damaged or are running low on fuel,
- Enemy bombers continue towards their target with a number of fighters remaining in support. Bombers are able to protect themselves at each tick through their **defend** procedure. In this procedure a bomber selects any two fighters within a one-patch radius and fires upon them. To reflect the lower probability of hitting a fighter the damage inflicted is a random float up to .05, and
- When bombers reach their target they "unload" their bombs and return home. It should be noted that this step is simply a checkpoint with no consideration given to the amount of bombs that hit the target in this iteration of the model.

As detailed above, to achieve the objectives of the research question there was a certain amount of abstraction undertaken. However, while the actual movements of the aircraft might not match the exact characteristic of an air battle, the actions are supportable given the objectives of the agents and basic air battle tactics. There will always be the need for some abstraction in an ABM; otherwise you have you have moved beyond an ABM into an engineering model.

Verification of the model's behavior was undertaken by performing parameter sweeps on extreme values, with the results analyzed to ensure that the model was performing as per design. Extensive visual inspections were also undertaken, with the various agent classes color-coded based on status to ensure updating occurred as per the design.

3   Experiments

To understand the possible influences on the losses for both sides, a full factorial experiment (Experiment 1) combined with an analysis of variance (ANOVA) as outlined in [8] was undertaken. The design matrix, seen in Table 3, was used and generated 128 combinations, with each combination run 50 times in the simulation. From these settings the largest battle was 300 RAF fighters up against 1,200 Luftwaffe planes. While a battle like this did not occur, it highlights the benefits of creating a simulation capable of exploring the outcomes of such a battle. The mean of both the input and output variables from each combination was taken to form the values used in the ANOVA model. A principle component analysis (PCA) was undertaken on the data as well.

Table 3. Design matrix for the full factorial experiment.

Variable	Low setting	High setting
numbaer_of_waves	1	3
number_of_wings	1	5
squadrons_per_wing	1	5
ration_fighters_bombers	3	5
ratio_to_RAF	1	4
number_of_home_bases	2	4
number_of_targets	1	3

The settings in Table 3 are supported by the descriptions of various battles provided in [1,2,5]. In particular, the following points are relevant:

- The 'Big Wing' debate is all about determining whether 1 or 5 squadrons was the correct number of squadrons per wing. In addition, 11 Group had the flexibility of sending multiple wings, while 12 Group was restricted to 1. To maintain symmetry the range was set at 1 and 5, but it must be acknowledged that the RAF never deployed 5 wings of 5 squadrons,
- The size of the Luftwaffe force to the RAF varied throughout the course of the battle. Small raids, a ratio_to_RAF of 1, were used at the commencement of the battle before larger raids (a ratio of 4) were employed later in the battle,
- As mentioned previously the German's varied the ratio of fighters to bombers within the range of the experiment,
- The range of waves and targets is consistent with records of the battle, and
- Each RAF group had their planes spread across multiple bases, meaning that an intercepting wing was unlikely to be all from the same base; hence this variable ranges from 2 to 4. The author will concede that a combination of 1 squadron scrambling from 4 bases would not have occurred. However, the implications are minor, if any in this version of the model.

To assess the effectiveness of the 'Big Wing' approach, the results from 1 wing of 5 squadrons (1W5Ss) was compared against results from 5 wings of 1 squadron (5Ws1S) in Experiment 2. Each strategy was tested against an increasing German force ratio (r2RAF), with the ratio beginning at 1, moving to 4 in increments of 0.1. Fifty runs of the model were made at each ratio setting[5].

---

[5] The other settings used were 3 homebases, ratio_fighters_bombers 3, number_of_waves 2, number of targets 1 and ratio_spitfires_hurr 1.

This scenario may not be 100 % consistent with how 11 Group used their forces. However, to create a valid comparison, the author felt it was appropriate and necessary to ensure the British force size was consistent at 60 RAF fighters.

An ordinary least squares (OLS) model as per Eq. 3 was fitted to the output of Experiment 1 and 2. Equation 3 provides the model for the British loss rate[6]:

$$\log\left(-\frac{dB}{dt}\right) = \log g + g1 \log GermanForces + b1 \log BritishForces \qquad (3)$$

This approach is consistent with fitting the data to the aimed fire Lanchester model and replicates the analysis provided in [5]. An analysis of covariance (ANCOVA) was undertaken to establish whether a statistical difference existed between the resulting models from Experiment 2. All analysis was undertaken in R [9].

4   Results

Figure 3 presents the Biplot resulting from the PCA analysis. From the chart it can be seen that the first component (PC1), which had an explanatory power of 33 %, relates mostly to the size of the forces engaged in the battle (RAFSize and GermanSize). Both the number of wings deployed and the number of squadrons per wing make a contribution. The second component (PC2), which explained 16.3 % of the data, relates primarily to the ratio of the two force (r2RAF) contrasted against the number of German losses. This indicates that as the ratio of German planes to the British increased, their losses tended to decrease. This finding is inconsistent with what the Lanchester model prescribes. Further tests explore this finding.

Also from Fig. 3 it can be seen that there is a clear division between where the data for raids with a 1:1 ratio sits (bottom half) compared to a 4:1 ratio (top half). The implications being that the British needed to match the force size of the Germans because while it increased the overall size of the battle, their losses were relatively lower when their ratio was closer to the Germans.

Table 4 presents the results of applying Eq. 3 to the full experimental data set. It should be noted that despite using the logs of the variables, both models failed the test for normality with regards to their residuals; hence the results are not robust. The British model, which returned an R^2 of 96.3 %, is consistent with the Lanchester model in that the British losses scale positively with increasing force sizes from both sides, albeit at a rate less than one (the assumption of the aimed fire model). The results for the German losses are not consistent with the Lanchester model, with the model returning a negative coefficient for the impact of an increase German force. The interpretation of this result is that the German's benefited from safety in numbers – an increasing return to scale for safety. This result was most likely driven by the improved defensive performance of massed bombers and is consistent with the interpretation of the PCA analysis. The R^2 for the German model was 60.2 %.

---

[6] For Experiment 2 the British force was held constant, therefore the b1 term was dropped.

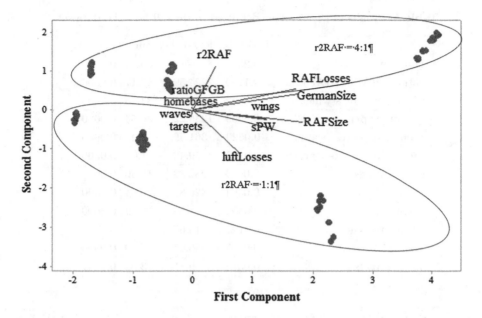

Fig. 3. Biplot resulting from the PCA analysis of the data from Experiment 1.

The results of the ANOVA and the subsequent OLS coefficients as per the approach of [8] are contained in Table 5. The dependent variable for the model was the British loss ratio (actual losses / the number of sorties), not the log of the actual losses, as per the previous model. The rationale for the change is that the ratio normalizes the outcome across the various settings, thus enabling the identification of the key drivers. The R^2 of the regression model was 98.1 %, with residuals meeting normality requirements.

From Table 5 it can be seen that there is significant interaction between r2RAF and the other variables, supporting the hypothesis that the FC needed to consider more than just force size in determining their strategies. This result

Table 4. The results of fitting an OLS model to the data from Experiment 1.

Side	Variable	Estimate	Std.Error	t value	Pr(> |t|)
British	(Intercept)	−2.2732	0.0584	−38.90	0.0000
losses	g1	0.8784	0.0502	17.49	0.0000
(Log)	b1	0.7854	0.0588	13.36	0.0000
German	(Intercept)	−0.0529	0.1158	−0.46	0.6488
losses	b2	1.5201	0.1165	13.04	0.0000
(Log)	g2	−0.8842	0.0995	−8.88	0.0000

Table 5. Results of the effect model fitted to the full factorial data set.

	Estimate	F-Value	t value	Pr(> |t|)
(Intercept)	0.2361	——	86.33	0.0000
ratio_to_RAF (r2RAF)	0.1290	2224.59	47.17	0.0000
number_of_wings(wings)	0.0945	1194.25	34.56	0.0000
squadrons_per_wing (sPW)	0.0999	1335.22	36.54	0.0000
number_of_waves (waves)	−0.0520	361.59	−19.02	0.0000
number_of_targets (targets)	−0.0192	49.48	−7.03	0.0000
r2RAF:wings	0.0459	282.33	16.80	0.0000
r2RAF:sPW	0.0564	425.88	20.64	0.0000
r2RAF:waves	−0.0352	165.83	−12.88	0.0000
r2RAF:targets	−0.0108	15.67	−3.96	0.0001
wings:sPW	0.0205	56.07	7.49	0.0000
waves:targets	0.0083	9.11	3.02	0.0031

is consistent with the influence of `r2RAF` in (PC2), as seen in Fig. 3. Other observations from Table 5 are:

1. Negative values for both `r2RAF:waves` and `r2RAF:targets` suggest that if an incoming raid is spread out, it benefited the British through a lower loss ratio;
2. Increasing the number of `wings` and `sPW` increased the British loss ratio as the Germans increased their force. This result provides mixed evidence in answering the 'Big Wing' debate. Experiment 2 provides greater insight on this point, and
3. The composition of the raiding party, the ratio of German fighters to bombers, the number of RAF home bases, were not significant factors.

Table 6 provides the results of fitting an OLS model explaining British losses as per Eq. 3 for the different strategies. The data was generated from Experiment 2 with the data illustrated in Fig. 4.

From Table 7 the results from the analysis of covariance (ANCOVA) and indicates that the interaction of the German force's size, and the number of

Table 6. Results of the effect model fitted to the full factorial data set.

Model	Variable	Estimate	Std.Error	t value	R^2
5Ws1S	(Intercept)	−0.6933	0.0622	−11.14	0.9682
	g1	0.8584	0.0289	29.69	
1W5Ss	(Intercept)	−1.0761	0.0616	−17.47	0.9777
	g1	1.0195	0.0286	35.64	

Table 7. Results of the ANCOVA testing for the significance of the two strategies.

	Estimate	F-Value	t value	Pr(> |t|)
(Intercept)	−1.0761	0.0619	−17.38	0.0000
g1	1.0195	0.0288	35.45	0.0000
Number of Wings (NW)	0.3828	0.0876	4.37	0.0001
LGF:NW	−0.1612	0.0407	−3.96	0.0002

wings (GF:Wing), is significant. This supports the hypothesis that the number of wings employed did indeed impact the loss rate of the British.

Figure 4 illustrates the results of Experiment 2 by showing the relationship between the British and German losses versus the size of the German force, remembering that the German force increased against a set number of British fighters (60). Consistent with the findings from Experiment 1, an increasing German force results in greater British losses but lower German losses.

The results of Experiment 2 suggest that the rate of British losses scales at greater than one on average when the 'Big Wing' (1W5Ss) is employed, and less than one for the smaller wings (5W1S). This finding in isolation is indeed

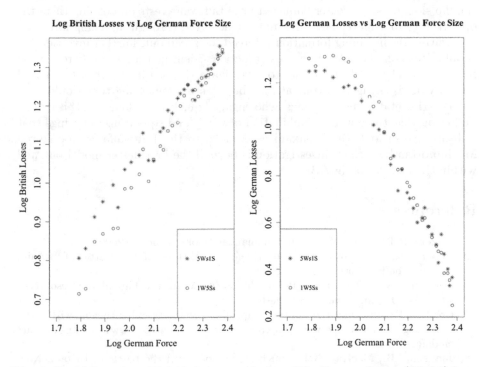

Fig. 4. (Left) Log plot of British Losses vs the log of the German forces. **(Right)** Log plot of German Losses vs the log of the German forces.

supportive of the strategy of Park. However, the smaller wing approach has a higher intercept value, with the interpretation being that the 'Big Wing' has a lower fixed cost yet higher variable cost of doing battle, while the smaller wing has the opposite. A similar analysis was undertaken on the German losses (Fig. 4) and there was no significant difference in the damage the British inflicted on the Germans by the two formations. The conclusion being that the British were limited in their ability to inflict greater losses on the Germans. Indeed, from the findings of Experiment 1, increased British successes were reliant on the German's waves spreading out.

Combining this inference with those from Experiment 1, it can be concluded that for the ranges that were tested for, the loss ratio of the British was higher under the smaller wing approach due to the average cost of the smaller wings being higher. Additionally, given there was no benefit from attacking in a smaller wing, it appears that when facing a German force equal to four times larger than the RAF force on average, the 'Big Wing' was the right approach.

5   Conclusion

The results obtained from the first known ABM of the Battle of Britain are supportive of the 'Big Wing', albeit only in terms of minimizing British losses. On the flip side, causing greater damage to the Luftwaffe rests on denying them the opportunity to achieve safety in numbers, achieved through matching force size or ensuring the incoming formation is forced to spread out. Further investigation should focus on the role of the cost functions identified for the different wing formations. The need also exists to investigate the possibility that the actual time a wing is engaged in combat may be a factor, something that would have been detrimental to smaller wings, who engaged quicker and longer in this model. Following this, the optimal combination of wings and squadrons per wings that reduces British losses and maximizes damage to the Luftwaffe can be solved for. Importantly, such an investigation is beyond the Lanchester model but well within the abilities of an ABM.

References

1. Bickers, R.T.: Battle of Britain. Salamander Books, London (2000)
2. Bungay, S.: The Most Dangerous Enemy: A History of the Battle of Britain. Aurum, London (2009)
3. Churchill, W.: The few (1940). http://www.winstonchurchill.org/resources/ speeches/1940-finest-hour/113-the-few
4. Gowlett, P.: Assessing the military impact of capability enhancement with Netlogo using the Falklands war as a case-study (2013). http://www.mssanz.org.au/ modsim2013
5. Johnson, I.R., MacKay, N.J.: Lanchester models and the battle of Britain. Nav. Res. Logistics 58(3), 210–222 (2011)
6. Lanchester, F.W.: Aircraft in Warfare: The Dawn of the Fourth Arm. Constable, London (1916)

7. MacKay, N., Price, C.: Safety in numbers: ideas of concentration in royal air force fighter defence from lanchester to the battle of britain. J. Hist. Assoc. **96**(323), 304–325 (2011)
8. NIST/SEMATECH: Nist/sematech e-handbook of statistical methods (2015). http://www.itl.nist.gov/div898/handbook/
9. R Core Team: R: A language and environment for statistical computing. R Foundation for Statistical Computing, Vienna (2015). http://www.R-project.org
10. Sarkar, D.: Bader's Duxford Fighters: The Big Wing Controversy. Ramrod Publications, St. Peter's, Worscester (1997)
11. Wilensky, U.: NetLogo (1999). http://ccl.northwestern.edu/netlogo/

How Testable Are BDI Agents?
An Analysis of Branch Coverage

Michael Winikoff[(✉)]

University of Otago, Dunedin, New Zealand
michael.winikoff@otago.ac.nz

Abstract. Before deploying a software system, it is important to assure that it will function correctly. Traditionally, this assurance is obtained by testing the system with a collection of test cases. However, since agent systems exhibit complex behaviour, it is not clear whether testing is even feasible. In this paper we extend our understanding of the feasibility of testing BDI agent programs by analysing their testability with respect to the *all edges* test adequacy criterion, and comparing with previous work that considered the *all paths* criterion. Our findings include that the number of tests required with respect to the all edges criterion is much lower than for the all paths criterion. We also compare BDI program testability with testability of (abstract) procedural programs.

1   Introduction

When any software system is deployed, it is important to have assurance that it will function as required. Traditionally, this assurance, encompassing both validation and verification[1], is obtained by testing, and there has been work on tools and techniques for testing agent-based systems (e.g. [9,11,14,15,24]). However, there is a general intuition that agents exhibit behaviour that is complex. More precisely, due to the need to handle dynamic and challenging environments, agents need to be able to achieve their objectives flexibly and robustly, which requires richer and more complex possible behaviours than traditional software. Therefore, a key question is *whether agent systems are harder, and possibly even infeasible, to assure by testing.*

Before proceeding further we need to define what we mean by a program being testable. Rather than define testability as a binary property, we define it as a numerical measure of the effort required to test a program[2]. Specifically, given a program and a *test adequacy criterion* [13], we consider the testability of

---

[1] More precisely: "software quality assurance (SQA) is a set of activities that define and assess the adequacy of software processes to provide evidence that establishes confidence that the software processes are appropriate and produce software products of suitable quality for their intended purposes." (ISO/IEC TR 19759:2015(E), page 10–5).

[2] We focus on system testing. See [20, Sect. 7] for a discussion of different forms of testing.

© Springer International Publishing AG 2016
N. Osman and C. Sierra (Eds.): AAMAS 2016 Ws Best Papers, LNAI 10002, pp. 90–106, 2016.
DOI: 10.1007/978-3-319-46882-2_6

a program to be the smallest number of tests that would be required to satisfy the criterion. For example, given the (very simple!) program "**if** c **then** s_1 **else** s_2", then we need two tests to cover all edges in the control-flow graph corresponding to this program, which satisfies the "all edges" test adequacy criterion (defined below).

The *all paths* and *all edges* test adequacy criteria are defined with respect to a control-flow graph. A given program P corresponds to a graph where nodes are statements (or, for agents, actions), and edges depict the flow of control: a node with multiple outgoing edges corresponds to a choice in the program. A single test corresponds to a path through the program's control-flow graph from its starting node to its final node (we assume that there is a unique start node S and a unique end node E, which can be easily ensured). The *all paths* criterion is satisfied iff the set of tests in the test suite T cover all *paths* in the control flow graph. The *all edges* criterion is satisfied iff the set of paths in the test suite T covers all *edges* in the control-flow graph [13]. The all edges criterion is also referred to as "branch coverage".

Given the importance of assurance, and the focus on testing as a means of obtaining assurance[3], there has been surprisingly little work that has considered whether testing agent systems is even feasible. In fact, the only work that we are aware of that considers this question is the recent work by myself & Cranefield[4] [20,21], which investigated the testability of Belief-Desire-Intention (BDI) agent programs with respect to the *all paths* test adequacy criterion. Winikoff & Cranefield concluded that BDI agent programs do indeed give rise to a very large number of possible paths (see left part of Table 1), and therefore they concluded that whole BDI programs are likely to be infeasible to assure via testing[5]. However, they do acknowledge that the all paths criterion is known to be overly conservative, i.e. it requires a very large number of tests. Specifically, all paths *subsumes* a wide range of other criteria, including all edges (e.g. see Fig. 7 of Zhu *et al.* [25] and Fig. 6.11 (page 480) of Mathur [13]). This means that the question of whether (whole) BDI agent programs can be feasibly tested is still open. This paper aims to address this question by considering testability with respect to the *all edges* [13] test adequacy criterion. The all edges criterion is regarded as "*the generally accepted minimum*" [12]. In essence, previous work [20] has provided an *upper* bound ("if we use a strong criterion, then it's this hard"). This paper provides a *lower* bound ("if we use a weaker criterion, than it's this hard").

---

[3] There is also a body of work on formal methods (primarily model checking) as a means of assurance [3,6–8,10,16,23]. However, despite considerable progress, these are not yet ready to handle realistic programs (e.g. see [8]).

[4] To avoid confusion between this paper and the earlier work, I will refer to my earlier work with Stephen Cranefield as "Winikoff & Cranefield" in the remainder of this paper.

[5] They also compared BDI programs with procedural programs, and found that BDI programs are *harder* to test than equivalently sized procedural programs, with respect to the all paths criterion.

The remainder of this paper is structured as follows. We (briefly) review BDI agent programs in Sect. 2. Section 3 is the core of the paper: it derives equations that compute for a given BDI program P the number of tests that are required to satisfy the all edges criterion. We then use these equations to compare testability (with respect to all edges) with testability with respect to all paths (Sect. 4). We also compare all edges testability for BDI programs with all edges testability for (abstract) procedural programs, in order to answer the question of whether BDI programs are *harder* to test than procedural programs with respect to the all edges criterion (Sect. 5). Finally, in Sect. 6 we conclude.

2   Belief-Desire-Intention (BDI) Agents

The Belief-Desire-Intention (BDI) model [4,5,18] is widely-used, and is realised in many agent-oriented programming languages (AOPLs) (e.g., [1,2]). It provides a human-inspired metaphor and mechanism for practical reasoning, in a way that is appropriate for achieving robust and flexible behaviour in dynamic environments.

A BDI agent program Π consists of a sequence of plans $\pi_1 \ldots \pi_n$ where each plan π_i consists of a triggering goal[6] g_i a context condition c_i and plan body b_i. The plan body is a sequence of steps $s_1^i \ldots s_{m_i}^i$ with each step being either an action or a sub-goal.

Due to space limitations, we give an informal summary of the semantics. Formal semantics can be easily defined following (e.g.) [17,19,22]. These semantics are common to the family of BDI programming languages (e.g. PRS, dMARS, JAM, AgentSpeak, JACK). A BDI program's execution begins with a goal g being posted. The first step is to determine the subset of *relevant* plans $\Pi_R \subseteq \Pi$ which is those plans π_i where the plan's trigger g_i can be unified with g. The second step is to determine the subset of *applicable* plans $\Pi_A \subseteq \Pi_R$ which is those plans π_i where the plan's context condition c_i holds with respect to the agent's current beliefs. The third step is to select one of the applicable plans $\pi_j \in \Pi_A$. The body b_j of the selected plan π_j is then executed. The execution is done step-by-step, interleaved with further processing of goals (and belief updates as information from the environment is received).

An important aspect of BDI execution is failure handling. A step in a plan body can fail. For an action, this can be because the action's preconditions do not hold, or due to the action simply not proceeding as planned (the environment is not always benign!). For a sub-goal, failure occurs when there is no applicable plan. When a plan step fails, the execution of the sequence of steps is terminated, and the plan is deemed to have failed.

A common way of dealing with the failure of a plan π_i which was triggered by goal g is to *repost* the goal g, and select another plan instance. More precisely, Π_A is re-computed (since the agent's beliefs might have changed in the interim),

---

[6] For the purposes of this paper we ignore other possible plan triggers provided by some AOPLs, such as the addition/removal of belief, and the removal of goals.

but with π_i excluded. A plan (instance) that has failed cannot be selected again when its triggering goal is reposted.

For the purposes of the analysis of this paper we consider a BDI agent program to be defined by the grammar below. This grammar simplifies from real BDI agent programs in a number of ways. Firstly, instead of a plan body having sub-goals g, with the relevant and applicable plan sets being derived from the plan library Π, we instead associate with each (sub-)goal g a set of plans[7] denoted $g^{\mathcal{P}}$ (where $\mathcal{P}$ is a set of plan instances). Because we have done this, we do not need to represent the plan library: a BDI program is simply a single (possibly quite complex) expression in the grammar below. Secondly, we follow CAN [22] in using an auxiliary "backup plan" construct to capture failure handling. Finally, we elide conditions: since the all edges criterion considers control-flow, we do not need to model the conditions that are used to decide which edge to take in the control flow graph.

We therefore define a BDI program P using the grammar:

$$P :: = a \mid g^{\{P^*\}} \mid P_1; P_2 \mid P_1 \triangleright P_2$$

where a is an action (and we use $a_1, a_2, a_3, \ldots$ to distinguish actions), $g^{\mathcal{P}}$ is a (sub-)goal with associated plans $\mathcal{P} = \{P_1, \ldots, P_n\}$ (a set of plans), $P_1; P_2$ is a sequence, and $P_1 \triangleright P_2$ represents a "backup plan": if P_1 succeeds, then nothing else is done (i.e. P_2 is ignored), but if P_1 fails, then P_2 is used. Any BDI program with given top-level goal can be mapped into a BDI program in this grammar. Note that this grammar does not capture some of the constraints of BDI programs (e.g. that a goal cannot directly post a sub-goal).

3   All-Edge Coverage Analysis

This section is the core of the paper. It derives equations that answer the question: "how many test cases (paths) are required to cover all edges in the control-flow graph corresponding to a given BDI program?".

Recall that a BDI agent program P can be either an action a, a sub-goal $g^{\mathcal{P}}$, a sequence (";"), or an alternative ("$\triangleright$"). We consider each of these cases in turn. For each case we consider how the construct is mapped to a control-flow graph, and then how many paths are required to cover all edges in the graph.

One important feature of BDI programs is that the execution of a BDI program (or subprogram) can either succeed or fail. A failed execution triggers failure handling. We represent this by mapping a program P to a graph (see right) where there

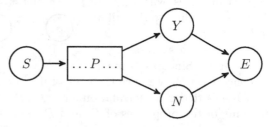

---

is a start node S, the program P is mapped to a graph that is reachable from S, and that has *two* outgoing edges: to Y (corresponding to a successful execution) and N (corresponding to a failed execution). There are edges from Y and N to the end node E.

Note that there is an important difference between the notion of a test for a conventional program and for an agent system. In a conventional program a test corresponds to the setting up of initial conditions, and then the program is started and runs. However, in an agent system (or, more generally a reactive system), the running system continues to interact with its environment, and so a test is not just the initial conditions, but also comprises the ongoing interactions of the system with its environment. One consequence of this is that conditions are controllable. If an agent system tests condition c at a certain point in time, and then tests that condition again later, then in general the environment might have changed c, and so we assume that all conditions can be controlled by the test environment. This means that, for instance, if we have a test (i.e. path) that involves two subsequent parts of the graph, G_1 and G_2, then the specific path taken through G_2 can be treated as being independently controllable from that taken through G_1.

We now seek to derive equations that calculate the smallest number of paths from S to E required such that all edges appear at least once in the set of paths.

In order to do this, it turns out that we need to also capture how many of these paths correspond to successful executions (go via Y) and how many go via N. Notation[8]: we define $\mathrm{p}(P)$ to be the number of paths required to cover all edges in the graph corresponding to program P. We also define $\mathrm{y}(P)$ (respectively $\mathrm{n}(P)$) to be the number of these paths that go via Y (respectively N). By construction we have that $\mathrm{p}(P) = \mathrm{y}(P) + \mathrm{n}(P)$.

Let us now consider each case in turn. The base case of a single action a is straightforward. In the graph above it corresponds to the sub-graph P being a single node a. To cover all edges in the graph we need two test cases: one path S-a-Y-E and one S-a-N-E. This reflects that an action a can either succeed or fail, and therefore requires two tests to cover these possibilities. Formally we have that $\mathrm{p}(a) = 2$, and that $\mathrm{y}(a) = \mathrm{n}(a) = 1$.

Next we consider $P_1; P_2$. Suppose that a sub-program P_1 requires $\mathrm{p}(P_1)$ tests (i.e. paths) to cover all edges, with $\mathrm{n}(P_1)$ of these tests leading to the failure of P_1, and the remaining $\mathrm{y}(P_1)$ tests leading to successful execution of P_1. Since P_1 is put in

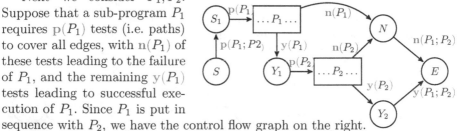

sequence with P_2, we have the control flow graph on the right.

We seek to derive an equation for $\mathrm{p}(P_1; P_2)$ (and for $\mathrm{y}(P_1; P_2)$ and $\mathrm{n}(P_1; P_2)$) in terms of the properties of P_1 and P_2. Let us firstly consider the case where $\mathrm{y}(P_1) \le \mathrm{p}(P_2)$. In this case if we have enough tests to cover the edges of the

---

[8] Colour is used to assist readability, but is not essential.

sub-graph corresponding to P_2, then these tests are also sufficient to cover all edges of P_1 that result in a successful execution of P_1 (which lead to P_2). So to cover all edges of P_1 we need to add in enough tests to cover those executions that are failed, i.e. $n(P_1)$. Therefore we have that:

$$p(P_1; P_2) = n(P_1) + p(P_2) \tag{1}$$

$$y(P_1; P_2) = y(P_2) \tag{2}$$

$$n(P_1; P_2) = n(P_1) + n(P_2) \tag{3}$$

We now consider the case where $y(P_1) \geq p(P_2)$. In this case if we have enough tests (i.e. paths) to cover the edges of the sub-graph corresponding to P_1, then these tests are also sufficient to cover all edges of P_2. We therefore have that $p(P_1; P_2) = p(P_1) = n(P_1) + y(P_1)$.

However, when considering $y(P_1; P_2)$ and $n(P_1; P_2)$ things become a little more complex. Since $y(P_1) > p(P_2)$, the edge from the sub-graph corresponding to P_1 that goes to the sub-graph corresponding to P_2 has more tests traversing it than are required to cover all edges of P_2. In effect, this leaves us with "excess" tests (paths), and we need to work out how many of these excess paths should be allocated to successful executions of P_2 (i.e. $y(P_2)$), and how many to $n(P_2)$.

Consider the following example. Suppose that $P_1; P_2$ is such that[9] P_1 requires 5 tests to cover all edges (four successful, and hence available to test P_2, and one unsuccessful), and where P_2 only requires 2 tests to cover all edges. In this situation there are two additional tests that are required to test P_1 and which proceed to continue executing P_2. These two extra tests could correspond to failed executions of P_2, to successful executions of P_2, or to one successful and one failed execution. This means that, if we annotate each edge with the number of times that it is traversed by the set of tests[10], then the edge from Y_1 to the P_2 sub-graph is traversed 4 times, since the edge from P_1 to Y_1 traversed 4 times. The edge from P_2 to Y_2 could have either a 1, 2, or 3, and similarly the edge from P_2 to N could have either 3, 2, or 1 (see Fig. 1 on the next page).

Returning to the analysis, in this case, where $y(P_1) > p(P_2)$, we define $\epsilon_1 + \epsilon_2 = y(P_1) - p(P_2)$. Then if we annotate each edge with the number of times that it is traversed by the tests, then the annotation on the edge from Y_1 to P_2 would be $p(P_2) + \epsilon_1 + \epsilon_2$. If we now consider the edges *from* the sub-graph corresponding to P_2, then the edge to N (the number of executions where P_2 failed) would be annotated with $n(P_2) + \epsilon_2$ and the edge to Y_2 would be annotated with $y(P_2) + \epsilon_1$. This gives us the following equations:

$$p(P_1; P_2) = n(P_1) + y(P_1) \tag{4}$$

---

[9] E.g. $P_1 = a_1 \triangleright a_2 \triangleright a_3 \triangleright a_4$ and $P_2 = a_5$.

[10] Note that for any internal node, the sum of annotations on incoming edges must equal the sum of annotations on outgoing edges, since all paths begin at S and terminate at E.

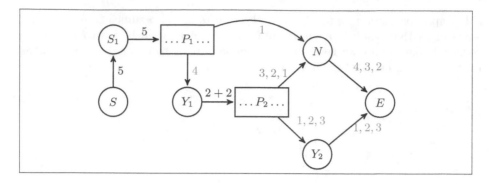

Fig. 1. Example for $P_1 = a_1 \triangleright a_2 \triangleright a_3 \triangleright a_4$ and $P_2 = a_5$.

$$y(P_1; P_2) = y(P_2) + \epsilon_1 \tag{5}$$

$$n(P_1; P_2) = n(P_1) + n(P_2) + \epsilon_2 \tag{6}$$
$$\text{where } \epsilon_1 + \epsilon_2 = y(P_1) - p(P_2)$$

Merging these cases with Eqs. 1, 2 and 3, we obtain the following. Derivation: for $y()$ and $n()$ observe that Eqs. 2 and 3 are in the case where $y(P_1) \leq p(P_2)$ and hence $\epsilon_1 = \epsilon_2 = 0$, reducing the equations below to Eqs. 2 and 3, and if $y(P_1) > p(P_2)$ then the equations below are identical to Eqs. 5 and 6. For $p(P_1; P_2)$ observe that if $y(P_1) \leq p(P_2)$ then the equation below reduces to Eq. 1, and that if $y(P_1) > p(P_2)$ then the equation below reduces to Eq. 4.

$$p(P_1; P_2) = n(P_1) + \max(y(P_1), p(P_2))$$
$$y(P_1; P_2) = y(P_2) + \epsilon_1$$
$$n(P_1; P_2) = n(P_1) + n(P_2) + \epsilon_2$$
$$\text{where } \epsilon_1 + \epsilon_2 = \max(0, y(P_1) - p(P_2))$$

Note that we don't have deterministic equations that compute $n(P_1; P_2)$ and $y(P_1; P_2)$. Instead, we have equations that permit a *range* of values, depending on how we choose to allocate the excess paths represented by $\epsilon_1 + \epsilon_2$ between the successful and unsuccessful executions of P_2.

Turning to $P_1 \triangleright P_2$ we perform a similar analysis. Note that the control glow graph for $P_1 \triangleright P_2$ has the same structure as that of $P_1; P_2$ except that N and Y are swapped (see Figure to the right). The simple case is when $n(P_1) \leq p(P_2)$, in which case the number of paths required to test (i.e. cover all edges of) P_2 also suffices to cover edges

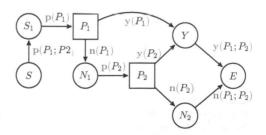

in P_1 when P_1 fails (for $P_1 \triangleright P_2$ it is when P_1 *fails* that P_2 is used). For this case

$$p(a) = 2 \quad y(a) = 1 \quad n(a) = 1$$
$$p(P_1; P_2) = n(P_1) + \max(y(P_1), p(P_2))$$
$$y(P_1; P_2) = y(P_2) + \epsilon_1$$
$$n(P_1; P_2) = n(P_1) + n(P_2) + \epsilon_2$$
$$\text{where } \epsilon_1 + \epsilon_2 = \max(0, y(P_1) - p(P_2))$$
$$p(P_1 \rhd P_2) = y(P_1) + \max(n(P_1), p(P_2))$$
$$y(P_1 \rhd P_2) = y(P_1) + y(P_2) + \epsilon_3$$
$$n(P_1 \rhd P_2) = n(P_2) + \epsilon_4$$
$$\text{where } \epsilon_3 + \epsilon_4 = \max(0, n(P_1) - p(P_2))$$
$$p(g^{\{P\}}) = \mathbf{1+}\, p(P) \quad y(g^{\{P\}}) = y(P) \quad n(g^{\{P\}}) = \mathbf{1+}\, n(P)$$
$$p(g^{\mathcal{P}}) = \mathbf{1+} \sum_{P_i \in \mathcal{P}} y(P_i) + \max(n(P_i), p(g^{\mathcal{P} \backslash \{P_i\}}))$$
$$y(g^{\mathcal{P}}) = \sum_{P_i \in \mathcal{P}} y(P_i) + y(g^{\mathcal{P} \backslash \{P_i\}}) + \epsilon_i$$
$$n(g^{\mathcal{P}}) = \mathbf{1+} \sum_{P_i \in \mathcal{P}} n(g^{\mathcal{P} \backslash \{P_i\}}) + \epsilon_i'$$
$$\text{where } \epsilon_i + \epsilon_i' = \max(0, n(P_i) - p(g^{\mathcal{P} \backslash \{P_i\}}))$$
$$p(\not{g}^{\mathcal{P}}) = \mathbf{1+} \sum_{P \in \mathcal{P}} p(P)$$
$$y(\not{g}^{\mathcal{P}}) = \sum_{P \in \mathcal{P}} y(P)$$
$$n(\not{g}^{\mathcal{P}}) = \mathbf{1+} \sum_{P \in \mathcal{P}} n(P)$$

Fig. 2. Equations to calculate $p(P)$, $y(P)$ and $n(P)$ when $\mathcal{P}$ is relevant plans. For applicable plans delete the grey shaded "$\mathbf{1+}$".

we therefore have $p(P_1 \rhd P_2) = y(P_1) + p(P_2)$ and $y(P_1 \rhd P_2) = y(P_1) + y(P_2)$ and $n(P_1 \rhd P_2) = n(P_2)$. Similar analysis for the more complex case gives the equations in Fig. 2.

Finally, we consider goals. We begin with the simple case: a goal with a single *relevant* plan $g^{\{P_1\}}$. In this case either the goal immediately fails (due to the plan's context condition failing), or the plan is executed. If the plan is executed, then the goal succeeds exactly when the plan succeeds. Therefore we have: $n(g^{\{P_1\}}) = 1 + n(P_1)$, and $y(g^{\{P_1\}}) = y(P_1)$, and $p(g^{\{P_1\}}) = 1 + p(P_1)$. In the case where P_1 is *applicable*, then the context condition cannot fail, and we simply have $n(g^{\{P_1\}}) = n(P_1)$ and $p(g^{\{P_1\}}) = p(P_1)$.

For a goal with two *relevant* plans $g^{\{P_1, P_2\}}$ (henceforth abbreviated g^2), there are three non-overlapping possibilities: the plan fails immediately (neither context condition is true), or the first plan is selected, or the second plan is selected. If a plan is selected, then the plan is executed with the other plan as a (possible) backup option. Informally we can describe this as

$$g^2 = \text{fail or } P_1 \rhd g^{P_2} \text{ or } P_2 \rhd g^{P_1}$$

(where g^P is short hand for $g^{\{P\}}$). Which leads to the following equations.

$$p(g^2) = 1 + p(P_1 \triangleright g^{P_2}) + p(P_2 \triangleright g^{P_1})$$
$$y(g^2) = y(P_1 \triangleright g^{P_2}) + y(P_2 \triangleright g^{P_1})$$
$$n(g^2) = 1 + n(P_1 \triangleright g^{P_2}) + n(P_2 \triangleright g^{P_1})$$

In the case where we are dealing with *applicable* plans, the only difference is that the "1+" in the equations for $p(g)$ and $n(g)$ is deleted, since the plan cannot fail. This can be generalised for a goal with k plans (details omitted) resulting in the equations in Fig. 2.

3.1   Removing Failure Handling

We now briefly consider what happens if we "turn off" failure handling, This is an interesting scenario to consider, because the all paths analysis of Winikoff & Cranefield [20] found that turning failure handling off reduced the number of tests required enormously. We use $\cancel{g}$ to denote a goal where failure handling is not used.

We firstly observe that without failure handling the equation for $\cancel{g}^{\{P\}}$ remains unchanged from $g^{\{P\}}$, since if the sole plan P fails, then there is no remaining plan available to recover.

However, for $\cancel{g}^{\{P_1,P_2\}}$ the equations are different. Instead of having (informally) $g^2 = $ fail or $P_1 \triangleright g^{P_2}$ or $P_2 \triangleright g^{P_1}$, we have simply $\cancel{g}^2 = $ fail or P_1 or P_2. Therefore the corresponding equations are simply: $p(\cancel{g}^2) = 1 + p(P_1) + p(P_2)$, and $y(\cancel{g}^2) = y(P_1) + y(P_2)$, and $n(\cancel{g}^2) = 1 + n(P_1) + n(P_2)$. These generalise for $\cancel{g}^P$ (where $\mathcal{P}$ denotes a set of plans), yielding the equations in Fig. 2. As before, for $\mathcal{P}$ being the *applicable* plans, remove the "$1 +$" from the equations.

3.2   Simplifying for Uniform Programs

In order to compare with the all paths analysis of Winikoff & Cranefield [20] we consider *uniform* BDI programs, as they did. A uniform BDI program is one where all plan bodies have j sub-goals, all goals have k plans, and the tree is uniformly deep.

Applying these assumptions allows the equations to be simplified, since all sub-goals of a plan (respectively plans of a goal) have identical structure, and are hence interchangeable.

For example, in the equation for $p(P_1; P_2)$, P_1 and P_2 are identical, so instead of $p(P_1; P_2) = n(P_1) + \max(y(P_1), p(P_2))$ we have $p(P; P) = n(P) + \max(y(P), p(P))$. Now, since $p(P) > y(P)$, we can replace $\max(y(P), p(P))$ with $p(P)$. Therefore, we have that $p(P; P) = n(P) + p(P)$. Since $p(P) = y(P) + n(P)$ this is just $n(P) + y(P) + n(P) = y(P) + 2n(P)$. This generalises to more than two sub-programs in sequence. Similar simplification can be applied to the other cases, yielding the equations shown in Fig. 3 (ignore the last four equations for the moment).

However, uniform programs (as used by the all paths analysis [20]) actually have a mixture of actions and goals in plans, i.e. a plan (that is not a leaf) is of the form $P = a; g; a; g; a$ (for $k = 2$), not $g; g$. This means we need to derive equations for this form.

We begin by deriving $p(a; g)$, $y(a; g)$ and $n(a; g)$, using the simplification that $\epsilon_1 = \epsilon_2 = 0$, since $y(P_1) = y(a) = 1$ and hence $p(P_2) \geq 1$ so $\max(0, y(P_1) - p(P_2)) = 0$.

$$
\begin{aligned}
p(a; g) &= n(a) + \max(y(a), p(g)) &= 1 + p(g) \quad (\text{since } p(g) > y(a) = 1) \\
y(a; g) &= y(g) \; (\text{since } p(g) > y(a) = 1) \\
n(a; g) &= 1 + n(g)
\end{aligned}
$$

We then define $p^1 = a; g; a$ and derive $p(p^1)$, $y(p^1)$ and $n(p^1)$. In deriving $y(p^1)$ and $n(p^1)$ we derive the upper and lower bounds (recall that the equations in Fig. 2 specify a range, depending on how we split "excess" $(y(P_1) - p(P_2))$ between ϵ_1 and ϵ_2). We work out the upper bound for $y(P_1)$ (respectively $n(P_1)$) by assigning all the excess to ϵ_1 (respectively ϵ_2). We derive equations under the assumption that $y(a; g) > 1$, and hence $y(a; g) \geq p(a) = 2$. This assumption holds when goals have more than one plan (i.e. $j > 1$), which is the case in Table 1.

$$
\begin{aligned}
p((a; g); a) &= n(a; g) + \max(y(a; g), p(a)) \\
&= n(a; g) + y(a; g) &= p(a; g) &= 1 + p(g) \\
y((a; g); a) &\leq y(a) + \max(0, y(a; g) - p(a)) \\
&= 1 + y(a; g) - 2 &= y(g) - 1 \\
y((a; g); a) &\geq y(a) &= 1 \\
n((a; g); a) &\leq n(a; g) + n(a) + \max(0, y(a; g) - p(a)) \\
&= (1 + n(g)) + 1 + (y(a; g) - 2) &= n(g) + y(g) &= p(g) \\
n((a; g); a) &\geq n(a; g) + n(a) &= (1 + n(g)) + 1 &= 2 + n(g)
\end{aligned}
$$

We then note that $p^2 = a; g; a; g; a$ can be defined as $p^2 = (a; g); p^1$, and, more generally, $p^{k+1} = (a; g); p^k$.

$$
\begin{aligned}
p(p^{k+1}) &= n(a; g) + \max(y(a; g), p(p^k)) \\
&= n(a; g) + p(p^k) \quad (\text{since } p(p^k) \geq y(a; g)) \\
&= 1 + n(g) + p(p^k) \\
&\text{which can be generalised to} \\
&= k \times (1 + n(g)) + 1 + p(g) \\
y(p^{k+1}) &\leq y(p^k) + \max(0, y(a; g) - p(p^k)) \\
&= y(p^k) \quad (\text{since } p(p^k) \geq y(a; g)) \\
&\text{so eventually we just get } y(p^1) \text{ which is } \ldots \\
&= y(g) - 1 \\
y(p^{k+1}) &\geq y(p^k) \quad \geq y(p^{k-1}) \quad \geq 1 \\
n(p^{k+1}) &= n(a; g) + n(p^k) + \max(0, y(a; g) - p(p^k))
\end{aligned}
$$

$$\begin{aligned}
&= && (1 + \mathrm{n}(g)) + \mathrm{n}(p^k) \text{ (since } \mathrm{p}(p^k) \geq \mathrm{y}(a;g)) \\
&= && k \times (1 + \mathrm{n}(g)) + \mathrm{n}(p^1)
\end{aligned}$$

The yields the last four equations of Fig. 3, which are required to calculate the testability of uniform BDI programs. Note that in the last equation, since $\mathrm{n}(p^1) \geq 2 + \mathrm{n}(g)$ and $\mathrm{n}(p^1) \leq \mathrm{p}(g)$, we also have a range for $\mathrm{n}(p^k)$.

4   All-Edges vs. All-Paths

In the previous section we derived equations that tell us how many tests (paths) are required to ensure adequate coverage of a BDI program with respect to the all *edges* criterion. We now use these equations to compare the all edges criterion against the all paths criterion. We know that the all paths criterion requires more tests to be satisfied, but how many more? Since comparing (complex) formulae is not easy, we follow the approach of Winikoff & Cranefield, and instantiate the formulae with a number of plausible values, to obtain actual numbers that can be compared. We use the same scenarios (i.e. parameters) that they used.

$$\mathrm{p}(P_1;\ldots;P_j) = \mathrm{y}(P) + j \times \mathrm{n}(P)$$
$$\mathrm{y}(P_1;\ldots;P_j) = \mathrm{y}(P)$$
$$\mathrm{n}(P_1;\ldots;P_j) = j \times \mathrm{n}(P)$$
$$\mathrm{p}(P_1 \triangleright \ldots \triangleright P_k) = \mathrm{n}(P) + k \times \mathrm{y}(P)$$
$$\mathrm{y}(P_1 \triangleright \ldots \triangleright P_k) = k \times \mathrm{y}(P)$$
$$\mathrm{n}(P_1 \triangleright \ldots \triangleright P_k) = \mathrm{n}(P)$$
$$\mathrm{p}(g^{\{P\}}) = 1 + \mathrm{p}(P)$$
$$\mathrm{y}(g^{\{P\}}) = \mathrm{y}(P)$$
$$\mathrm{n}(g^{\{P\}}) = 1 + \mathrm{n}(P)$$
$$\mathrm{p}(g^{P}) = 1 + |\mathcal{P}| \times (\mathrm{y}(P) + \mathrm{p}(g^{\mathcal{P}\setminus\{P_i\}}))$$
$$\mathrm{y}(g^{P}) = |\mathcal{P}| \times (\mathrm{y}(P) + \mathrm{y}(g^{\mathcal{P}\setminus\{P_i\}}))$$
$$\mathrm{n}(g^{P}) = 1 + |\mathcal{P}| \times \mathrm{n}(g^{\mathcal{P}\setminus\{P_i\}})$$
$$\mathrm{p}(\not g^{P}) = 1 + |\mathcal{P}| \times \mathrm{p}(P)$$
$$\mathrm{y}(\not g^{P}) = |\mathcal{P}| \times \mathrm{y}(P)$$
$$\mathrm{n}(\not g^{P}) = 1 + |\mathcal{P}| \times \mathrm{n}(P)$$
$$\mathrm{p}(p^{k+1}) = k \times (1 + \mathrm{n}(g)) + 1 + \mathrm{p}(g)$$
$$\mathrm{y}(p^{k+1}) \leq \mathrm{y}(g) - 1$$
$$\mathrm{y}(p^{k+1}) \geq 1$$
$$\mathrm{n}(p^{k+1}) = k \times (1 + \mathrm{n}(g)) + \mathrm{n}(p^1)$$

Fig. 3. Equations to calculate $\mathrm{p}(P)$, $\mathrm{y}(P)$ and $\mathrm{n}(P)$, simplified for uniform programs, where p^{k+1} denotes a program of the form $a; g; a; \ldots a; g; a$ with $k + 1$ goals ($k \geq 0$).

In order to derive the All Edges numbers in Table 1 the equations of Fig. 2 were implemented as a Prolog program that computed (non-deterministically) the values of $p(P)$, $y(P)$ and $n(P)$ for any given BDI program P. Additionally, code was written to generate a uniform BDI program P, given values for j, k, and d. This was used to generate the full uniform program P for the first three cases in Table 1, and then compute $p(P)$ for the generated BDI program. The last case exhausted Prolog's stack.

Additionally, the equations of Fig. 3 were implemented as a Scheme program that computed $p()$, $y()$, and $n()$ for given values of j, k, and d. These were used to calculate values of $p()$. These values matches those computed by the Prolog program for the first three cases, and provided the values for the fourth case ($d = 3$, $j = 3$, $k = 4$ for which Prolog ran out of stack space).

Table 1 contains the results for these illustrative comparison cases (ignore the rightmost column for now). The left part of the Table (Parameters, Number of goals, plans, and actions, and All Paths) are taken from the all paths analysis of Winikoff & Cranefield [20]. The right part (All Edges) is the new numbers from this work.

Comparing the results we make a number of observations. Firstly, as expected, the number of tests required to adequately test a given BDI program P with respect to the all edges test adequacy criterion is lower than the number of tests required with respect to the all paths criterion. However, what is interesting is that the numbers are very much lower (e.g. a few thousand compared with more than 2×10^{107}). Specifically, the number of tests required with respect to the all edges criterion is sufficiently small to be feasible. For instance, in the third case ($j = 2$, $k = 3$, $d = 4$) where the (uniform) BDI program has 259 goals and 518 plans, corresponding to a non-trivial agent program, the number of required test cases is less than 1600.

However, it is worth emphasising that the all edges criterion, even for traditional software, is regarded as a *minimum*. Additionally, it can be argued that agents, which are situated in an environment that is typically non-episodic, might be more likely than traditional software to be affected by the history of their interaction with the environment [20, Sect. 1.1], which means that the all paths criterion is more relevant (since a path includes history, and requiring all paths insists that different histories are covered when testing).

We now turn to consider the four cases under All Edges, i.e. the effects of disabling failure handling, and allowing goals to fail even when there are remaining plans. Whereas a key finding of Winikoff & Cranefield was that failure handling made an enormous difference, in our analysis we found the opposite. This does not reflect a disagreement with their analysis, but a difference in the characteristics of all paths vs. all edges. Adding failure handling has the effect of extending paths that would otherwise fail. This means that enabling failure handling increases the number of paths. However, for the all edges criterion, we do not need to cover all paths, only all edges, so the additional paths created by enabling failure handling do not require a commensurate increase in the number of tests required to cover all edges.

Table 1. Comparison of All Paths and All Edges analyses. The first number under "actions" (e.g. 62) is the number of actions in the tree, the second (e.g. 13) is the number of actions in a single execution where no failures occur. For All Edges there are four numbers: the first two are the (normal) case where failure handling is used to re-post a goal in the event that a plan fails. The next two are the case where failure handling is disabled, so if a plan fails, the parent goal fails as well. The columns labelled "relev." and "applic." are where the plans associated with a goal are respectively the *relevant* plans (so a goal can fail even though there are still untried plans), and the *applicable* plans.

Params			Number of ...			All Paths		All Edges				All Edges $q(Q)$
								$p(g)$		$p(\not g)$		
j	k	d	goals	plans	actions	$n^{\checkmark}(g)$	$n^{\times}(g)$	relev.	applic.	relev.	applic.	
2	2	3	21	42	62 (13)	6.33×10^{12}	1.82×10^{13}	141	78	85	64	62
3	3	3	91	273	363 (25)	1.02×10^{107}	2.56×10^{107}	6,391	2,961	469	378	363
2	3	4	259	518	776 (79)	1.82×10^{157}	7.23×10^{157}	1,585	808	1,037	778	776
3	4	3	157	471	627 (41)	3.13×10^{184}	7.82×10^{184}	10,777	4,767	799	642	627

Finally, we consider the difference between the set of plans associated with a goal being the *relevant* and being the *applicable* plan set. Interestingly, this makes a difference, and surprisingly, in some cases it makes more of a difference than enabling failure handling! For example, in the third example case ($j = 2$, $k = 3$, $d = 4$) where *more* tests are required without failure handling (1037) than with failure handling, but where the plans are the applicable plan set (808). Note that the all paths analysis considered the j plans associated with each goal to be *applicable*.

5   BDI vs. Procedural

The previous section considered the question of whether testing BDI agent programs was *hard*. We now consider the question of whether it is *harder*, i.e. we compare the number of tests required to adequately test a BDI agent program (with respect to the all edges criterion) with the number of tests required to adequately test an equivalent-sized (abstract) procedural program.

We choose to compare equivalently-sized programs for the simple reason that, in general, a larger program (procedural or BDI) will require more tests. So in order to compare procedural and BDI programs we need to keep the size fixed. The particular measure of size that we use is the number of primitive elements, actions for BDI programs, primitive statements for procedural programs.

Following Winikoff & Cranefield [20] we define an abstract procedural program as (we use Q to avoid confusion with BDI programs P):

$$Q:: = s \mid Q + Q \mid Q; Q$$

In other words, the base case is a statement s, and a compound program can be a combination of programs either in sequence ($Q_1; Q_2$), or as an alternative choice

$(Q_1 + Q_2)$. Note that for our analysis we do not need to model the condition on the choice, so the program "**if** c **then** Q_1 **else** Q_2" is simply represented as a choice between Q_1 and Q_2, i.e. $Q_1 + Q_2$. Note that loops are modelled as a choice between looping and not looping (following standard practice [13, p. 408] we only consider loops to be executed once, or zero times). Mapping these programs to control-flow graphs is straightforward, and a program is mapped to a single-entry and single-exit graph.

We now consider how many tests (i.e. paths) are required to cover all edges in the graph corresponding to a procedural program Q. We denote this number (i.e. the testability of program Q with respect to the all edges criterion) by $\mathbf{q}(Q)$. There are three cases. In the base case, a single statement, a single path suffices to cover both edges. In the case of an alternative, each path either traverses the sub-graph corresponding to Q_1, or the sub-graph corresponding to Q_2. Therefore the number of paths required to cover all edges in the graph corresponding to $Q_1 + Q_2$ is the *sum* of the number of paths required for each of the two sub-graphs, i.e. $\mathbf{q}(Q_1 + Q_2) = \mathbf{q}(Q_1) + \mathbf{q}(Q_2)$. Turning to a sequence $Q_1; Q_2$, suppose that we require $\mathbf{q}(Q_1)$ tests to cover all edges in Q_1, and, respectively, $\mathbf{q}(Q_2)$ paths to cover all edges in Q_2. Note that each path traverses the sub-graph corresponding to Q_1, and then continues to traverse the sub-graph corresponding to Q_2. This means that each path "counts" towards both Q_1 and Q_2, so the smallest number of paths that might be able to cover all edges is just the maximum of the number of paths required to test each of the two sub-graphs $(\mathbf{q}(Q_1; Q_2) = \max(\mathbf{q}(Q_1), \mathbf{q}(Q_2)))$.

However, this assumes that paths used to cover the part of the control-flow graph corresponding to Q_1 can be "reused" effectively to cover the Q_2 part of the graph. This may not be the case, and since conditions are not controllable (the environment cannot change conditions while the program is running), we cannot make this assumption. So although it might be possible that only $\max(\mathbf{q}(Q_1), \mathbf{q}(Q_2))$ tests (i.e. paths) would suffice to cover all edges in the control flow graph corresponding to $Q_1; Q_2$, it may also be the case that more tests are required. In the worse case it might be that the set of tests designed to cover all edges of Q_1 all take the same path through Q_2, in which case we would require an additional $\mathbf{q}(Q_2) - 1$ tests to cover the rest of the sub-graph corresponding to Q_2. This yields the following definition:

$$\mathbf{q}(s) = 1$$
$$\mathbf{q}(Q_1; Q_2) \geq \max(\mathbf{q}(Q_1), \mathbf{q}(Q_2))$$
$$\mathbf{q}(Q_1; Q_2) \leq \mathbf{q}(Q_1) + \mathbf{q}(Q_2) - 1$$
$$\mathbf{q}(Q_1 + Q_2) = \mathbf{q}(Q_1) + \mathbf{q}(Q_2)$$

We define the *size* of a program Q (denoted by $|Q|$) as being the number of statements. It can then be shown that for a procedural program Q of size m it is the case that $\mathbf{q}(Q) \leq m$.

Lemma 1. $\mathbf{q}(Q) \leq |Q|$. *Proof by Induction: Base case: size 1, so $Q = s$, and $\mathbf{q}(s) = 1 \leq 1$. Induction: suppose $\mathbf{q}(Q) \leq |Q|$ for $|Q| < m$, need to show it* *also holds for $|Q| = m$. Observe that $\mathbf{q}(Q_1; Q_2) < \mathbf{q}(Q_1 + Q_2)$, so we only need to show that $\mathbf{q}(Q_1 + Q_2) \leq |Q_1| + |Q_2|$, and the case for $\mathbf{q}(Q_1; Q_2)$ then follows. So, consider the case where $Q = Q_1 + Q_2$, hence $\mathbf{q}(Q) = \mathbf{q}(Q_1) + \mathbf{q}(Q_2)$. By the induction hypothesis we have that $\mathbf{q}(Q_1) \leq |Q_1|$ and $\mathbf{q}(Q_2) \leq |Q_2|$ and so $\mathbf{q}(Q_1 + Q_2) = \mathbf{q}(Q_1) + \mathbf{q}(Q_2) \leq |Q_1| + |Q_2| = |Q|$.* □

In other words, the number of paths (tests) required to cover all edges is at most the number of statements in the program. By contrast, to cover all paths, the number of tests required is approximately $3^{m/3}$ [20, page 109].

The rightmost column of Table 1 shows the number of tests (paths) required to test a procedural program Q of the same size as the BDI program in question for that row. Following Winikoff & Cranefield, we define size in terms of the number of actions (BDI) and statements (procedural), so, for example, the first row of Table 1 concerns a BDI goal-plan tree containing 62 actions (with $j = k = 2$ and $d = 3$), and a procedural program containing 62 statements.

We observe that the case with no failure handling and where $\mathcal{P}$ is *applicable* plans (i.e. the rightmost of the four numbers) is very close to $\mathbf{q}(Q)$. On the other hand, enabling failure handling does, for some cases, result in significantly more tests being required to adequately test the program. For example, 6,391 vs. 363, or 10,777 vs. 627. Both these cases have $j = 3$, whereas for the other two cases where $j = 2$ the difference is smaller. So we conclude that, especially where failure handling exists (which is the case for most BDI agent programming languages), and where goals have multiple plans available, then testing a BDI agent program is indeed harder than testing an equivalently-sized procedural program.

6   Conclusion

We considered the question of whether testing of BDI agent programs is feasible by quantifying the number of tests required to adequately test a given BDI agent program with respect to the all edges criterion. Our findings extend the earlier analysis of this question with respect to the all paths criterion to give a more nuanced understanding of the difficulty of testing BDI agents.

One key conclusion is that the number of tests required to satisfy the all edges criterion is not just lower (as expected) but very much lower (e.g. $> 2 \times 10^{107}$ vs. around $6,400$). Indeed, the number of tests required is sufficiently small to be feasible, although we do need to emphasise that all edges is generally considered to be a *minimal* requirement, and that there are arguments for why it is less appropriate for agent systems.

We also found that the introduction of failure handling did not make as large a difference for the all edges criterion, as it did for the all paths analysis.

When comparing BDI programs to procedural programs, our conclusion lends strength to the earlier result of Winikoff & Cranefield. They found that BDI agent programs were *harder* to test than equivalently sized procedural programs (with respect to the all paths criterion). We found that this is also the case for the all edges criterion, but only where goals had more than two plans.

Our overall conclusion is that BDI programs do indeed seem to be *harder* to test than procedural programs of equivalent size. However, whether it is feasible to test (whole) BDI programs remains unsettled. The all paths analysis (which is known to be pessimistic) concluded that BDI programs could not be feasibly tested. On the other hand, the all edges analysis (known to be optimistic) concluded that BDI programs could be feasibly tested. Further work is required.

Other future work includes applying these calculations to real programs, and continuing the development of formal methods for assuring the behaviour of agent-based systems [3,6–8,10,16,23].

References

1. Bordini, R.H., Dastani, M., Dix, J., El Fallah Seghrouchni, A. (eds.): Multi-Agent Programming: Languages, Platforms and Applications. Springer, Heidelberg (2005)
2. Bordini, R.H., Dastani, M., Dix, J., El Fallah Seghrouchni, A. (eds.): Multi-Agent Programming: Languages, Tools and Applications. Springer, Heidelberg (2009)
3. Bordini, R.H., Fisher, M., Pardavila, C., Wooldridge, M.: Model checking AgentSpeak. In: Autonomous Agents and Multiagent Systems (AAMAS), pp. 409–416 (2003)
4. Bratman, M.E.: Intentions, Plans, and Practical Reason. Harvard University Press, Cambridge (1987)
5. Bratman, M.E., Israel, D.J., Pollack, M.E.: Plans and resource-bounded practical reasoning. Comput. Intell. **4**, 349–355 (1988)
6. Dastani, M., Hindriks, K.V., Meyer, J.-J.C. (eds.): Specification and Verification of Multi-agent systems. Springer, Berlin/Heidelberg (2010)
7. Dennis, L.A., Fisher, M., Lincoln, N.K., Lisitsa, A., Veres, S.M.: Practical verification of decision-making in agent-based autonomous systems. In: Automated Software Engineering, 55 pages (2014)
8. Dennis, L.A., Fisher, M., Webster, M.P., Bordini, R.H.: Model checking agent programming languages. Autom. Softw. Eng. J. **19**(1), 3–63 (2012)
9. Ekinci, E.E., Tiryaki, A.M., Çetin, Ö., Dikenelli, O.: Goal-oriented agent testing revisited. In: Luck, M., Gomez-Sanz, J.J. (eds.) AOSE 2008. LNCS, vol. 5386, pp. 173–186. Springer, Heidelberg (2009). doi:10.1007/978-3-642-01338-6_13
10. Fisher, M., Dennis, L., Webster, M.: Verifying autonomous systems. Commun. ACM **56**(9), 84–93 (2013)
11. Gómez-Sanz, J.J., Botía, J., Serrano, E., Pavón, J.: Testing and debugging of MAS interactions with INGENIAS. In: Luck, M., Gomez-Sanz, J.J. (eds.) AOSE 2008. LNCS, vol. 5386, pp. 199–212. Springer, Heidelberg (2009). doi:10.1007/978-3-642-01338-6_15
12. Jorgensen, P.: Software Testing: A Craftsman's Approach, 2nd edn. CRC Press, Boca Raton (2002)
13. Mathur, A.P.: Foundations of Software Testing. Pearson (2008). ISBN 978-81-317-1660-1
14. Nguyen, C.D., Perini, A., Tonella, P.: Experimental evaluation of ontology-based test generation for multi-agent systems. In: Luck, M., Gomez-Sanz, J.J. (eds.) AOSE 2008. LNCS, vol. 5386, pp. 187–198. Springer, Heidelberg (2009). doi:10.1007/978-3-642-01338-6_14

15. Padgham, L., Zhang, Z., Thangarajah, J., Miller, T.: Model-based test oracle generation for automated unit testing of agent systems. IEEE Trans. Softw. Eng. **39**, 1230–1244 (2013)
16. Raimondi, F., Lomuscio, A.: Automatic verification of multi-agent systems by model checking via ordered binary decision diagrams. J. Appl. Logic **5**(2), 235–251 (2007)
17. Rao, A.S.: AgentSpeak(L): BDI agents speak out in a logical computable language. In: Velde, W., Perram, J.W. (eds.) MAAMAW 1996. LNCS, vol. 1038, pp. 42–55. Springer, Heidelberg (1996). doi:10.1007/BFb0031845
18. Rao, A.S., Georgeff, M.P.: Modeling rational agents within a BDI-architecture. In: Allen, J., Fikes, R., Sandewall, E. (eds.) Principles of Knowledge Representation and Reasoning, Proceedings of the Second International Conference, pp. 473–484. Morgan Kaufmann (1991)
19. Vieira, R., Moreira, Á., Wooldridge, M., Bordini, R.H.: On the formal semantics of speech-act based communication in an agent-oriented programming language. J. Artif. Intell. Res. (JAIR) **29**, 221–267 (2007)
20. Winikoff, M., Cranefield, S.: On the testability of BDI agent systems. J. Artif. Intell. Res. (JAIR) **51**, 71–131 (2014)
21. Winikoff, M., Cranefield, S.: On the testability of BDI agent systems (extended abstract). In: Journal Track of the International Joint Conference on Artificial Intelligence (IJCAI), pp. 4217–4221 (2015)
22. Winikoff, M., Padgham, L., Harland, J., Thangarajah, J.: Declarative & procedural goals in intelligent agent systems. In: Proceedings of the Eighth International Conference on Principles of Knowledge Representation and Reasoning (KR), pp. 470–481. Morgan Kaufmann, Toulouse (2002)
23. Wooldridge, M., Fisher, M., Huget, M.-P., Parsons, S.: Model checking multi-agent systems with MABLE. In: Autonomous Agents and Multi-Agent Systems (AAMAS), pp. 952–959 (2002)
24. Zhang, Z., Thangarajah, J., Padgham, L.: Automated unit testing for agent systems. In: Second International Working Conference on Evaluation of Novel Approaches to Software Engineering (ENASE), pp. 10–18 (2007)
25. Zhu, H., Hall, P.A.V., May, J.H.R.: Software unit test coverage and adequacy. ACM Comput. Surv. **29**(4), 366–427 (1997)

Dynamics of Fairness in Groups of Autonomous Learning Agents

Fernando P. Santos[1,2($\boxtimes$)], Francisco C. Santos[1,2], Francisco S. Melo[1],
Ana Paiva[1], and Jorge M. Pacheco[2,3]

[1] INESC-ID and Instituto Superior Técnico, Universidade de Lisboa,
Taguspark, Av. Prof. Cavaco Silva, 2780-990 Porto Salvo, Portugal
fernando.pedro@tecnico.ulisboa.pt
[2] ATP-Group, 2780-990 Porto Salvo, Portugal
[3] CBMA e Departamento de Matemática e Aplicações, Universidade do Minho,
Campus de Gualtar, 4710-057 Braga, Portugal

Abstract. Fairness plays a determinant role in human decisions and
definitely shapes social preferences. This is evident when groups of individuals need to divide a given resource. Notwithstanding, computational
models seeking to capture the origins and effects of human fairness often
assume the simpler case of two person interactions. Here we study a
multiplayer extension of the well-known Ultimatum Game. This game
allows us to study fair behaviors in a group setting: a proposal is made
to a group of Responders and the overall acceptance depends on reaching
a minimum number of individual acceptances. In order to capture the
effects of different group environments on the human propensity to be
fair, we model a population of learning agents interacting through the
multiplayer ultimatum game. We show that, contrarily to what would
happen with fully rational agents, learning agents coordinate their behavior into different strategies, depending on factors such as the minimum
number of accepting Responders (to achieve group acceptance) or the
group size. Overall, our simulations show that stringent group criteria
leverage fairer proposals. We find these conclusions robust to (*i*) asynchronous and synchronous strategy updates, (*ii*) initially biased agents,
(*iii*) different group payoff division paradigms and (*iv*) a wide range of
error and forgetting rates.

1 Introduction

Fairness plays a central role in human decision-making and it often directs the
actions of people towards unexpected outcomes. This fact has puzzled academics
from multiple fields and the subject comprises a fertile ground of multidiscipli-
nary research [9,10]. A neat way to verify that humans often give up their own
material gains in order to achieve fair outcomes is achieved by observing how
people play a very simple game named the Ultimatum Game (UG) [13]. In
this game, two players interact with each other. The Proposer is endowed with
some resource and has to propose a division with the Responder. After that, the
Responder has to state her acceptance or rejection. If the proposal is rejected,

© Springer International Publishing AG 2016
N. Osman and C. Sierra (Eds.): AAMAS 2016 Ws Best Papers, LNAI 10002, pp. 107–126, 2016.
DOI: 10.1007/978-3-319-46882-2_7

none of the players earn anything. If the proposal is accepted, they will divide the resource as it was proposed. In the context of UG, the outcome of any accepted proposal stands as a social optimum (in the Pareto sense, i.e., no other player can improve her payoff without damaging the payoff of others) however, only the egalitarian division, in which both the Proposer and the Responder earn a similar reward, is considered a fair result.

A first approach, attempting to predict the behavior of people in this game, relies on the assumption that each player is a rational agent that seeks to unconditionally maximize the rewards. In this case, it is easy to notice that the Responder should always accept any offer; wherefore, the Proposer should never fear to have a proposal rejected and should always propose the minimum possible. This indeed constitutes the sub-game perfect equilibrium of the UG [27]. A vast number of works, however, report experiments with people in which the rational sub-game prediction is not played and fair outcomes are verified [13,26,35,46]. Humans tend to reject low proposals and manage to offer high/fair divisions. Offers are higher than expected even in the so-called Dictator games, where the Responders do not have the opportunity to reject and proposals are always accepted [10,16].

If one intends to model, explain and tentatively predict the behavior of people in this game, new mathematical and computational tools have to be employed, other than the game theoretical sub-game perfect equilibrium. For instance, by relaxing the rational assumption made about human decision making and by simply undertaking that strategies are adopted or renounced by individual [11,22,43] or social learning [31,33,41], various mechanisms can be tested and different conclusions can be obtained. In the second case, assuming that agents co-habit a population and adopt strategies with a probability that grows with the success those strategies are perceived to consent, the dynamics of strategy adoption interestingly resemble a process of gene replication and the evolving behavior of agents can be modeled by tools from Evolutionary Game Theory (EGT) [50]. Interestingly, EGT can also be used to study individual learning dynamics [1].

UG has been studied in the context of EGT and it has been shown that when Proposers collect pieces of information about opponents' previous actions, it is worth for the Responders to cultivate a fierce bargainer reputation [25]. This explains the long-term benefits of Responders that acquire an intransigent image by rejecting unfair offers. Other models attribute the evolution of fairness to repeated interactions [49], to empathy [29] or even simply to environmental noise and stochasticity [32,37]. A slightly different approach suggests that fair Proposers and Responders may emerge due to the topological arrangement of their network of contacts: if individuals are arranged in lattices [30,45] or complex networks [17,42] clusters of fairness may emerge.

While the UG is ubiquitous in real-life encounters, there is a wide range of human interactions that a pairwise interaction model does not enclose. It is perfectly straightforward to realize that also UG instances take place in groups, with proposals being made to assemblies [38]. Take the case of pervasive democratic institutions, economic and climate summits, markets, auctions, or the ancestral activities of proposing divisions regarding the loot of group hunts and fisheries. All those examples go beyond a pairwise interaction. More specifically, the relation of groups and the possibility of fair allocations is a topic utterly relevant in the context of group buying [19,20], collective bargaining of work contracts or coalition policy making [14] and indeed, there is a growing interest in doing experiments with multiplayer versions of fairness games [3,6,7,9,12,23,39]. A simple extension of UG may turn it adequate to study a wide variety of ubiquitous group encounters. This extension, the Multiplayer UG (MUG), allows to study the traditional UG in a context where proposals are made to groups that should decide about its acceptance or rejection [38]. In the context of this game, some questions need to be addressed: What is the role of the specific group environment on people's behavior? What is the impact of group acceptance rules (i.e., the minimum number of accepting Responders to obtain group acceptance) on individual offers? What is the role of group size on fairness?

If one assumes that agents always opt for the payoff maximizing strategy, the previous questions have trivial answers: proposals in MUG are accepted regardless of the group particularities and any effect of group size or group acceptance rules in the preferred people's behavior should be neglected. However, abandoning this strong rationality assumption, and acknowledging that unexpected behaviors often result from an adaptive process of evolution and learning, turns plausible that different group environments can shape decision making and nurture fair outcomes. As mentioned before, the use of multiagent learning techniques can, for that end, unveil important characteristics of human interactions that are neglected by typical equilibrium analysis. Here we seek to analyze the role of different group environments on the emergence of fair outcomes, by combining MUG with agents that adapt their behavior through reinforcement learning [44]. We implement and test with the well-known Roth-Erev reinforcement learning algorithm [35]. We show that group size and different group acceptance rules impact, in a nontrivially manner, the learned strategies and the associated fairness: increasing the minimum number of accepting Responders to achieve group acceptance has the effect of increasing the offered values and consequently fairness; secondly, the effect of group size strongly depends on the group acceptation threshold.

For simplicity and readability purposes, in Table 1 we provide a list of the nomenclature used through this document. In Sect. 2, we present the MUG [38] and we review the equilibrium notions of classical game theory, namely, the subgame perfection. In Sect. 3 we present the Roth-Erev learning model that we use thorough this work. After that, in Sect. 4, we present the results showing that, within a population of adaptive agents, group environment (group acceptance rules and group size) indeed plays a fundamental role in the employed strategies. In Sect. 5 we discuss the obtained results and provide a set of concluding remarks.

Table 1. Glossary

Symbol	Meaning
p	Offer by Proposer
q	Acceptance threshold of Responder
$\Pi_P(p_i, q_{-i})$	Payoff earned by a Proposer
$\Pi_R(p_j, q_{-j})$	Payoff earned by a Responder
$\Pi(p_i, q_i, p_{-i}, q_{-i})$	Payoff being Proposer and Responder
$a_{p_i, q_{-i}}$	Group acceptance flag
$Q(t)$	Propensity matrix at time t
λ	Forgetting rate
ϵ	Local experimentation
$\rho_{ki}(t)$	Probability that k uses strategy i
$\bar{p}, \bar{q}$	Average p, q population-wide
$i_{p,q}$	Integer representation of strategy (p, q)
R	Number of runs
Z	Population size
N	Group size
M	Group acceptance rule
T	Number of time steps
R	Number of runs

2   Multiplayer Ultimatum Game

Often people incur in interactions that are fundamentally rooted in proposals made to groups. These proposals can naturally be accepted or rejected, depending on the subsequent bargaining and group acceptance rules. The outcome of this interaction can favor unequally each part involved and is thereby likely that concerns about fairness puzzle each player mood. The role played by the group in this interaction is overlooked by the traditional two-person UG. Thereby, here we present and analyze the Multiplayer Ultimatum Game (MUG) which allows us to test the effect of different group environments on the behaviors adopted by people and the associated fairness levels [38].

In the UG, we can assume that the strategy of the Proposer is the fraction of resource offered to the Responder (p) and the strategy of the Responder is the personal threshold (q) used to decide about acceptance or rejection [25, 30]. Only whenever $p \geq q$ the proposal is accepted. Considering that the amount being divided sums to 1, an accepted proposal of p endows the Proposer with $1 - p$ and the Responder with p. If the proposal is rejected, none of the individuals earn anything. The UG can now be extended to a N-person game if we account for the existence of a group composed by $N-1$ Responders [36,38]. The group decision making can be arbitrarily complex yet, we simplify this process by assuming that each of the $N-1$ Responders accepts or rejects the proposal and the overall group acceptance depends on a group acceptance rule: if the number of acceptances equals or exceeds a minimum number of accepting Responders, M, the proposal is accepted by the group. In this case, the Proposer keeps what she did not offer $(1-p)$ and the offer is divided by the Responders (in two possible ways, as detailed next); otherwise, if the number of acceptances remains below M, the proposal is rejected by the group and no one earns anything. The accepted proposal can be (i) evenly divided by all the Responders or (ii) only divided by the accepting Responders.

The payoff function describing the gains of a Proposer i, with strategy p_i, facing a group of Responders with strategies $q_{-i} = \{q_1, ..., q_j, ..., q_{N-1}\}, j \neq i$ reads as

$$\Pi_P(p_i, q_{-i}) = (1 - p_i)a_{p_i,q_{-i}} \tag{1}$$

Where $a_{p_i,q_{-i}}$ summarizes the group acceptance of the proposal made by agent i (p_i), standing as

$$a_{p_i,q_{-i}} = \begin{cases} 1, & \text{if } \sum_{q_j \in q_{-i}} \Theta(p_i - q_j) \geq M. \\ 0, & \text{otherwise.} \end{cases} \tag{2}$$

$\Theta(x)$ is the Heaviside unit step function, having value 1 whenever $x \geq 0$ and 0 otherwise. This way, $\Theta(p_i - q_j) = 1$ if agent j accepts agent's i proposal and $\sum_{q_j \in q_{-i}} \Theta(p_i - q_j)$ is the number of Responders (within those using strategies $q_{-i} = \{q_1, ..., q_j, ..., q_{N-1}\}, j \neq i$) accepting proposal p_i.

Similarly, the payoff function describing the gains of a Responder belonging to a group with a strategy profile $q_{-j} = \{q_1, ..., q_k, q_i, ..., q_{N-1}\}, k \neq j$, listening to a Proposer j with strategy p_j, is, in the case of proposals evenly divided by all, given by

$$\Pi_R(p_j, q_{-j}) = \frac{p_j}{N-1} a_{p_j,q_{-j}}. \tag{3}$$

In the case of proposals divided by the accepting Responders, the payoff of a Responder (with strategy q_i) is given by

$$\Pi_R(p_j, q_{-j}) = \frac{p_j \Theta(p_j - q_i)a_{p_j,q_{-j}}}{\sum_{q_k \in q_{-j}} \Theta(p_j - q_k)} \tag{4}$$

This equation implies that a Responder only earns something if both she and the group accept that proposal. In turn, Eq. (3) implies that only the group has to accept a proposal, for any Responder to earn something.

We can assume that these games occur in groups where each individual acts once as Proposer and $N-1$ times as Responder. This way, the overall payoff of an individual with strategy (p_i, q_i), playing in a group with strategy profile (p_{-i}, q_{-i}), is given by

$$\Pi(p_i, q_i, p_{-i}, q_{-i}) = \Pi_P(p_i, q_{-i}) + \sum_{p_j \in p_{-i}} \Pi_R(p_j, q_{-i}) \tag{5}$$

The interesting values of M range between 1 and $N-1$. If $M = 0$, no Responders are needed to accept a proposal and so, all proposals would be accepted. With $M > N - 1$ all proposals are rejected irrespectively of the strategies used by the players.

2.1   Sub-game Perfect Equilibrium

In order to derive the sub-game perfect equilibrium of MUG, let us introduce some canonical notation. A game given in a sequential form has a set of stages in which a specific player (chosen by a *player function*) should act. A *history* stands as any possible sequence of actions, given the turns assigned by the player function. Roughly speaking, a *terminal history* is a sequence of actions that go from the beginning of the game until an end, after which there are no actions to follow. Each *terminal history* will prescribe different outcomes to the players involved, given a specific *payoff* structure that fully translates the preferences of the individuals. This way, a *sub-game* is composed by the set of all possible histories that may follow a given non-terminal history. A strategy profile is a *sub-game perfect equilibrium* if it also the Nash equilibrium of every sub-game [27].

Let us turn to the specific example of MUG to clarify this idea. In this game, the Proposer does the first move and the Responders should, secondly, state acceptance or rejection. The game has two stages and any terminal history is composed by sets of two actions, one taken by a single individual (Proposer, with possibility to suggest any division of the resource) and the second by the group (acceptance or rejection).

Picture the scenario in which groups consist of 5 players, where one is the Proposer, the other 4 are the Responders and M = 4 (different M would lead to the same conclusions). Let us evaluate two possible strategy profiles: $s_1 = (0.8, 0.8, 0.8, 0.8, 0.8)$ and $s_2 = (\mu, 0, 0, 0, 0)$, where the first value is the offer by the Proposer and the remaining 4 are the acceptance thresholds by the Responders. Both strategy profiles are Nash Equilibria of the whole game. In the first case, the Proposer does not have interest in deviating from 0.8: if she lowers this value, the proposal will be rejected and thus she will earn 0; if she increases the offer, she will keep less to herself. The same happens with the Responders: if they increase the threshold, they will earn 0 instead of 0.2, and if they decrease it, nothing happens (non-strict equilibrium). The exact same reasoning can be made for s_2, assuming that $\mu/(N-1)$ is the smallest possible division of the resource.

Regarding sub-game perfection, the conclusions are different. Assume the *history* in which the Proposer has chosen to offer μ (let us call the sub-game after this history, in which only one move is needed to end the game, h). In this case, the payoff yielded by s_1 is $(0, 0, 0, 0, 0)$ (every Responder rejects a proposal of μ) and the payoff yielded by s_2 is $(1-\mu, \mu/(N-1), \mu/(N-1), \mu/(N-1), \mu/(N-1))$. So it pays for the Responders to choose s_2 instead of s_1, which means that s_1 is not a Nash Equilibrium of the sub-game h. Indeed, while any strategy profile in the form $s = (p, p, p, p, p), \mu < p \le 1$ is a Nash Equilibrium of MUG, only $s^* = (\mu, 0, 0, 0, 0)$ is the sub-game perfect equilibrium. As described in the introductory section, a similar conclusion, yet simpler and more intuitive, could be reached through backward induction.

3   Learning Model

The use of multiagent learning algorithms can unveil fundamental properties of human interactions that are overlooked if one would assume that individuals always behave following fully rational behaviors [8,11,22,35,43]. Particularly, the Roth-Erev algorithm was used with remarkable success in modeling the process of human learning when playing well-known interaction paradigms such as the Ultimatum Game [35]. We use the Roth-Erev algorithm to analyze the outcome of a population with learning agents playing MUG in groups of size N. In this algorithm, at each time-step t, each agent k is defined by a propensity vector $Q_k(t)$. Over time, this vector is updated given the payoff gathered after each play. Successfully employed actions will grant larger payoffs that, when added to the corresponding propensity value, will increase the probability of repeating that strategy in the future (as will be made clear below). We consider that games take place within a population with Z ($Z > N$) adaptive agents. Agents earn payoff following an anonymous random matching model [11], i.e., we sample random groups without any kind of preferential arrangement or reciprocation mechanism. We consider MUG with discretized strategies. We round the possible values of p (proposed offers) and q (individual threshold of acceptance) to the closest multiple of $1/D$, where D measures the granularity of the strategy space considered. We map each pair of decimal values p and q into an integer representation, thereafter $i_{p,q}$ is the integer representation of strategy (p, q) and p_i (or q_i) designates the p (q) value corresponding to the strategy with integer representation i.

The core of the learning algorithm takes place in the update of the propensity vector of each agent, $Q(t + 1)$, after a play at time-step t. Denoting the set of possible actions by $A, a_i \in A : a_i = \{p_i, q_i\}$, and the population size by Z, the propensity matrix, $Q(t) \in R_+^{Z \times |A|}$, is updated following the base rule

$$Q_{ki}(t+1) = \begin{cases} Q_{ki}(t) + \Pi(p_i, q_i, p_{-i}, q_{-i}) & \text{if } k \text{ played } i \\ Q_{ki}(t) & \text{otherwise} \end{cases} \qquad (6)$$

The above update can be enriched with human learning features: *forgetting rate* $(\lambda, 0 \leq \lambda \leq 1)$ and *local experimentation error*, $(\epsilon, 0 \leq \epsilon \leq 1)$ [35], leading to an update rule slightly improved,

$$Q_{ki}(t+1) = \begin{cases} Q_{ki}(t)\bar{\lambda} + \Pi(p_i, q_i, p_{-i}, q_{-i})(1 - \epsilon) & k \text{ played } i \\ Q_{ki}(t)\bar{\lambda} + \Pi(p_i, q_i, p_{-i}, q_{-i})\frac{\epsilon}{4} & k \text{ pl. } i_p \pm 1 \\ Q_{ki}(t)\bar{\lambda} + \Pi(p_i, q_i, p_{-i}, q_{-i})\frac{\epsilon}{4} & k \text{ pl. } i_q \pm 1 \\ Q_{ki}(t)\bar{\lambda} & \text{otherwise} \end{cases} \qquad (7)$$

where $\bar{\lambda} = 1 - \lambda$ and $i_p \pm 1$ ($i_q \pm 1$) corresponds to the index of the p (q) values of the strategies adjacent to p_i (q_i), naturally depending on the discretization chosen. The introduction of local experimentation errors is convenient as they prevent the probability of playing the less used strategies (however close to the used ones) from going to 0. Moreover, those errors may introduce the spontaneous trial of novel strategies, a feature that is both human-like and showed to improve the performance of autonomous agents [40]. The forgetting rate is convenient to inhibit the entries of Q from growing without bound: when the propensities reach a certain value, the magnitude of the values forgotten, $Q_{ki}(t)\lambda$, approach those of the payoffs being added, $\Pi(p_i, q_i, p_{-i}, q_{-i})$.

When an agent is called to pick an action, she will do so following the probability distribution dictated by the normalization of her propensity vector. The probability that individual k picks the strategy i at time t is given by

$$\rho_{ki}(t) = \frac{Q_{ki}(t)}{\sum_n Q_{ni}(t)} \tag{8}$$

The initial values of propensity, $Q(0)$, have a special role in the convergence to a given propensity vector and on the exploration *versus* exploitation dilemma. If the norm of propensity vectors in $Q(0)$ is high, the initial payoffs obtained will have a low impact on the probability distribution. Oppositely, if the norm of propensity vectors in $Q(0)$ is small, the initial payoffs will have a big impact on the probability of choosing the corresponding strategy again. Convergence will be faster if the values in $Q(0)$ are low, yet in this case agents will not initially explore a wide variety of strategies. Here we consider three variants of initially attributed values to $Q(0)$: (*i*) random initial propensity, where each entry $Q_{ki}(0)$ assumes real values randomly sampled (uniformly) from the interval $[0, Q(0)_{max}]$; (*ii*) propensity values initially high on the strategy $p = q = 0$ – specifically, we attribute a random value between 0 and 1 to the propensities corresponding to the strategies $p \neq 0$, $q \neq 0$ and we attribute the value $Q(0)_{max}$ to the propensity corresponding to the strategy $p = q = 0$; (*iii*) values of propensity initially high on the strategy $p = q = 1$ and low on strategies $p \neq 1$, $q \neq 1$.

All together, the individual learning algorithm can be intuitively perceived: when individual k uses strategy i she will reinforce the use of that strategy provided the gains that she obtained; higher gains will increase to a higher extent the probability of using that strategy in the future. The past use of the remaining strategies, and the obtained feedbacks, will be forgotten over time; similar strategies to the one employed (which in the case of MUG are just the adjacent values of proposal and acceptance threshold) will also be reinforced, yet to a lower extent. This learning algorithm is rather popular, providing a canonical method of reinforcement learning that was successfully applied in the past to fit the way that people learn to play social dilemmas [8,35]. It is noteworthy that two important properties of human learning are captured by this model: the Law of Effect [47] and the Power Law of Practice [24]. The first poses that humans (and animals) tend to reinforce the use of previously successfully employed strategies; the Power Law of Practice states that the learning curve of a given task by a human is initially steep and, over time, gets flat. Indeed, by using the Roth-Erev algorithm, larger payoffs reinforce to a larger extent

---

Algorithm 1. Roth-Erev reinforcement learning algorithm in an adaptive population and considering **synchronous** update of propensities.

$Q(0) \leftarrow initialization;$
for $t \leftarrow 1$ **to** T, *total number of time-steps* **do**

> $tmp \leftarrow \{0, ..., 0\}$　　/* keeps the temporary payoffs of the current time step to allow for synchronous update of propensities */;
> **for** $k \leftarrow 1$ **to** Z **do**
> > 1. *pick random group with individual k;*
> > 2. *collect strategies (Eq. 8);*
> > 3. *calculate payoff of k (Eq. 5);*
> > 4. *update $tmp[k]$ with payoff obtained;*
>
> *update $Q(t)$ given $Q(t-1)$ and tmp (Eq. 7);*
> *save $\bar{p}$ (Eq. 9);*
> *save $\bar{q}$ (Eq. 9);*

---

the usage of a given strategy (alongside preventing the usage of the remaining strategies) and, following Eq. (8), payoffs have a larger relative impact on the probability of picking a strategy at the beginning of the learning process, when $Q_{ki}(t)$ values are lower.

Algorithm 2. Roth-Erev reinforcement learning algorithm in an adaptive population and considering **asynchronous** update of propensities.

$Q(0) \leftarrow initialization;$
for $t \leftarrow 1$ **to** T, *total number of time-steps* **do**

> **for** $i \leftarrow 1$ **to** Z **do**
> > 1. *pick random individual k and random group with k;*
> > 2. *collect strategies (Eq. 8);*
> > 3. *calculate payoff of k (Eq. 5);*
> > 4. *update Q_k with the payoff obtained;*
>
> *save $\bar{p}$ (Eq. 9);*
> *save $\bar{q}$ (Eq. 9);*

The remaining algorithm is summarized in Algorithms 1 and 2. In Algorithm 1 we detail the synchronous version of the algorithm. In this case, we guarantee that during each time step every agent has the opportunity to update her propensity values. Moreover, during a given time step, all agents play and the obtained payoff is kept in a temporary registry, so that all agents update their propensities at once, after a time step elapses.

In Algorithm 2 we summarize the asynchronous version of the propensity updates. In this case, Z (the population size) agents are randomly selected to update their propensity values during one time step, without any guarantee that all agents are given this opportunity and that no agents are repeatedly selected. Additionally, when an agent plays, the corresponding propensity value is immediately updated, precluding any kind of synchronism in the propensity update process.

We keep track of the average values of p and q in the population, designating them by $\bar{p}$ and $\bar{q}$. Provided a propensity matrix, they are calculated as

$$\bar{p} = \frac{1}{Z} \sum_{1 < k < Z} \sum_{1 < i < |A|} \rho_{ki} p_i$$

$$\bar{q} = \frac{1}{Z} \sum_{1 < k < Z} \sum_{1 < i < |A|} \rho_{ki} q_i \qquad (9)$$

In the next section, we present and discuss the results stemming from our experiments.

4   Results

Through the simulation of the multiagent system described in the previous section, we first show that different group acceptance rules have a considerable impact on the average values of offers (p) and acceptance thresholds (q) learned by the population. As the time-series in Fig. 1 (left column) show, when MUG takes place in groups of size $N = 8$ and for $M = 1$ (top), $M = 4$ (middle) and $M = 7$ (bottom), agents learn the strategies that allow them to maintain high acceptance rates and high average payoffs. Notwithstanding, the offered values are higher and fairer if M increases. An average p of 0.2 ($M = 1$) endows Proposers with an average payoff of 0.8, while each Responder keeps 0.2. Oppositely, an average value of p close to 0.7 ($M = 7$) provides the more equalitarian outcome of endowing Proposers with 0.3 and Responders with 0.7. Recall that the sub-game perfect equilibrium always predicts that Proposers would keep almost all the sum and Responders would earn something close 0.

In Fig. 1 we additionally portray the variance of strategies at an individual (middle column) and population level (right column). Initially, propensity values are attributed randomly, sampled from a uniform distribution from 0 to $Q(0)_{max}$. This way, the variance of propensity is initially high, at an agent level. However, the average values of p and q used by each agent are approximately 0.5 for

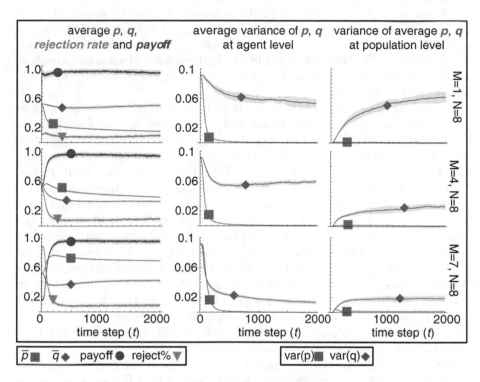

Fig. 1. Left column: time series reporting the evolution of average strategies (p and $\bar{q}$), average payoff population-wide (*payoff*) and proposals rejection rate (*reject%*). Each plot depicts the average over 100 runs (the corresponding standard deviation, often negligible, is represented by a background shadow), each starting with a random propensity matrix where each entry is sampled from a uniform distribution over the interval $[0, Q(0)_{max}]$. For group size $N = 8$ and for the thresholds $M = 1$, $M = 4$ and $M = 7$, the rejection rate converges to a value near the minimum, thereby, the average payoff in the population approximates the maximum possible. The average strategy values do not inform us about the predictability of agents' actions (the spread of the distribution of individual propensity values) neither about the diversity level of strategies occurring at a population level (spread of average strategies considering all agents), thereby, we present the variance of propensity at an individual (middle column) and population (right column) level. We observe that, as time steps go by, all agents learn to always use (approximately) the same proposal values (p), an evidence that stems from the low average variance of propensities both within each agent and across all the population. Contrarily, the variance of the propensity values of q remain high. This variance is considerable lower when M is high, reflecting the larger pressure that is exerted upon q. In these specific plots, we assume synchronous propensity updates and offers divided by all the Responders. Other parameters: population size $Z = 100$, granularity $D = 20$, forgetting rate $\lambda = 0.01$, local experimentation rate $\epsilon = 0.01$, total number of time-steps $T = 20000$ $Q(0)_{max} = 20$.

everyone, which results in an initially low variance of average strategies, at a population level. As time goes by (higher values of t), all the agents adapt in order to always use the same values of p, resulting in a low variance of propensity both at agent and population level. Oppositely, different agents learn to use different ranges of q. This is depicted by the high variance of propensity both at an individual and population level: in what concerns q, agents are unpredictable and populations are diverse.

We can have a better intuition for the evolving distribution of strategies within a population if we observe a snapshot, for one specific run, of the propensity distribution over the space of possible p and q values. The corresponding results are pictured in Figs. 2 ($M = 1$), 3 ($M = 4$) and 4 ($M = 7$) for time-steps $t = 200$, $t = 500$, $t = 1000$, $t = 3000$, $t = 19000$. Each small square corresponds to a pair (p, q) and a darker square means that more agents have a propensity vector with a high value in that position. Figures 2, 3 and 4 show that, over time, agents learn to use a p value that grows with M. Concerning q, the learned values have a sizeable variance within the same population. This variance decreases with M, an effect already visible in Fig. 1. The reasoning for this result is straightforward: as M increases, a proposal is only accepted if more Responders accept it. In the limiting case of $M = N - 1$, all Responders have to accept an offer in order for it to be accepted by the group, thereby, the pressure for having low acceptance thresholds (q) is high. When M is low, a lot of q values in the group of Responders turn to be irrelevant. In this case, the pressure for q values to converge to confined domain is softened.

So far we considered that propensity values are initially attributed at random. This naturally casts doubt on whether populations of initially unfair agents are also able to learn to be fair and adapt their behaviour given different values of M. This way, we explicitly consider the effect of initially biased agents. At $t = 0$ we input in each agent a propensity vector that induces them to use a specific strategy with high probability (darker squares in the bottom-left (middle panel) or top-right (bottom panel) corners of each figure at $t = 200$). We consider the two extreme cases of high and low p, q values. In the middle panels of Figs. 2, 3 and 4, a lot of propensity is initially placed in the strategies $p = q = 0$, for all agents (extremely unfair agents). In the bottom panels, a lot of propensity is initially placed in the strategies $p = q = 1$ (extremely altruistic agents). We show that, despite this initial bias, agents learn to use approximately the same strategies, in the long run. Moreover, we conclude again that the learned strategies strongly depend on M.

Indeed, if we systematically increase M, the proposed values rise concomitantly. In Fig. 5 we observe this effect in four different conditions: (i) synchronous updates of propensities (Algorithm 1) and payoff divided by all Responders (Eq. 3); (ii) synchronous updates of propensities and payoff divided by accepting Responders (Eq. 4); (iii) asynchronous updates of propensities (Algorithm 2) and payoff divided by all Responders; (iv) asynchronous updates of propensities and payoff divided by accepting Responders. Interestingly, when the payoff is only divided by the accepting Responders, the average values of q and p decrease.

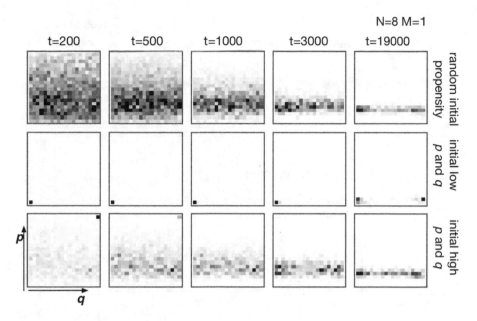

Fig. 2. Snapshots of the population composition regarding the average values of p and q to be played given $Q(t)$. Each plot represents the space of all possible combination of p and q, assuming that $D = 20$ and thereby, p and q rounded to the closest multiple of $1/20$. We represent the state of the population for five distinct time-steps (from left to right: $t = 200$, $t = 500$, $t = 1000$, $t = 3000$, $t = 19000$) and given three different $Q(0)$ conditions: on top, initial propensity values uniformly distributed; on the middle, initial propensity $Q_{k0}(0) = 50$ and $Q_{k,i\neq0}(0) = U(0,1)$, where $U = (0,1)$ is a random real sampled uniformly from the interval $[0,1]$; on bottom, initial propensity $Q_{k(D+1)^2-1}(0) = 50$ and $Q_{k,i\neq(D+1)^2-1}(0) = U(0,1)$. Irrespectively of the initial conditions, for $M = 1$ agents learn to use low values of p. Each square within the 2D-plots represents a specific combination of (p,q). If the square is darker it means that more individuals use, with high probability, a strategy corresponding to that location. Other parameters: group size $N = 8$, group acceptance threshold $M = 1$, initial propensities maximum $Q(0)_{max} = 50$, population size $Z = 100$, granularity $D = 20$, forgetting rate $\lambda = 0.01$, local experimentation rate $\epsilon = 0.01$, total number of time-steps $T = 20000$.

This result is plausible because, when the number of accepting Responders in a group stands above M and the offer is divided by all the Responders, only the q of those that accepted the proposal has indeed an impact in the obtained payoff; all the agents with a high q receive the same payoff as the accepting agents with low q. However, when the payoff is divided by solely the accepting Responders (low q), the agents with a high q that individually reject a proposal can be impaired even if the proposal is accepted by the group. This way, the pressure for q to decrease is higher in the condition where proposals are only divided by the accepting Responders. Alongside, the values of p also decrease. Consistently with this hypothesis, when M is higher the difference in both payoff division paradigms is alleviated. On the other hand, there is no significant difference in

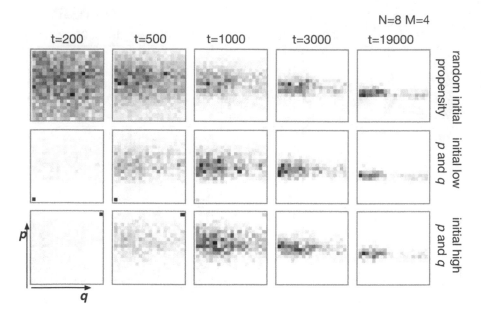

Fig. 3. Snapshots of the population composition regarding the average values of p and q to be played given $Q(t)$. For an interpretation of this Fig., please see the caption of Fig. 2. Other parameters: group size $N = 8$ and group acceptance threshold $M = 4$.

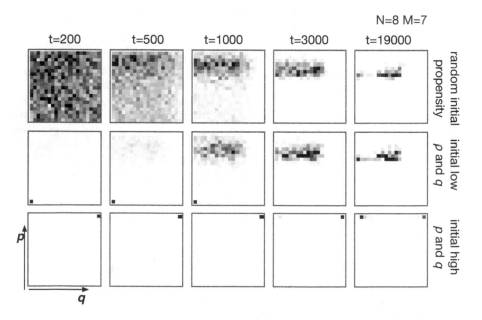

Fig. 4. Snapshots of the population composition regarding the average values of p and q to be played given $Q(t)$. For an interpretation of this Fig., please see the caption of Fig. 2. Other parameters: group size $N = 8$ and group acceptance threshold $M = 7$.

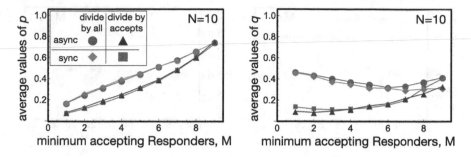

Fig. 5. The average values of p and q for group size $N = 10$ with M assuming all possible non-trivial values $1 \le M \le N - 1$. Each point in the plot corresponds to a time and ensemble average: (i) time average over the last half of the time-steps, i.e., we wait for a transient time for propensity values to stabilise and (ii) we take the average of 100 runs, each one starting from a random $Q(0)$ propensity matrix. The variance over different runs is negligible. On the left, we represent the average values of proposal and on the right we depict the average threshold acceptance values. In each case, we consider all the combinations of (i) asynchronous or synchronous propensity updates with (ii) payoff divided by all the Responders or payoff only divided by the accepting Responders. Other parameters: population size $Z = 100$, granularity $D = 20$, forgetting rate $\lambda = 0.01$, local experimentation rate $\epsilon = 0.01$, total number of time-steps $T = 10000$, number of runs $R = 100$, initial propensities maximum $Q(0)_{max} = 20$.

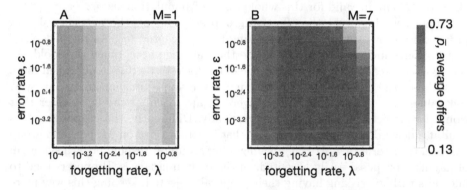

Fig. 6. Average values of p and q for different combinations of λ (forgetting rate) and ϵ (local experimentation error). In this case, we assume synchronous propensity updates and offers divided by all the Responders. For all the tested combinations, we always obtain a higher value of p whenever M increases and all other parameters stand fixed. Other parameters: group size $N = 8$, population size $Z = 100$, granularity $D = 20$, total number of time-steps $T = 10000$, number of runs $R = 100$, initial propensities maximum $Q(0)_{max} = 20$.

the learned strategies when considering asynchronous or synchronous propensity updates.

It is noteworthy that the relation between high M and fair proposals remains valid for a wide range of combinations of λ (forgetting rate) and ϵ (local

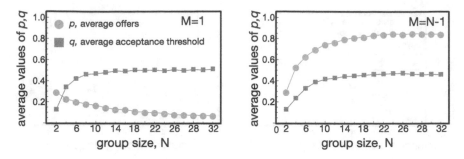

Fig. 7. Average values of p and q for different combinations of group sizes, N (2 to 32), and group acceptance rules, M (left panel: $M = 1$ i.e., just a single individual acceptance to render a proposal accepted; right panel: $M = N - 1$, unanimity of individual acceptances to overall accept a proposal). In this case, we assume synchronous propensity updates and offers divided by all the Responders. Other parameters: population size $Z = 100$, granularity $D = 20$, forgetting rate $\lambda = 0.01$, local experimentation error $\epsilon = 0.01$, total number of time-steps $T = 10000$, number of runs $R = 100$, initial propensities maximum $Q(0)_{max} = 20$.

experimentation error) (Fig. 6). We additionally tested for $N = 7$, $M = 1, 3, 6$ and $Z = 20, 30, 50, 200, 300, 500$ and verified that the conclusions regarding the effect of M remain valid for this whole range of population sizes.

Finally, we highlight the effect of group size (N) on the average value of proposals made ($\bar{p}$) and proposals willing to be accepted ($\bar{q}$). As Fig. 7 depicts, larger groups induce individuals to rise their average acceptance threshold. As the group of Responders grows and the offers have to be divided between more individuals, the pressure to learn optimal low q values is alleviated. This way, the values of q should increase, on average, approaching the 0.5 barrier that would be predicted if they behaved erratically. Differently, the proposed values exhibit a dependence on the group size that is conditioned on M. For mild group acceptance criteria (e.g. $M = 1$), having a big group of Responders is a synonym of having a proposal easily accepted. In these circumstances, Proposers tend to offer less without risking having their proposals rejected, keeping this way more for themselves and exploiting the Responders. Oppositely, when groups agree upon stricter acceptance rules (e.g., $M = 7$), having a big group of Responders means that more people need to be convinced of the advantages of a proposal. This way, Proposers have to adapt, increase the offered values and sacrifice their share in order to have their proposals accepted.

5   Discussion and Conclusion

In this work we model an adaptive population with agents interacting through MUG. Agents learn over time following the Roth-Erev reinforcement learning algorithm. This individual learning algorithm was shown to mimic quite well the learning process of humans while playing social dilemmas [8,35]. Indeed, our main goal is to capture, in a computational model, the role of group acceptance rules and the own group sizes on human behavior. While the role of different group environments is overlooked by an approach that takes all agents as being fully rational, we show that, in the context of learning agents, some particularities of the group setting importantly change the learned behaviors: increasing the minimum number of accepting Responders to obtain group acceptance has the effect of increasing the offered values; the effect of group size depends on the group decision rule in a way that big groups combined with soft group criteria are a fertile ground for selfish Proposers to thrive and, oppositely, big groups that require a large number of Responders to accept a proposal induce Proposers to offer more.

The individual learning model that we implement is close to a trial and error mechanism that individuals may use to successively adapt to the environment, given the feedback provided by their own actions. A different approach implements a system of social learning [38] in which individuals learn by observing the strategies of others and accordingly imitate the strategies perceived as best [31,33,41]. These two learning paradigms (individual and social) can lead to very different outcomes concerning the learned strategies and the long-term behaviour of the agents [4,48]. Interestingly, our results are in line with some of the results obtained in the context of evolutionary game theory and social learning [38]. It is remarkable, however, that an individual learning approach does not rely on information about others' complete strategy set and performances. Agents' learning only requires knowledge about the used strategy and the received payoff. This way, the individual learning method that we employ is suitable to model MUG situations where, reasonably, others' strategies are unknown and the only feedback obtained is the overall group acceptance or rejection.

As stated, we simulate a population of learning agents as a proxy to better understand human behaviour. In AI, algorithms of reinforcement learning are typically implemented in order to equip artificial agents with autonomy and optimality, characteristics often attributed to human intelligence. This way, human behavior is taken as an inspiration to design artificial agents. This work (following others [4,8,22,35,43]) intends to close the loop by experimenting with artificial agents new interactions and behaviors that tentatively allow to gain knowledge about the way that humans act: the emergent behavior of artificial agents is taken as an inspiration to understand human behavior. Interestingly, by telling us something about emergent human behavior, our results can again be used to aid the design of artificial agents that are both efficient and believable when used in human-agent interactions [2,5]. Take the example of automatic negotiation [18,21,34]. What would be the requirements of artificial agents designed to negotiate with a human in an environment that is surely dynamic? Should they behave assuming human rationality and predicting sub-game perfect equilibrium (see Sect. 2.1)? Should they act accordingly with the behaviors that emerge after a learning process? Here we clearly show that the proposal and acceptance threshold of those agents should be implemented as a function of the specific group environment where agents are going to act. These conclusions could hardly be obtained after assuming agents rationality.

Finally, a note on further applications of the game we test with. As Hamilton states, "The theory of many person games may seem to stand to that of two-person games in the relation of sea-sickness to a headache" [15,28]. Indeed, here we see that a multiplayer version of the Ultimatum Game, while still reasonably simple and general, brings attached a set parameters whose effect is certainly not trivial to understand [36,38]. The interaction paradigm that we consider is prevalent in numerous daily situations and human activities, thereby, the study of MUG using different modeling tools and assumptions is both a challenge and opportunity to address stimulating open questions. For instance, how will the group size affect the social pressure on the rejecting Responders? How to manage individual reputations if only the general group verdict is known, rather than individual decisions? What would change if Proposers were allowed to target offers to specific Responders and how would M impact that behavior? How should agents be selected to be Proposers from within a group, given their previous actions? We hope that the adaptive learning agents and multiagent systems community feels tempted to address those (and many other) questions that MUG instigates.

Acknowledgments. This research was supported by Fundação para a Ciência e Tecnologia (FCT Portugal) through grants SFRH/BD/94736/2013, PTDC/EEI-SII/5081/2014, PTDC/MAT/STA/3358/2014 and by multi-annual funding of CBMA and INESC-ID (under the projects UID/BIA/04050/2013 and UID/CEC/50021/2013 provided by FCT).

References

1. Bloembergen, D., Tuyls, K., Hennes, D., Kaisers, M.: Evolutionary dynamics of multi-agent learning: a survey. J. Artif. Intell. Res. **53**, 659–697 (2015)
2. Blount, S.: When social outcomes aren't fair: the effect of causal attributions on preferences. Organ. Behav. Hum. Decis. Process. **63**(2), 131–144 (1995)
3. Bornstein, G., Yaniv, I.: Individual and group behavior in the ultimatum game: are groups more rational players? Exp. Econ. **1**(1), 101–108 (1998)
4. Cimini, G., Sánchez, A.: Learning dynamics explains human behaviour in prisoner's dilemma on networks. J. R. Soc. Interface **11**(94), 20131186 (2014)
5. de Melo, C.M., Carnevale, P., Gratch, J.: The effect of expression of anger and happiness in computer agents on negotiations with humans. In: The 10th International Conference on Autonomous Agents and Multiagent Systems, International Foundation for Autonomous Agents and Multiagent Systems, pp. 937 944 (2011)
6. Duch, R., Przepiorka, W., Stevenson, R.: Responsibility attribution for collective decision makers. Am. J. Polit. Sci. **59**(2), 372–389 (2015)
7. Elbittar, A., Gomberg, A., Sour, L.: Group decision-making and voting in ultimatum bargaining: an experimental study. B.E. J. Econ. Anal. Policy **11**(1), 53 (2011)
8. Erev, I., Roth, A.E.: Predicting how people play games: reinforcement learning in experimental games with unique, mixed strategy equilibria. Am. Econ. Rev. **88**, 848–881 (1998)
9. Fischbacher, U., Fong, C.M., Fehr, E.: Fairness, errors and the power of competition. J. Econ. Behav. Organ. **72**(1), 527–545 (2009)

10. Forsythe, R., Horowitz, J.L., Savin, N.E., Sefton, M.: Fairness in simple bargaining experiments. Games Econ. Behav. **6**(3), 347–369 (1994)
11. Fudenberg, D., Levine, D.K.: The Theory of Learning in Games. MIT press, Cambridge (1998)
12. Grosskopf, B.: Reinforcement and directional learning in the ultimatum game with responder competition. Exp. Econ. **6**(2), 141–158 (2003)
13. Güth, W., Schmittberger, R., Schwarze, B.: An experimental analysis of ultimatum bargaining. J. Econ. Behav. Organ. **3**(4), 367–388 (1982)
14. Hagan, J.D., Everts, P.P., Fukui, H., Stempel, J.D.: Foreign policy by coalition: deadlock, compromise, and anarchy. Int. Stud. Rev. **3**(2), 169–216 (2001)
15. Hamilton, W.D.: Innate social aptitudes of man: an approach from evolutionary genetics. In: Fox, R. (ed.) Biosocial Anthropology, pp. 133–155. Wiley, New York (1975)
16. Hoffman, E., McCabe, K., Smith, V.L.: Social distance and other-regarding behavior in dictator games. Am. Econ. Rev. **86**, 653–660 (1996)
17. Iranzo, J., Román, J., Sánchez, A.: The spatial ultimatum game revisited. J. Theor. Biol. **278**(1), 1–10 (2011)
18. Jennings, N.R., Faratin, P., Lomuscio, A.R., Parsons, S., Wooldridge, M.J., Sierra, C.: Automated negotiation: prospects, methods and challenges. Group Decis. Negot. **10**(2), 199–215 (2001)
19. Jing, X., Xie, J.: Group buying: a new mechanism for selling through social interactions. Manage. Sci. **57**(8), 1354–1372 (2011)
20. Kauffman, R.J., Lai, H., Ho, C.-T.: Incentive mechanisms, fairness and participation in online group-buying auctions. Electron. Commer. Res. Appl. **9**(3), 249–262 (2010)
21. Lin, R., Kraus, S.: Can automated agents proficiently negotiate with humans? Commun. ACM **53**(1), 78–88 (2010)
22. Macy, M.W., Flache, A.: Learning dynamics in social dilemmas. Proc. Natl. Acad. Sci. **99**, 7229–7236 (2002)
23. Messick, D.M., Moore, D.A., Bazerman, M.H.: Ultimatum bargaining with a group: underestimating the importance of the decision rule. Organ. Behav. Hum. Decis. Process. **69**(2), 87–101 (1997)
24. Newell, A., Rosenbloom, P.S.: Mechanisms of skill acquisition and the law of practice. Cogn. Skills Acquisition **1**, 1–55 (1981)
25. Nowak, M.A., Page, K.M., Sigmund, K.: Fairness versus reason in the ultimatum game. Science **289**(5485), 1773–1775 (2000)
26. Oosterbeek, H., Sloof, R., Van De Kuilen, G.: Cultural differences in ultimatum game experiments: evidence from a meta-analysis. Exp. Econ. **7**(2), 171–188 (2004)
27. Osborne, M.J.: An Introduction to Game Theory. Oxford University Press, New York (2004)
28. Pacheco, J.M., Santos, F.C., Souza, M.O., Skyrms, B.: Evolutionary dynamics of collective action. In: Chalub, F.A.C.C., Rodrigues, J.F. (eds.) The Mathematics of Darwin's Legacy, pp. 119–138. Springer, Basel (2011)
29. Page, K.M., Nowak, M.A.: Empathy leads to fairness. Bull. Math. Biol. **64**(6), 1101–1116 (2002)
30. Page, K.M., Nowak, M.A., Sigmund, K.: The spatial ultimatum game. Proc. R. Soc. Lond. B Biol. Sci. **267**(1458), 2177–2182 (2000)
31. Pinheiro, F.L., Santos, M.D., Santos, F.C., Pacheco, J.M.: Origin of peer influence in social networks. Phys. Rev. Lett. **112**(9), 098702 (2014)

32. Rand, D.G., Tarnita, C.E., Ohtsuki, H., Nowak, M.A.: Evolution of fairness in the one-shot anonymous ultimatum game. Proc. Natl. Acad. Sci. **110**(7), 2581–2586 (2013)
33. Rendell, L., Boyd, R., Cownden, D., Enquist, M., Eriksson, K., Feldman, M.W., Fogarty, L., Ghirlanda, S., Lillicrap, T., Laland, K.N.: Why copy others? insights from the social learning strategies tournament. Science **328**(5975), 208–213 (2010)
34. Rosenfeld, A., Zuckerman, I., Segal-Halevi, E., Drein, O., Kraus, S.: Negochat-a: a chat-based negotiation agent with bounded rationality. Auton. Agent. Multi-Agent Syst. **30**(1), 60–81 (2016)
35. Roth, A.E., Erev, I.: Learning in extensive-form games: experimental data and simple dynamic models in the intermediate term. Games Econ. Behav. **8**(1), 164–212 (1995)
36. Santos, F.P., Santos, F.C., Melo, F.S., Paiva, A., Pacheco, J.M.: Learning to be fair in multiplayer ultimatum games. In: Proceedings of the 2016 International Conference on Autonomous Agents and Multiagent Systems, International Foundation for Autonomous Agents and Multiagent Systems, pp. 1381–1382 (2016)
37. Santos, F.P., Santos, F.C., Paiva, A.: The evolutionary perks of being irrational. In: Proceedings of the 2015 International Conference on Autonomous Agents and Multiagent Systems, International Foundation for Autonomous Agents and Multiagent Systems, pp. 1847–1848 (2015)
38. Santos, F.P., Santos, F.C., Paiva, A., Pacheco, J.M.: Evolutionary dynamics of group fairness. J. Theor. Biol. **378**, 96–102 (2015)
39. Segal-Halevi, E., Hassidim, A., Aumann, Y.: Waste makes haste: bounded time protocols for envy-free cake cutting with free disposal. In: Proceedings of the 2015 International Conference on Autonomous Agents and Multiagent Systems, International Foundation for Autonomous Agents and Multiagent Systems, pp. 901–908 (2015)
40. Sequeira, P., Melo, F.S., Paiva, A.: Emergence of emotional appraisal signals in reinforcement learning agents. Auton. Agents Multi-Agent Syst. **29**(4), 537–568 (2014)
41. Sigmund, K.: The Calculus of Selfishness. Princeton University Press, Princeton (2010)
42. Sinatra, R., Iranzo, J., Gomez-Gardenes, J., Floria, L.M., Latora, V., Moreno, Y.: The ultimatum game in complex networks. J. Stat. Mech. Theory Exp. **2009**(09), P09012 (2009)
43. Skyrms, B.: Signals: Evolution, Learning, and Information. Oxford University Press, Oxford (2010)
44. Sutton, R.S., Barto, A.G.: Reinforcement Learning: An Introduction. MIT Press, Cambridge (1998)
45. Szolnoki, A., Perc, M., Szabó, G.: Defense mechanisms of empathetic players in the spatial ultimatum game. Phys. Rev. Lett. **109**(7), 078701 (2012)
46. Thaler, R.H.: Anomalies: the ultimatum game. J. Econ. Perspect. **2**, 195–206 (1988)
47. Thorndike, E.L.: Animal intelligence: an experimental study of the associative processes in animals. In: The Psychological Review: Monograph Supplements, (4), i (1898)
48. Van Segbroeck, S., De Jong, S., Nowé, A., Santos, F.C., Lenaerts, T.: Learning to coordinate in complex networks. Adapt. Behav. **18**(5), 416–427 (2010)
49. Van Segbroeck, S., Pacheco, J.M., Lenaerts, T., Santos, F.C.: Emergence of fairness in repeated group interactions. Phys. Rev. Lett. **108**(15), 158104 (2012)
50. Weibull, J.W.: Evolutionary Game Theory. MIT Press, Cambridge (1997)

Using Stackelberg Games to Model Electric Power Grid Investments in Renewable Energy Settings

Merlinda Andoni$^{(\boxtimes)}$ and Valentin Robu

Institute of Sensors, Signals and Systems, Heriot-Watt University, Edinburgh, UK
{ma146,v.robu}@hw.ac.uk

Abstract. Often renewable generators cluster in remote regions (such as windy islands) located away from demand centres. Suitability of these locations in terms of renewable resources, is often coupled with insufficient grid capacity, which leads to the application of generation curtailment, when power generated exceeds local aggregate demand. This work studies the effect of curtailments schemes on the strategic interaction of different investors. Our work uses a game-theoretic approach to study the profitability and decision making on future renewable investment, for a variety of different schemes. Next, we study the effect of curtailment and line access rules in power grid expansion. We model the interplay between a private line investor and local generators as a Stackelberg game and determine the generation capacity and profits at equilibrium. Finally, we examine a UK-based network upgrade case-study and show how results can be utilised to set a grid access payment mechanism, ensuring both the implementation of transmission and local generation investments.

Keywords: Generation incentives · Renewable energy · Stackelberg game · Transmission investment

1 Introduction

Renewable energy sources (RES) are a key technology for the transition to low-carbon economy and sustainability [24]. In recent years, this problem has begun to attract considerable attention from the artificial intelligence and multi-agent community, as part of the computational sustainability agenda [6,30,31]. In practical developments, in many countries, the implementation of incentive mechanisms such as feed-in tariffs (FITs) or renewable obligations (ROs) have led fast increases of installed renewable generation capacity. This capacity is typically provided by local generators (such as wind turbines or PV panels) embedded in local distribution networks. While this is a beneficial development from the point of view of decarbonisation goals, it places great strains on existing electricity grids, and raises a new set of challenges [5,9].

Often, most favourable locations for generation, where renewable resources are abundant or generators meet least planning resistance, are far away from

© Springer International Publishing AG 2016
N. Osman and C. Sierra (Eds.): AAMAS 2016 Ws Best Papers, LNAI 10002, pp. 127–146, 2016.
DOI: 10.1007/978-3-319-46882-2_8

the electricity demand centres, where power is most needed. High volumes of RES generators coupled with insufficient grid infrastructure, can often lead to *generation curtailment*. Generators are required to reduce their power outputs, due to technical reasons, in the discretion of the system operator, resulting in 'waste' energy [25]. In many countries including the UK, when generators operate at areas with network constraints, they are usually compensated for the reduced profits when imposed to curtailment, leading to increasing energy costs.

For this reason, new approaches are required to deal with the issue of curtailment, such as the introduction of Active Network Management (ANM) techniques and new commercial agreements between RES generators and system operators. In this context, generators are offered a non-firm connection and agree to the rules, order and frequency of curtailment.

Different curtailment strategies are used in ANM schemes or proposed by the power systems literature [4,7,13]. Related work so far views these schemes from a technical scope, focusing on which curtailment schemes are easier to implement and guarantee operational stability. However, it has become apparent that other than the financial incentives available (the level of ROs or FITs), the curtailment level and strategy selected by the system operator can be crucial for the decision making of investors, whether to invest in new renewable generation capacity [2].

Curtailment can be mitigated by building or reinforcing distribution or transmission lines between remote locations where capacity (such as wind turbines) can be installed, and areas of high demand. This can be expensive and technically challenging, especially as these lines often have to be deployed in harsh environments, such as at considerable depth on the sea floor.

The starting point of our work was motivated by the practical problem of reinforcing transmission/distribution lines in outlying islands and remote regions of Scotland. The Orkney Islands (in north-eastern Scotland) are a classical example of active network management scheme running in practice, where both installed renewable generation and curtailment levels are among the highest in the UK [13].

In many countries, public funding has been used by transmission system or local distribution network operators (TSO/DNOs) to reinforce such power lines. This is, however, expensive and increasingly harder to justify (since only a few companies benefit from what is essentially a public investment), and often leads to considerable delays in capacity being installed. Recently, system operators have started a debate on finding new ways to incentivies privately built lines [11], paid by the renewable generation companies [15], possibly partially supported by TSOs/DNOs. This raises the crucial issue of the line access rules to be applied to the new transmission lines, as well as the interplay between the line access and the curtailment mechanism.

While lines with completely private access (so called 'single merchant access') lines are possible, it would be beneficial if new power lines are built (partially) by private investors, keeping the access to this infrastructure public. Power lines can be built under *'common access'* line rules, where a line investor is granted approval to install the power line, however he has to permit access to other generators or competitors, who are subject to a transmission fee per energy unit transported through the transmission link. The level of the payment mechanism is capped by the independent system regulator. We show in this work that the interaction between line access rules and the curtailment scheme selected can bring up complicated problems, especially as different players (local RES generators, line investor or system operator) desire to optimise different goals. We show that for 'common access' line rules and a fair curtailment policy, the line investor and local generators interplay results to a complex Stackelberg game, where the generation capacities built and associated profits depend on the strategic interaction of these players.

Specifically, the case study we use in this paper, is the grid reinforcement between Hunterston and Crossaig, in the remote Kintyre peninsula in Western Scotland. This remote region is a good example of a location with high wind generation potential, where it became clear that private line investment would be needed to export the renewable energy generated. However, the 'single merchant' access mechanism used had the unintended effect that each new renewable development built its own separate line, which met only the capacity required for its own wind farm. This resulted in no less than three separate line reinforcements being built or under construction between the same two locations. Obviously, this is a hugely expensive and wasteful process, as power lines have to be laid subsea, for a distance of over 20 miles.

While the marginal cost of building a larger capacity line is cited as a possible explanation, a less obvious, but potentially key reason is that each producer had no incentive to build a larger capacity line which permitted access to rival competitors. The main analytical result of this paper suggests that, in such cases, it is possible for Ofgem (the UK system regulator) to encourage private line investors - possibly, with subsidies or public support - to build larger capacity lines under a 'common access' rule, as long as transmission charges, in the equilibrium of the game, are set in such ways that allow sufficient profits.

The main contribution of our work can be summarised as follows:

- First, we provide a study of the most prevailing curtailment strategies and show how these rules affect the viability of a RES investment, at a certain location. Moreover, we use a competitive analysis approach to determine the level of RES capacity built at a single location with network constraints.
- Second, we consider a two-location setting of a demand and a RES generation site and study the transmission interconnection installation as a Stackelberg game, between the line investor and local RES generators, and we characterise the equilibrium of the game.
- Next, we perform a case study analysis and apply our model to a network upgrade project in the UK. The financial parameters used for this are realistic, and in fact much of this information was released by Ofgem and Scottish Southern Energy (SSE), the local DNO, as part of a public consultation exercise [27].

Finally, we emphasize that, while the numerical application is specific to the UK case, our analysis and equilibrium results are general, and the underlying problem of renewable generation and demand not being co-located occurs in many other places around the globe, facing similar challenges.

The remainder of this paper is organised as follows: Sect. 2 presents the literature review and Sect. 3 elaborates on different curtailment rules. Effects on renewable capacity investment are shown in Sect. 4 and on transmission investment in Sect. 5. Numerical results of the network upgrade case study are presented in Sect. 6, while Sect. 7 concludes.

2   Related Work

The issue of curtailment has been studied by both academic and commercial studies [2,4,7,13], focusing mainly on the technical and legal implications of different schemes. Our work aims to determine the effects of different policies in the incentives and decision-making of generation capacity and power grid infrastructure investors.

Different players and their strategic interaction can be simulated with agent-based modeling. In [3], renewable and grid infrastructure investment are jointly considered, whereas [20] studies the effects of generation capacity to transmission planning. [19] examines network reinforcements performed by system operators or private investors and shows that, the optimal results derived can vary widely, due to different underlying goals. Their work is focused, however, on using Mathematical Program with Equilibrium Constraints (MPEC) to solve power flows, and curtailment strategies were not considered. In [23], the authors consider privately installed power lines and show how group formation can be used to reduce the system's losses. The main focus in this work is the coalition formation and its results in configurations of multiple-location settings, not the effects of transmission access rules, which are the scope of our work.

Several works consider transmission planning or expansion at congested areas of the power network. Joskow and Tirole [10] analyse a two-node network market behaviour, for settings of players with different market power and allocation of transmission rights. Our work follows a different approach, since we specify our analysis on the transmission access rules and curtailment imposed, rather than analysing the market behaviour in areas of network constraints.

Several works use Stackelberg game analysis to model network expansion with economic analysis and social welfare [26], Locational Marginal Pricing [28] or stochastic renewable generation [32].

Moreover, Stackelberg games have been used to model energy trading with microgrids [1,17]. Zheng et al. (2015) propose a novel, crowdsourced funding model for renewable energy investments, using a sequential game-theoretic approach [33]. However, transmission issues were not considered.

In addition, Stackelberg games have been extensively used to model security games [22] or test designing [18].

3 Curtailment Rules

The most significant criteria for determination of the curtailment rules include ease of implementation, fairness, efficiency, transparency and reliability. A review of different schemes is presented in [4,7,8,12]. The generators can be allocated to a curtailment scheme, according to their technical characteristics, rated capacity or chronological order of their regulatory approval.

In our work, we focus on two mechanisms that are widely used in commercial ANM schemes in the UK[1] or proposed in the literature: last-in-first out (LIFO), where the last generator granted a connection to the scheme is curtailed first, and Pro Rata (or proportional), where curtailment is shared equally according to the size or power output of generators.

Another important category are *Rota*-based schemes, where generators are curtailed on a rotational basis or a predetermined rota, as specified by the system operator. However, Rota does not account for the size of the generators, disadvantaging the smaller units. For this reason, we propose a new Rota-type curtailment rule we call *Fractional Round Robin* (FRR), where the required curtailed power is allocated to the generators on a sequential order in direct relation to their size. This scheme provides similar fairness properties to the Pro Rata rule and provides the benefit of reducing the frequency of curtailment. Note that, such schemes might require modified pitch-controlled wind turbines, able to receive power set-points from the system operator, thus the frequency of curtailment is also significant for the generators imposed to curtailment.

We illustrate the effects of these schemes with a simplified example. Consider a network with no export capability, comprising three wind generators of unequal rated capacities, e.g. $P_{N_1} = 3$ MW, $P_{N_2} = 5$ MW and $P_{N_3} = 2$ MW. The subscript denotes the order of connection to the power grid, with the first generator being the earlier distributed generation (DG) connection. Moreover, for example simplicity, let's assume the actual power output at time interval t, equals their nominal capacities i.e. $P_{G,t} = 10$ MW, while the total demand at time t at this location is $P_{D,t} = 7$ MW. Hence, given that excess energy cannot be exported, a total of $P_{C,t} = P_{G,t} - P_{D,t} = 3$ MW needs to be curtailed.

With LIFO, the third generator is completely curtailed, the second is curtailed by 1 MW and the first is not affected. By contrast, with Pro Rata the required curtailment is distributed proportionally among the generators, as:

$$P_{C_i,t} = \frac{P_{C,t}}{P_{G,t}} P_{G_i,t} \tag{1}$$

This results in 0.9 MW, 1.5 MW and 0.6 MW curtailed from the generator 1, 2 and 3 respectively. With a simple Rota strategy, the generators take turns each time curtailment is required. With FRR, on the other hand, we account for the size (i.e. rated capacity) of a generator. This means for instance that,

---

[1] LIFO is used in: https://www.ssepd.co.uk/OrkneySmartGrid/ and www.ninessma rtgrid.co.uk/our-project/ Pro Rata is used in: http://innovation.ukpowernetworks. co.uk/innovation/en/Projects/tier-2-projects/Flexible-Plug-and-Play-(FPP)/.

on average, every 10 times a curtailment of 3 MW is needed, the first generator will be curtailed 3 times, the second 5 times and the third 2 times. It can be shown that for a sufficiently long period of time (several years lifetime of the wind turbine), the curtailment rate under FRR converges to the proportional curtailment rate with Pro Rata.

To ease understanding, in Sect. 3.1 we provide an example implementation of curtailment schemes, to show how they can affect the viability of RES investments. We note that several prior works have discussed the effect of the curtailment strategies applied on building generation capacity. In [13], the effects of several curtailment strategies on the capacity factor (CF) of wind generators based in Orkney, Scotland are examined. It is shown that LIFO leads to lower CF for 'later' connections, when compared to Pro Rata and Rota, and therefore might discourage new generation capacity investment [14]. A related study by UK Power Networks observes that the most important factor in the decision-making procedure of a new investor, especially if a LIFO scheme is used, is the CF of the last generator connected [16]. A LIFO scheme discourages new investment by shutting out newer entrants, essentially leading to unexploited network capacity. Hence, the focus of the analysis in our work will be on 'fair' schemes, such as Pro Rata or FRR.

3.1 Effects of Curtailment Strategies on Renewable Capacity Utilisation - An Illustration

Based on the example network of 10 MW total power in Sect. 3, we simulated a curtailment process over the course of one year, to illustrate the effect of different schemes on the capacity factor (CF), a crucial indicator for performance. CF is a widely used parameter in electrical engineering, and is a ratio of the actual energy generated by a certain resource, to the maximum energy level it could generate, if operating under nominal conditions. Note that, the CF of a typical wind turbine (even if output is never curtailed) depends on wind conditions at the site's location and in the UK is in the range of 30 %.

Our one-year simulation process performs 8,760 hourly iterations. Every hour, a curtailment event is decided on with a probability of curtailment p_c (here, for simplicity we have $p_c = 0.2$, but in practice this parameter would wary on the network congestion conditions of a specific location). For time intervals when a curtailment event occurs, the total curtailment is determined probabilistically among four levels: of $P_C = 1.5$ MW, 3 MW, 4.5 MW and lastly $P_C = 6$ MW, with probabilities of 40 %, 30 %, 20 % and 10 %, respectively (these numbers follow a realistic distribution, as small curtailment events are much more frequent in practice). Finally, according to the applied strategy, the curtailment is allocated to the three generators.

Results are shown in Fig. 1. First, note that under the LIFO scheme, Generator 1 is not affected, whereas Generators 2 and 3 experience severe CF reduction of 15.10 % and 56.53 %, respectively. CF is affected equally for all generators at 24.34 % with Pro Rata, and similar results are derived for FRR, as expected. Results show, there is a clear market advantage of early connections when LIFO

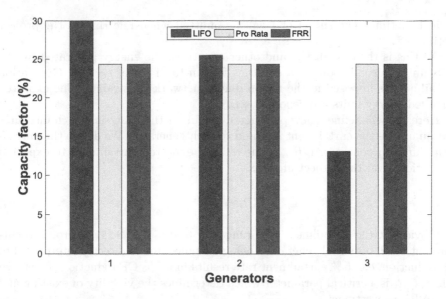

Fig. 1. Curtailment mechanisms effects on the CF of wind generators under LIFO, Pro Rata and FRR

is applied, which is detrimental both for the economic performance of 'late' generators and future investment. With Pro Rata and FRR, CF will continue to decrease if other plants are built, therefore, the commercial and legal clauses of access to the distribution network will differ.

Next, we determine given a congested location, an upper level of tolerable curtailment, which enables renewable capacity investment to be profitable.

4 Renewable Investment in Single Locations

Consider n RES generators at a single location of the distribution network with network constraints. Generator i is expected to produce $\mathsf{E}(E_{G_i,t})$ energy units, in a time interval of length t, according to the available resource on site location, without curtailment. It is important to note that, while for a particular period such as an hour or a day the expected generation is uncertain, for the overall lifetime of a renewable project (typically 20–25 years), the total expected generation can be estimated with relatively high certainty from the weather and wind patterns at a particular location. Hence, the term $\mathsf{E}()$ which denotes 'expected', will be omitted from this point on, in order to simplify the notation. The cost of expected generation per unit c_{G_i} with constant depreciation, is defined as

$$c_{G_i} = \frac{I_{G,i} + M_{G_i}}{E_{G_i}} \qquad (2)$$

where I_{G_i} the cost of building the plant (initial investment), M_{G_i} the cost of operation and maintenance and E_{G_i} the expected generation, throughout the project lifetime. The subscript t will be omitted when referring to the project lifetime.

As this is the case in UK and other countries, the energy generated by the RES unit is usually sold at a constant feed-in-tariff price, p_G [21]. Generation curtailment is imposed in the region due to network constraints. The expected curtailed energy units are denoted as E_{C_i}.

Here, we will define a new parameter, useful for the analysis, which measures and quantifies the curtailment imposed to each generator. We define the *curtailment rate* of i generator CR_i, as the ratio of expected curtailment to expected generation, over the project lifetime:

$$CR_i = \frac{E_{C_i}}{E_{G_i}} \tag{3}$$

Obviously, the curtailment rate ranges from $0 \le CR_i < 1$ i.e. from no curtailment to all potential generation being curtailed and is directly interpreted to CF reduction, e.g. 5 % curtailment rate results in a 5 % CF reduction. As shown below, CR_i is a critical parameter which determines the viability of existing and future RES investment.

4.1   Individual Generator Incentives

Lemma 1. *A generation capacity investment is viable, if and only if the curtailment rate of i generator CR_i is smaller or equal to a threshold τ_G*

$$CR_i \le \tau_G \tag{4}$$

where

$$\tau_G = 1 - \frac{c_G}{p_G} \tag{5}$$

Proof. The profit Π of generator i with curtailment, is given by $\Pi_i = (E_{G_i} - E_{C_i}) \cdot p_G - E_{G_i} \cdot c_{G_i} \ge 0$. Dividing the profit function by $E_{G_i} \cdot c_{G_i}$ and then substituting CR_i by (3) gives $CR_i \le 1 - \frac{c_{G_i}}{p_G}$. We can assume this threshold is location-specific: all generators at this location have approximately the same access to land and required technology. If this is not true, τ_G would depend on the costs c_{G_i} of each generator.   □

As shown here, the profitability of a RES development depends on the relation of the generation cost with the FIT price. The smaller the cost ratio, larger amounts of curtailment can be tolerated by the power producers. However, the rules of curtailment remain under the control of the mechanism designer (local DNO or regulator). Hence, a natural question to ask is *which curtailment rule maximises the local generation capacity?* This question is of interest in itself, but as we will see, it also plays a role in modeling investment decisions of new transmission.

4.2   Total Generation Capacity

Consider a perfectly competitive setting, in which all generators do not have the market power to influence the price equilibrium. Using assumptions of competitive equilibrium (Cournot) analysis, any investor will be able to install an additional generation unit, as long as its marginal profit exceeds its marginal cost. As discussed above, renewable resources and technology are roughly equal for all investors, so we can assume marginal costs are the same and, moreover, the decision to invest is taken if the curtailment rate does not exceed a certain location-dependent threshold τ_G (c.f. Lemma 1). Given these assumptions, the curtailment strategy selected by the system operator, can impact the total generation capacity installed.

Lemma 2. *In a perfectly competitive equilibrium setting, the local generation capacity installed is maximised under proportional curtailment strategies.*

Proof. The problem of maximising the generation capacity installed is equivalent to maximising the total energy generated at a single location and it can be formulated as the optimisation problem

$$\max \left(\sum_{i=1}^{n} E_{G_i} \right) = max(E_{G_1} + ... + E_{G_i} + ... + E_{G_n}) \tag{6}$$

subject to a set of n constraints (one for each generator), as derived from Lemma 1, above:

$$\frac{E_{C_i}}{E_{G_i}} \leq \tau_G, \forall i = 1 \dots n \tag{7}$$

The curtailed energy units E_{C_i}, are equal to the energy it could be generated, minus the amount actually required (demand), $E_{C_i} = E_{G_i} - E_{D_i}$. Furthermore, the total generation which can be purchased from renewable sources at this location (or exported at another location) is bounded across all the n generators to some quantity E_D (total demand), where $E_D = \sum_{i=1}^{n} E_{D_i}$. The constraints in (7), can hence be written as $E_{G_i} \leq \frac{E_{D_i}}{1 - \tau_G}, \forall i = 1 \dots n$. The initial maximisation target can be decomposed without loss of generality into n individual maximisation problems, therefore $\max \left(\sum_{i=1}^{n} E_{G_i} \right) = \sum_{i=1}^{n} \max (E_{G_i})$ and given the set of n constraints, will be maximised when all the constraints are equal, i.e. $E_{G_i} = \frac{E_{D_i}}{1 - \tau_G}, \forall i = 1 \dots n$. Expressed back in terms of curtailment rate, the solution of the problem is given when all curtailment rates CR_i of the generators are equal to each other and to the threshold τ_G:

$$\frac{E_{C_1}}{E_{G_1}} = \frac{E_{C_2}}{E_{G_2}} = ... = \frac{E_{C_i}}{E_{G_i}} = ... = \frac{E_{C_n}}{E_{G_n}} = \tau_G \tag{8}$$

Essentially, this condition will be satisfied by proportional or 'fair' curtailment strategies, i.e. those mechanisms which divide existing demand, hence curtailment, equally across all participants and can be expressions of either Pro Rata or FRR type of strategy.   □

5 Transmission Investment in Multiple Locations

In this section, we turn our attention to the central problem of this paper, namely how the applied line access and curtailment rules influence the decision to build or reinforce transmission lines.

In our analysis, we consider two locations: A is a net consumer (demand exceeds supply, e.g. a mainland location with industry or significant population density) and B is a net energy producer (favourable RES conditions, e.g. a remote region rich in wind resource). In practice, there would be some local demand and supply, considered here negligible, and installation of new RES capacity would not be feasible without network upgrade. Location A has a net demand of $E_{D,A}$, equal to local generation minus local demand. Moreover, we consider two players: a player who is the line investor, who can be merchant-type or a utility company and is building the $A - B$ interconnection (and, possibly, additional renewable generation capacity at B), and a local player, who represents the other renewable generators or investors located at B (this second player can be thought of as the local community). Note that in Scotland, but also in several other countries such as Denmark, local groups often group together to make land available and invest in local renewable generation projects.[2]

We consider two separate models for the multi-location problem, distinguished by how strategically the local investors respond to the actions of the utility company (i.e. the 'line player'). In the first model (Sect. 5.1), we formalise the decision of the line investor to build the line, but assuming the local players do not react to this line being built, by building extra capacity themselves. In the second model, local investors can and do react to this extra line capacity being built. Hence, the line investor has to account for this reaction of the other generator when building the line, leading to a Stackelberg game. This case is examined in Sect. 5.2.

5.1 Implementation in Areas with High Curtailment

Driven by favourable RES conditions, assume several investors have installed considerable volumes of RES capacity $E_{G_2,B}$ at location B, which is required to be curtailed by $E_{C_2,B}$ energy units. Local generators at B act in a perfectly competitive setting or Cournot equilibrium.

A new transmission line will export the renewable energy installed by the line investor $E_{G_1,B}$, but will also take advantage of the curtailed energy by local generators. The power line cost, over project lifetime, is estimated as:

---

[2] In Scotland, Community Energy Scotland (CES) is an umbrella organisation representing the interests of such groups.

$$C_T = I_T + M_T \tag{9}$$

where I_T the cost of building the line (or initial investment) and M_T the cost of operation and maintenance. Note that C_T refers to the total costs over the project lifetime, while c_G in (2), refers to the cost per energy unit.

The monetary value of the transmission line is proportional to the energy flowing from B to A, charged under 'common access' rules with p_T transmission fee per energy unit. Similarly to the previous analysis, we ask: *How does the curtailment rate affect the viability of the transmission line investment?*

Lemma 3. *A transmission capacity investment is viable if and only if the curtailment rate of local generators $CR_{2,B}$ (before the line is built) is greater or equal to a threshold τ_T*

$$CR_{2,B} \geq \tau_T \tag{10}$$

where

$$\tau_T = \frac{C_T - E_{D,A} \cdot (p_G - c_{G_1})}{c_{G_1} \cdot E_{G_2,B}} \tag{11}$$

Proof. The line investor has two streams of revenue, the curtailed energy produced by local generators and the energy generated from additional capacity, which lead to a profit function of

$$\Pi_1 = E_{C_2,B} \cdot p_T + E_{G_1,B} \cdot (p_G - c_{G_1}) - C_T \geq 0$$

The latter combined with the capacity of the line $E_{D,A} = E_{G_1,B} + E_{C_2,B}$ and divided by the expected energy from local generators $E_{G_2,B}$, results in the curtailment rate of local producers at B:

$$CR_{2,B} \geq \frac{C_T - E_{D,A} \cdot (p_G - c_{G_1})}{(p_T - p_G + c_{G_1}) \cdot E_{G_2,B}} \tag{12}$$

For local generators, the curtailed energy before the line is built is essentially wasted. Recall that (see Lemma 1), local generator investments are still profitable, as long as $CR_i \leq \tau_G$. This means the line investor can actually impose a large transmission fee, which approaches the FIT price $p_T \to p_G$, in order to maximise its own profits. Considering this in (12), we derive the desired conclusion.   □

Note that in this section, we assumed the local investors are not players who have the possibility to react by increasing their own generation once the new line gets built. In practice, they do, of course, hence the decision of the line investor must include an element of 'strategic foresight' to include the reaction of the other investors when deciding whether to build the line. This model is essentially a Stackelberg game, and is examined in the next section.

5.2   Transmission Investment as a Stackelberg Game

In this section, we determine the equilibrium strategies of the line investor and local investors, who are able to react to the new line being built. For simplicity, we assume there is no renewable capacity installed at location B prior to the construction of the transmission line.

Crucially, in this setting, the line investor has a 'first mover' advantage, as only he can build the grid infrastructure, which is expensive and technically challenging and only a limited set of investors (such as DNO-approved or DNO themselves), have the technical expertise and regulatory approval to carry it out. The line investor (*leader*) can assess and evaluate the reaction of other investors to determine his strategy, namely the capacity of the power line and the level of renewable capacity to be installed, with the ultimate target to influence the equilibrium price. Other investors (*followers*) can only act after observing the leader's strategy. In practice, the leader can be thought of as a major utility company developing a wind investment project, while the follower investors can be thought of as the local community on the island, who do not have the technical/financial capacity to build a line, but may have access to cheaper land, it is easier to get community permission to build turbines etc., hence may have a lower per unit generation cost. This two-stage process is analysed as a Stackelberg game [29].

Equilibrium is found by backward induction. First of all, the leader estimates the best response of local generators, given its own output and then decides his strategy with profit maximisation criteria. The renewable generation capacity installed by the follower will be a function of the generation capacity installed by the line investor. At a second stage, the follower observes this strategy and decides his generation capacity, according to its best response, i.e. maximising his own profit, as anticipated and predicted by the leader. The solution of this process is the Stackelberg equilibrium of the transmission investment game.

The network access arrangements play here a crucial role for the market equilibrium formed. We examine in the following sections, the effects of two representative curtailment rules, LIFO and proportional schemes, which can be expressions of both Pro Rata or FRR.

LIFO Scheme

Lemma 4. *The transmission investment game between the line investor and local generators with LIFO curtailment results in the expected generation at Stackelberg equilibrium:*

$$E_{G_1,B}^* = E_{D_A} \tag{13}$$

$$E_{G_2,B}^* = 0 \tag{14}$$

and associated profits

$$\Pi_1^* = (p_G - c_{G_1}) \cdot E_{D_A} \tag{15}$$

$$\Pi_2^* = 0 \tag{16}$$

Proof. The capacity of the transmission line is bound by the demand at mainland, therefore total generation capacity at location B, $(E_{G_{1,B}} + E_{G_{2,B}})$ cannot exceed E_{D_A}. Any generation capacity built exceeding the demanded energy, has to be curtailed. Taking this into account, the profit functions of the two players are

$$\Pi_1 = p_T \cdot E_{D_A} + (p_G - p_T - c_{G_1}) \cdot E_{G_{1,B}} - C_T$$
$$\Pi_2 = (E_{D_A} - E_{G_{1,B}}) \cdot (p_G - p_T - c_{G_2})$$

Clearly, under a LIFO scheme the line investor (who acts first) is protected from any curtailment, hence it can build all generation capacity to cover demand E_{D_A} itself and maximise its profits. The local investors would take all curtailment in the LIFO scheme, as they represent 'late' connections and have low priority, hence there is no incentive for them to invest in new capacity.   □

To conclude, LIFO always protects the line investor, giving it absolute advantage.

Pro Rata or FRR Scheme. The main difference from LIFO, is that Pro Rata or FRR rules are imposed to all generators, regardless of their order of connection. Therefore, more total capacity $E_{G,B} = E_{G_{1,B}} + E_{G_{2,B}}$ than the energy demanded at A can potentially be installed, as long as the curtailment rate or energy curtailed $E_{C,B} = E_{G,B} - E_{D,A}$ allows the investments to be profitable. The curtailment rate at location B is given by

$$CR_B = 1 - \frac{E_{D,A}}{E_{G_{1,B}} + E_{G_{2,B}}} \tag{17}$$

Using the curtailment rate from (17), the general profit functions of the players, which are functions of both players energy outputs, i.e. $\Pi(E_{G_{1,B}}, E_{G_{2,B}})$, can be written as:

$$\Pi_1 = \left(\frac{p_G \cdot E_{D,A}}{E_{G_{1,B}} + E_{G_{2,B}}} - c_{G_1} \right) \cdot E_{G_{1,B}}$$
$$+ \frac{p_T \cdot E_{D,A}}{E_{G_{1,B}} + E_{G_{2,B}}} \cdot E_{G_{2,B}} - C_T \tag{18}$$

$$\Pi_2 = \left[\frac{(p_G - p_T) \cdot E_{D,A}}{E_{G_{1,B}} + E_{G_{2,B}}} - c_{G_2} \right] \cdot E_{G_{2,B}} \tag{19}$$

Before stating our main Stackelberg equilibrium result, we need to define the best responses of the players.

Proposition 1. *Given the output of the leader $E_{G_{1,B}}$, the best response of the follower which maximises his profit is*

$$E^*_{G_{2,B}} = \sqrt{\frac{(p_G - p_T) \cdot E_{D,A} \cdot E_{G_{1,B}}}{c_{G_2}}} - E_{G_{1,B}} \tag{20}$$

Proof. Let the value of $E_{G_2,B}$ which maximises the profit of the follower be:

$$E_{G_2,B}{}^* = \underset{E_{G_2,B}}{argmax} \; \Pi_2$$

Setting as zero the partial derivative of Π_2 in (19), with respect to $E_{G_2,B}$ and rearranging, we get (20).   □

Proposition 2. *Given the output of the follower $E^*_{G_2,B}$, the best (i.e. profit-maximising) response of the leader is:*

$$E^*_{G_1,B} = \frac{(p_G - p_T) \cdot c_{G_2} \cdot E_{D,A}}{4 \cdot c_{G_1}{}^2}$$

Proof. Let the value of $E_{G_1,B}$ which maximises the profit of the follower be

$$E_{G_1,B}{}^* = \underset{E_{G_1,B}}{argmax} \; \Pi_1$$

Substituting (20) in (18) and then setting as zero the partial derivative of Π_1 with respect to $E_{G_1,B}$ gives the stated expression.   □

Lemma 5. *The transmission investment game between the line investor and local generators with Pro Rata, results in expected generation at Stackelberg equilibrium:*

$$E^*_{G_1,B} = \frac{(p_G - p_T) \cdot c_{G_2} \cdot E_{D,A}}{4 \cdot c_{G_1}{}^2} \qquad (21)$$

$$E^*_{G_2,B} = \frac{(p_G - p_T) \cdot (2 \cdot c_{G_1} - c_{G_2}) \cdot E_{D,A}}{4 \cdot c_{G_1}{}^2} \qquad (22)$$

and associated profits

$$\Pi_1{}^* = \frac{(p_G - p_T) \cdot c_{G_2} \cdot E_{D,A}}{4 \cdot c_{G_1}} + p_T \cdot E_{D,A} - C_T \qquad (23)$$

$$\Pi_2{}^* = \frac{(2 \cdot c_{G_1} - c_{G_2})^2 \cdot (p_G - p_T) \cdot E_{D,A}}{4 \cdot c_{G_1}^2} \qquad (24)$$

Proof. Replacing Proposition 2 in (20), the optimum output of local generators $E^*_{G_2,B}$ is found, i.e. (22). Finally, substituting the energy outputs at equilibrium (21) and (22) in (18) and (19), we derive the equilibrium profits $\Pi_1{}^* = max \; \Pi_1$ and $\Pi_2{}^* = max \; \Pi_2$.   □

By adding up (21) and (22), we see the total generation installed at B depends on the energy demand, the transmission fee and the line investor's generation cost, as:

$$E^*_{G_B}{}^* = E^*_{G_1,B} + E^*_{G_2,B} = \frac{(p_G - p_T)E_{D,A}}{2c_{G_1}} \qquad (25)$$

Finally note that a curtailment scheme is required if and only if total generation capacity exceeds the net demand at A, $E_{G_1,B} + E_{G_2,B} > E_{D,A}$ (otherwise there is no strategic interaction and no game, as both players can sell all their generated power). This constraint yields the following conditions, which must hold for the setting to actually be game-theoretic (and for our analysis to be relevant):

$$c_{G_2} < p_G - p_T \tag{26}$$

$$c_{G_1} < \frac{p_G - p_T}{2} \tag{27}$$

6   Network Upgrade Case Study

In this section, we apply the theoretical Stackelberg model stated in the previous section (c.f. Lemma 5), to a case study of a grid reinforcement project under development in Western Scotland.

The power grid in the Kintyre peninsula was originally designed and built to serve a typical rural area of low demand. Wind energy development, quickly led to substantial volumes of renewable investment in the region. Future renewable connections in this area are estimated to exceed 793 MW. Scottish Southern Energy (SSE), the local DNO, proceeded to a grid reinforcement project connecting the Kintyre peninsula to the Scottish mainland in Hunterston, partially via a sub-sea link (see Fig. 2). The project will allow 150 MW additional renewable capacity [27] with an estimated cost of £230 m.

Based on these project figures, we consider a simplified two-node network, in which the mainland energy demand being met by generation in Kintyre, equals the energy transmitted through the power line. With the majority of investment being wind projects, we estimate the total energy demand as

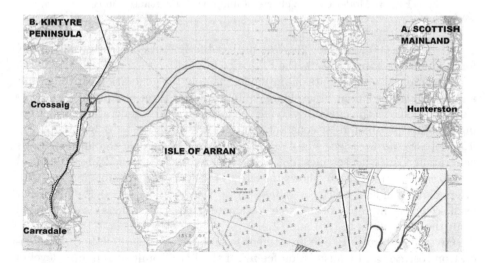

Fig. 2. Hunterston-Kintyre project map: power line connecting Scottish mainland (high demand area) to Kintyre peninsula (high renewables) [27]

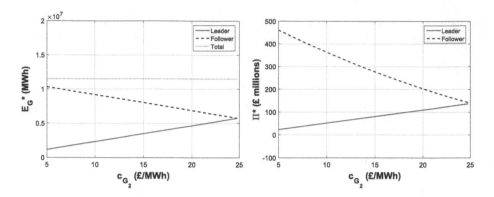

Fig. 3. Model results: effects of local generators' generation cost

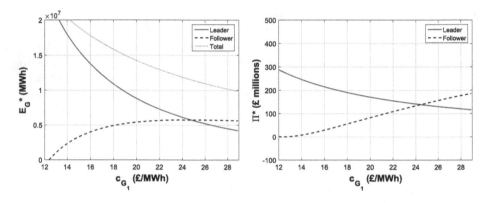

Fig. 4. Model results: effects of line investor's generation cost

$E_{D,A} = 9,855,000$ MWh for 25 years project lifetime. As currently valid in UK for medium size wind projects, the FIT price was set to $p_G = £82.60$/MWh [21].

We summarise the results of our model, namely the generation capacity built and associated profits at Stackelberg equilibrium, for three scenarios: *Scenario 1* (see Fig. 3) shows the effect of varying the local investors' generation cost, keeping all other parameters at constant values (set as $c_{G_1} = p_T = 0.3p_G$ and $c_{G_2} = 0 \ldots c_{G_1}$), *Scenario 2* (see Fig. 4) shows the effect of varying the line investor's generation cost (with settings: $c_{G_2} = p_T = 0.3p_G$ and $c_{G_1} = 0.125p_G \ldots 0.35p_G$) and *Scenario 3* (see Fig. 5) shows the effect of varying the transmission fee (with other parameters set at $c_{G_1} = 0.3p_G$, $c_{G_2} = 0.9c_{G_1}$ and $p_T = 0 \ldots 0.4p_G$). For each scenario, the range of the 'free' parameter (fixing the others) is determined from the constraints in (26) and (27).

Given a certain FIT, line investment feasibility depends directly on the generation cost c_{G_1} and transmission fee p_T. If the line is built, it sets up a level of total feasible generation investment at B, which combined with a proportional access rule, leads to larger volumes of capacity being built than actual demand

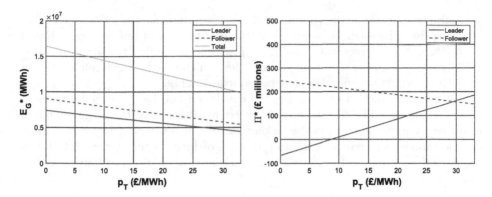

Fig. 5. Model results: effects of transmission fee

(see Fig. 3 and (25)), as long as the curtailment rate is kept under reasonable levels. Note this total level of generation does *not* depend on the generation costs of local investors, since they cannot act without the existence of the line (see Fig. 3). For all settings, the size of c_{G_2} relative to c_{G_1} determines how exportable level of generation capacity is shared among the two agents. Cheaper generation has an advantage in all three sets of results (c.f. Figs. 3, 4 and 5), although as the graphs show, the dependency is not necessarily linear.

Another conclusion is that transmission charges, agreed by the line investor and an independent regulatory authority, has to be set within a specific range. Low values of p_T may lead to transmission investment being aborted, somewhat larger values might theoretically be sufficient to achieve profitability for the line investor, however, hide the risk of 'free-riding' from local investors, who pay cheap for the benefits offered by the leader's costly investment. What the result in Fig. 5 shows is that there exists a range in which p_T can be set such as to assure the line gets built (i.e. when the leader's profits are above 0 – in our case, transmission charges need to be at least £8/MWh), but also not discourage other local renewable investors.

7 Conclusions and Future Work

Building a low-carbon and sustainable future demands further development of RES technologies, which require innovative incentive provision and deployment of new market models. We examine the combined effects of curtailment strategies and transmission access rules on generation capacity investment and foremost network expansion, which is essential aspect for renewable energy integration in practice. Our research focused on the effects of leading curtailment schemes to investors decisions and market behaviour. We model grid reinforcement invest-ment as a two-stage strategic game between the line investor and local gener-ators and determined output generation capacities and profits at equilibrium. One aspect our study highlights is that regulatory authorities who seek renew-able facilitation can promote grid infrastructure expansion, not only by providing subsidies or technical support, but by allowing 'common access' rules, as a tool to attract private investment and improve the profitability of line investors. Based on a UK grid reinforcement project, we proposed a method to calculate transmission charges, under 'common access' rules, which enables the implementation of both transmission and local generation investments.

Future work includes expanding the developed two-location model to more complex settings, in order to model the transmission investment game across multiple locations, such as in the Orkney Islands in Scotland. Moreover, a more detailed model will require the incorporation of future energy storage facilities co-located with renewable generation, which are capable of partially deferring curtailment.

Acknowledgments. The authors would like to thank Community Energy Scotland and SSE for all the information provided, the Scottish government for their financial support through a Local Energy Scotland Challenge grant, and the participants of the Ofgem consultation workshop on new business models for power systems for many inspiring discussions.

References

1. Asimakopoulou, G.E., Dimeas, A.L., Hatziargyriou, N.D.: Leader-follower strategies for energy management of multi-microgrids. IEEE Trans. Smart Grid **4**(4), 1909–1916 (2013)
2. Baringa Partners, UK Power Networks: Flexible Plug and Play Principles of Access Report: Final report on smart commercial arrangements for generators connecting under the Flexible Plug and Play Project. Technical report, December 2012
3. Baringo, L., Conejo, A.J.: Transmission and wind power investment. IEEE Trans. Power Syst. **27**(2), 885–893 (2012)
4. Bell, K., Green, R., Kockar, I., Ault, G., McDonald, J.: Project TransmiT: Academic Review of Transmission Charging Arrangements. Technical report, May 2011
5. Brouwer, A.S., van den Broek, M., Seebregts, A., Faaij, A.: Impacts of large-scale intermittent renewable energy sources on electricity systems and how these can be modeled. Renew. Sustain. Energy Rev. **33**, 443–466 (2014)
6. Chalkiadakis, G., Robu, V., Kota, R., Rogers, A., Jennings, N.R.: Cooperatives of distributed energy resources for efficient virtual power plants. In: 10th International Conference on Autonomous Agents and Multiagent Systems AAMAS 2011, International Foundation for Autonomous Agents and Multiagent Systems, Taipei, pp. 787–794, May 2011
7. Currie, R., O'Neill, B., Foote, C., Gooding, A., Ferris, R., Douglas, J.: Commercial arrangements to facilitate active network management. In: CIRED 21st International Conference on Electricity Distribution, CIRED, Frankfurt, June 2011
8. EirGrid, S.: Ensuring a secure, reliable and efficient power system in a changing environment. Technical report, June 2011
9. Holttinen, H., Meibom, P., Orths, A., Lange, B., O'Malley, M., Tande, J.O., Estanqueiro, A., Gomez, E., Söder, L., Strbac, G., Smith, J.C., van Hulle, F.: Impacts of large amounts of wind power on design and operation of power systems, results of IEA collaboration. Wind Energy **14**(2), 179–192 (2010)

10. Joskow, P., Tirole, J.: Transmission rights and market power on electric power networks. RAND J. Econ. **31**(3), 450–487 (2000)
11. Joskow, P., Tirole, J.: Merchant transmission investment. J. Ind. Econ. **53**(2), 233–264 (2005)
12. Kane, L., Ault, G.: A review and analysis of renewable energy curtailment schemes and principles of access: transitioning towards business as usual. Energy Policy **72**, 67–77 (2014)
13. Kane, L., Ault, G.: Evaluation of wind power curtailment in active network management schemes. IEEE Trans. Power Syst. **30**(2), 672–679 (2015)
14. Kane, L., Ault, G., Gill, S.: An assessment of principles of access for wind generation curtailment in active network management schemes. In: CIRED 22nd International Conference on Electricity Distribution, CIRED, Stockholm, June 2013
15. Kristiansen, T., Rosellon, J.: Merchant electricity transmission expansion: a European case study. Energy **35**(10), 4107–4115 (2010)
16. Laguna Estopier, A., Crosthwaite Eyre, E., Georgiopoulos, S., Marantes, C.: Flexible plug and play low carbon networks: commercial solutions for active network management. In: CIRED 22nd International Conference and Exhibition on Electricity Distribution. IET, Stockholm (2013)
17. Lee, J., Guo, J., Choi, J.K., Zukerman, M.: Distributed energy trading in microgrids: a game theoretic model and its equilibrium analysis. IEEE Trans. Industr. Electron. **62**(6), 3524–3533 (2015)
18. Li, Y., Conitzer, V.: Game-theoretic question selection for tests. In: IJCAI 23rd International Joint Conference on Artificial Intelligence, pp. 254–262. ACM, Beijing, August 2013
19. Maurovich-Horvat, L., Boomsma, T.K., Siddiqui, A.S.: Transmission and wind investment in a deregulated electricity industry. IEEE Trans. Power Syst. **30**(3), 1633–1643 (2015)
20. Motamedi, A., Zareipour, H., Buygi, M.O., Rosehart, W.D.: A transmission planning framework considering future generation expansions in electricity markets. IEEE Trans. Power Syst. **25**(4), 1987–1995 (2010)
21. Office of Gas and Electricity Markets (Ofgem): Tariff tables (2015). https://www.ofgem.gov.uk/environmental-programmes/feed-tariff-fit-scheme/tariff-tables. Accessed 20 Oct 2015
22. Paruchuri, P., Pearce, J.P., Marecki, J., Tambe, M., Ordonez, F., Kraus, S.: Efficient algorithms to solve Bayesian Stackelberg games for security applications. In: 23rd Conference on Artificial Intelligence, AAAI, Chicago, pp. 1559–1562, July 2008
23. Perrault, A., Boutilier, C.: Efficient coordinated power distribution on private infrastructure. In: International Conference on Autonomous Agents and Multiagent Systems (AAMAS 2014), International Foundation for Autonomous Agents and Multiagent Systems, Paris, pp. 805–812, May 2014
24. Ramchurn, S., Vytelingum, P., Rogers, A., Jennings, N.R.: Putting the smarts into the smart grid: a grand challenge for artificial intelligence. Commun. ACM **55**(4), 86–97 (2012)
25. Rogers, J., Fink, S., Porter, K.: Examples of wind energy curtailment practices. Technical report, July 2010
26. Sauma, E.E., Oren, S.S.: Proactive planning and valuation of transmission investments in restructured electricity markets. J. Regul. Econ. **30**(3), 261–290 (2006)
27. Scottish and Southern Energy Power Distribution (SSE): Kintyre-Hunterston (2015). https://www.ssepd.co.uk/KintyreHunterston. Accessed 5 Oct 2015

28. Shrestha, G.B., Fonseka, P.A.J.: Congestion-driven transmission expansion in competitive power markets. IEEE Trans. Power Syst. **19**(3), 1658–1665 (2004)
29. von Stackelberg, H.: Market Structure and Equilibrium. Springer Science & Business Media, Heidelberg (2010)
30. Vasirani, M., Kota, R., Cavalcante, R.L., Ossowski, S., Jennings, N.R.: An agent-based approach to virtual power plants of wind power generators and electric vehicles. IEEE Trans. Smart Grid **4**(3), 1909–1916 (2013)
31. Vytelingum, P., Voice, T.D., Ramchurn, S.D., Rogers, A., Jennings, N.R.: Agent-based micro-storage management for the smart grid. In: 9th International Conference on Autonomous Agents and Multiagent Systems (AAMAS 2010), International Foundation for Autonomous Agents and Multiagent Systems, Toronto, vol. 1, pp. 39–46, May 2010
32. van der Weijde, A.H., Hobbs, B.F.: The economics of planning electricity transmission to accommodate renewables: using two-stage optimisation to evaluate flexibility and the cost of disregarding uncertainty. Energy Econ. **34**(6), 2089–2101 (2012)
33. Zheng, R., Xu, Y., Chakraborty, N., Sycara, K.: A crowdfunding model for green energy investment. In: IJCAI Proceedings of the 24th International Joint Conference on Artificial Intelligence, pp. 2669–2675. AAAI Press, Buenos Aires, July 2015

Multi-scale Simulation for Crowd Management: A Case Study in an Urban Scenario

Luca Crociani[1], Gregor Lämmel[2(✉)], and Giuseppe Vizzari[1]

[1] Complex Systems and Artificial Intelligence Research Centre,
University Milano-Bicocca, Milan, Italy
{luca.crociani,giuseppe.vizzari}@unimib.it
[2] Institute of Transportation Systems, German Aerospace Center (DLR),
Berlin, Germany
gregor.laemmel@dlr.de

Abstract. Safety, security, and comfort of pedestrian crowds during large gatherings are heavily influenced by the layout of the underlying environment. This work presents a systematic agent-based simulation approach to appraise and optimize the layout of a pedestrian environment in order to maximize safety, security, and comfort. The performance of the approach is demonstrated based on annual "Salone del mobile" (Design Week) exhibition in Milan, Italy. Given the large size of the scenario, and the proportionally high number of simultaneously present pedestrians, the computational costs of a pure microscopic simulation approach would make this hardly applicable, whereas a multi-scale approach, combining simulation models of different granularity, provides a reasonable trade off between a detailed management of individual pedestrians and possibility to effectively carry out what-if analyses with different environmental configurations. The paper will introduce the scenario, the base model and the alternatives discussing the achieved results.

Keywords: Crowd management · Multi-agent simulation · Pedestrian simulation · Optimal environment layout

1 Introduction

The management of pedestrian crowds is a crucial task when organizing large gatherings such as festivals, sports events, or religious celebrations. Three main reasons for an active crowd management are: safety, security, and comfort.

- From safety point of view, situations that would lead to high pedestrian densities should be avoided, in particular for bidirectional pedestrian flows or for crossing pedestrian streams.
- Security considerations deal with unforeseen threats to the visitors that require, e.g. fast evacuations of large venues.
- Related to safety and security is the comfort of the visitors. Comfort considerations include the avoidance of long waiting times (e.g. at ticket counters) and the reduction of high density situations.

© Springer International Publishing AG 2016
N. Osman and C. Sierra (Eds.): AAMAS 2016 Ws Best Papers, LNAI 10002, pp. 147–162, 2016.
DOI: 10.1007/978-3-319-46882-2_9

Obviously, these three key concepts are closely related and should be seen as mutually dependent. The present work proposes an integrated simulation based appraisal and optimization approach to improve safety, security, and comfort of the visitors of large events. The current contribution demonstrates the approach based on an 'offline' scenario of the annually "Salone del mobile" exhibition in Milan, Italy. The overall event gathers more than 200000 visitors[1] every year. The location is the main exhibition area of Milan, but its importance and number of visitors led to the creation of a spin-off called "Fuori Salone" that organizes many related events in the city center during the fair week. The case study that will be analyzed in this paper describes the scenario of an important event belonging to the Fuori Salone, named "Tortona Design Week". It is located in the surrounding area of the Porta Genova train and metro station of Milan. The estimated number of visitors is also quite significant, around 115,000 for the 6 days of the event[2].

2   Related Works

In the simulation context (pedestrian) travel behavior is usually modeled at three different levels [22,31]. Plans and final objectives are formulated at the *strategic level*. At the *tactical level* a set of activities to complete the plan is created. The physical execution of the activities is performed at the *operational level*. Approaches to simulate the operational level can be divided into three classes.

– Macroscopic models treat the crowds as a flow of densities where individual pedestrians are not represented but rather considered as gas or liquids (see, e.g., [18,21]). For macroscopic models the computational burden increases rather with the size of the simulated area than with the number of simulated pedestrians. Thus, macroscopic models can be efficient for the simulation of large crowds in small spaces. However, since individual pedestrians are not represented by those models, scenarios with complex origin-destination-relations seem to be hard to model.
– In contrast, microscopic models are constructed from the individual's point of view, where each and every traveler follows his/her own plan. Some microscopic models treat space as a continuous entity (e.g. force based models [10,20]), others take a discretized view on environment (e.g. cellular automata (CA) [3,7]). Most microscopic models are built as a continuous simulations with a fixed time step size. Recently, a model with adaptive time step size has been proposed in order to speed up computation [35]. Another way to speed up the computation is to apply the concept of discrete event simulation [27].
– A third class of simulation models is often referred to as mesoscopic models. One example is the queue simulation model [28]: in this approach, pedestrians are still treated individually, but the environment is represented as a graph of

---

[1] http://salonemilano.it/en-us/VISITORS/Salone-Internazionale-del-Mobile/ Exhibition-fact-sheet.
[2] http://www.tortonadesignweek.com/.

interconnected FIFO queues. This implies a simplification of the environmental representation and a reduction of the computational costs for the management of the simulation process. The representation of the physical movement at the operational level is simplified and the approach is less effective at representing turbulences due to conflicts, for instance when the situation comprises crossing streams [30].

Hybrid coupling (or multi-scale modeling in general) has been applied to different scientific fields and it combines the advantages of models with different granularity in spatial representation, striving to achieve good overall computational properties with the possibility to zoom in spots requiring more details in the model. This is valid both for extremely small areas, like biological systems [13], that include a very high number of interacting entities in potentially small space, as well as for urban and territorial scale socio-economic systems [36].

In the transportation field, early approaches deal with the vehicular traffic only. Hybrid couplings of macroscopic and microscopic models are proposed by [4,15,19]. Examples for the hybrid couplings of mesoscopic and microscopic models are [5,6]. Approaches from pedestrian domain include [1,9]. A basic requirement for hybrid modeling, is a consistent transfer of travelers (e.g. pedestrians or vehicles) between the involved simulation models. In the pedestrian domain, this requires that fundamental properties like flow and speed are conserved over the models' boundaries. A respective approach is discussed in [30]. Recently, this approach has been demonstrated in a case study on an inter- and multi-model evacuation [25].

The strategic and tactical level of behavior deals with the navigation in complex environments and a key feature is the ability to find feasible paths from any origin to any destination. An apparent solution to this problem is the shortest paths solution. It can be computed e.g. by Dijkstra's shortest path algorithm [14]. However, since the shortest path solution neglects congestion, often longer but faster paths exists: although humans are not necessarily always able to find optimal solutions, the shortest path approach sometimes fails at representing the ability of some pedestrians to select a longer trajectory for preserving a higher walking speed. Those faster but longer paths can be found by an iterative best response dynamics [8]. In the pedestrian context a corresponding macroscopic modeling approach is proposed in [22]. A mesoscopic modeling approach is presented in [29]. In the microscopic context, applications of best response dynamics started only recently. An application to tactical level of behavior is discussed in [24]. A systematic approach where all three levels of behavior are explicitly modeled and paths finding is solved by an iterative approach is proposed in [11].

Pedestrian simulation models are often applied in the evacuation context. Newer works also deal with the appraisal of pedestrian environments regarding their performance under normal conditions, in order to optimize crowd management strategies (e.g. [12]).

3   A Multi-scale Model for the Simulation of Urban Scenarios

The development of a multi-scale model has been proposed for two main purposes. On one hand, the simulation system should provide a very detailed representation of parts of the scenario in which more complex behaviors can take place. On the other hand, a mesoscopic approach can be used to design and simulate large parts of the urban environment that are not affected by such complex dynamics but are still fundamental for the analysis of the overall scene.

Hence the system described here is composed of two models with two different scales of detail: (i) a 2d microscopic model based on a discrete representation for a detailed yet optimized reproduction of pedestrian environments; (ii) a queue model that is used for the simulation of other relevant city roads. Such integration between these models leads to a quite powerful approach capable of performing analysis in urban scenarios, considering multiple modes of transportation and performing simulations in a relatively fast way.

Considering computational costs is quite relevant since the multi-scale system applies an iterative approach to manage the agents' strategic model. The iterative approach moves the overall behavior either towards a Nash equilibrium or to the system optimum depending on the applied cost function. In this way it is possible both to predict what will happen in the scenario on a normal day (with the NE) and to have information about the minimum average travel time of the whole crowd (with the SO). One might argue that implementing the optimal flows configuration is still an issue, since it implies that some people take a detour without perceiving relevant congestion on the shorter way. The desired behavior could be induced by the usage of adaptive bottlenecks (e.g. automatic bollards) that make, depending on the current situation, detours more attractive to some of the people. The development of such a concept represents the overall idea behind this work and it will be subject of future research.

The components of the multi-scale model and their integration will be now briefly presented. For a in depth discussion of the CA-model, it is referred to [11].

3.1   The Discrete Microscopic Model

The model is a 2-dimensional Cellular Automaton with a square-cells grid representation of the space. The 0.4×0.4 m^2 size of the cells describes the average space occupation of a person [37] and reproduces a maximum pedestrian density of 6.25 persons/m^2, that covers the values usually observable in the real world. A cell of the environment can be basically of type *walkable* or of type *obstacle*, meaning that it will never be occupied by any pedestrians during the simulation.

Intermediate targets can also be introduced in the environment to mark the extremes of a particular region (e.g. rooms or corridors), and so decision points for the route choice of agents. Final goals of the discrete environment are its open edges, i.e., the entrances/exits of the discrete space that will be linked to roads. Since the concept of region is fuzzy and the space decomposition is a

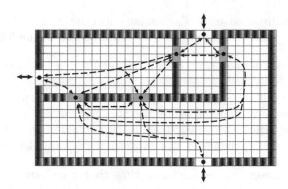

Fig. 1. Sample scenario with its network representation. While the blue cells represent intermediate targets, the outside arrows describe the links with the outside network that will be simulated with the mesoscopic model.

subjective task that can be tackled with different approaches, the configuration of their position in the scenario is not automatic and it is left to the user.

Employing the floor field approach [7] and spreading one field from each target –either intermediate of final– allows to build a network of the environment. In this graph, each node denotes one target and the edges identify the existence of a direct way between two targets (i.e. passing through only one region). To allow this, the floor field diffusion is limited by obstacles and cells of other targets. An example for an environment with the overlayed network is shown in Fig. 1. The open borders of the microscopic environment are the nodes that will be plugged to the other network of the mesoscopic model.

To integrate the network with the one of the mesoscopic model and to allow the reasoning at the strategic level, each edge a of the graph is firstly labeled with its length l_a, describing the distance between two targets δ_i, δ_j in the discrete space. This value is computed using the floor fields as:

$$l_a(\delta_1, \delta_2) = Avg\left(FF_{\delta_1}(Center(\delta_2)),\ FF_{\delta_2}(Center(\delta_1))\right) \qquad (1)$$

where $FF_\delta(x, y)$ gives the value of the floor field associated to a destination δ in position (x, y); $Center(\delta)$ describes the coordinates of the central cell of δ and Avg computes the average between the two values and provides a unique distance. Together with the average speed of pedestrians in the discrete space (explained below), l_a is used to calculate the free speed travel time of the link $T_a^{free} = \frac{l_a}{s_a}$.

With a simple probabilistic choice, similar to the one proposed in [7], the pedestrian movement towards one target is reproduced with the floor fields values. This allows to avoid obstacles and other pedestrians in a very simple way, but it is not enough to generate a plausible dynamics, i.e., by respecting the fundamental relation about local density and flow.

For the achievement of a realistic microscopic model, the idea of [16] has been extended to 2-dimensional models. The model works on the basis of 3 simple rules that allow the calibration to fit the fundamental diagram of 1-directional and 2-directional flow. The movement rules are summarized in the following:

- **Movement rule**: a pedestrian cannot change his/her position before τ_m seconds,
- **Jam rule**: if a cell is occupied at time t by the pedestrian p, every pedestrian $\bar{p} \neq p$ cannot occupy that cell before time $t + \tau_j$,
- **Counter-flow rule**: if two pedestrian in two consecutive cells at time t are in a head-on conflict, then they will swap their position at time $t + \tau_m + \tau_s$.

The first rule describes the minimum time that a pedestrian can employ to move forward of one cell, thus τ_m is the duration of the time-step. The second rule manages the dynamics in presence of jamming, implying additional time to move in case of congestion. In particular, this rule has been implemented by letting the agents produce a *trace* in their previous position, which will keep the cell occupied for τ_j seconds. This mechanism is able to translate back the effects of congestion as observed, generating the so-called *density waves*.

The third rule defines an agents position exchange mechanism, but the way that agents recognize others belonging to counter-flows needs clarification. The agents of this model, in addition to the floor field related to their current target, are able to perceive the fields of the persons they have in their neighborhood. With this information, they will be able to understand if the surrounding agents are –probably– moving in counter-direction. Hence they will be able to choose the movement in the occupied position by the counter-flow pedestrian and, if this will perform the same choice, start the position exchange at the end of the step. This action will need $\tau_m + \tau_s$ seconds. In [11] it is shown how, by varying the value of τ_m and τ_s with the local density, it is possible to fully calibrate this model to fit the fundamental diagrams of pedestrian 1-directional and 2-directional flow.

Summarizing, with these rules the model is able to produce feasible simulations of pedestrian motion in planar environments. Nonetheless, the simulation of a complex environment might need consideration of particular elements, such as stairs, which implies at least a lower speed of the agents. To overcome this issue, the environment definition has been enriched by introducing the possibility to mark the borders of stairs, which will affect the agents speed by multiplying their τ_m times 2, i.e., they will move one time-step over two. With the assumed $\tau_m = 0.25\,\mathrm{s}$, pedestrians will have a free flow speed of $1.3\,\mathrm{m/s}$ in flat spaces and of $0.65\,\mathrm{m/s}$ inside stairs, in accordance with the average speed observed in the real world. At the network level, the links describing the area of a staircase are labeled with a higher free speed travel time.

More advanced approaches to manage arbitrary speeds have already been proposed in the literature, using stochastic methods that do not imply a complete synchronization of the agents (e.g. [2]). For the model and the application here proposed, though, this simple and efficient approach is considered effective and further developments on this aspect might be subject of future directions.

Finally, in order to respect the dynamics among the mesoscopic and microscopic models, the connection at the borders of the pedestrian environment are managed with so-called *transition areas*, that temporary host the agents before entering the "real" environment. When the agents pass from the mesoscopic model to the discrete environment, thus, they temporary have a *double* presence in both model and this allows to extend the influence of eventual congestion from one model to the other one.

3.2 The Mesoscopic Model

The overall system is implemented within the MATSim framework[3]. The standard simulation approach in MATSim is based on a queueing model based on [34]. Originally, the model was designed for the simulation of vehicular traffic only, but later it has been adapted for the additional consideration of pedestrians [29]. The network is modeled as a graph whose links describe urban streets and the nodes describe their intersections. In the pedestrian context "streets" also include side walks, ramps, etc. Links behave like FIFO queues controlled by the following parameters:

- the length of the link l;
- the area of the link A;
- the free flow speed $\hat{v}$;
- the free speed travel time t_{min}, given by $l/\hat{v}$;
- the flow capacity FC;
- the storage capacity SC.

The dynamics, thus, follows the rules defined with these parameters. An agent is able to enter to a link l until the number of agents inside l is below its storage capacity. Once the agent is inside, it travels at speed $\hat{v}$ and it cannot leave the link before t_{min}. The congestion is managed with the flow capacity parameter FC, which is used to lock the agents inside the link to not exceed it.

3.3 Strategic Model

At the strategic level agents plan their paths through the environment. Normally, the aim of the strategic planning is to emulate the real-world pedestrians' behavior. A fair assumption is that pedestrians try to minimize the walking distance when planning their paths. In the simulation context the shortest path solution is straightforward to compute e.g. by Dijkstra's shortest path algorithm [14]. However, it is well known that the shortest path solution neglects congestion and thus the shortest path solution is not necessarily the fastest one. In particular commuters who repeatedly walk between two locations (e.g. from a particular track in a large train station to a bus stop outside the train station) often try to iteratively find faster paths. If all commuters display that same behavior they might reach a state where it is no longer possible to find any faster path. If this is the case, then the system has reached a state of a Nash [32] or user equilibrium w.r.t. individual travel times. This behavior can be emulated by applying an

---

[3] http://www.matsim.org.

iterative best-response dynamic [8] and has been widely applied in the context of vehicular transport simulations (see, e.g., [17,23,33]). In the pedestrian context this concept is still new albeit some preliminary works exist as discussed in Sect. 2. Related to the Nash equilibrium is the system optimum. But unlike the Nash equilibrium, the system optimum does not minimize individual travel times but the system (or average) travel time. Like the Nash equilibrium, the system optimum can also be achieved by an iterative best response dynamic, but based on the marginal travel time instead of the individual travel time. The marginal travel time of an individual traveler corresponds to the sum of the travel time experienced by her/him (internal costs) and the delay that he/she impose to others (external costs). While it is straightforward to determine the internal costs (i.e. travel time), the external costs calculation is not so obvious. An approach for the marginal travel time estimation and its application to a mesoscopic evacuation simulation is discussed in [26]. Based on this, [11] propose an adaption of the approach to microscopic simulation models. In the present work, the external costs are estimated in the same way as proposed in [11]. The following gives a brief description of the approach. As discussed both the mesoscopic and the microscopic model are mapped on the same global network of links and nodes. A link can either be in a congested or in an uncongested state. Initially, all links are considered as uncongested. A link switches from the uncongested state to the congested state once the observed travel time along the link is longer than the free speed travel time. Vice versa, a link in the congested state switches to the uncongested state as soon as the first pedestrian is able to walk along the link in free speed travel time. Every pedestrian that leaves a given link while it is in the congested state imposes external costs to the others. The amount of the external costs corresponds to the time span from the time when the pedestrian under consideration leaves the congested link till the time when the link switches to the uncongested state again.

In this work, the iterative search of equilibrium/optimum follows the logic of the iterative best response dynamic and it is described by the following tasks:

1. Compute plans for all agents.
2. Execute the multi-scale simulation.
3. Evaluate executed plans of the agents.
4. Select a portion of the agents population and re-compute their plans.
5. Jump to step 2, if the stop criterion has not been reached.

The stopping criterion is implemented as a predetermined number of iterations defined by the user. This is because the number of iterations needed for the system to reach a relaxed state depends on the complexity of the scenario and is not known a-priori. In the underlying context, one hundred iterations gives a good compromise between relaxation and runtime.

Initial plan computation is performed with a shortest path algorithm. In the subsequent iterations the agents try to find better plans based on the experienced travel costs. Depending on the cost function, the agents learn more convenient paths either for them individually (relaxation towards a Nash equilibrium) or for the overall population (relaxation towards the system optimum).

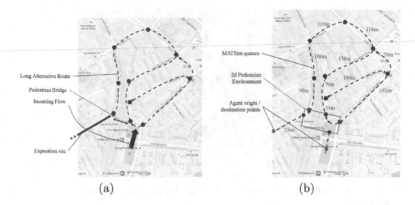

Fig. 2. (a) The location of the event and the possible paths from the train and subway stations. (b) Implementation of the scenario with the multi-scale simulation model (maps taken with Google Maps). (Color figure online)

4   Analysis of an Urban Scenario

4.1   The Scenario of the Tortona Design Week

The Tortona Design Week is a yearly exhibition that is organized in the surrounding area of the Porta Genova train station in Milan. The estimated number of visitors for the 6 days of the event is about 115,000 persons, mostly distributed with peaks on Friday and Saturday nights.

Figure 2(a) illustrates the real world scenario with the location of the event and the directions of flows. The larger part of the incoming flow of pedestrians arrives from the station square, where also the entrance/exit of a subway station is located. The main issue of this scenario is given by the connection between the square and the event location. In the direct surrounding, in fact, this is only possible through a three meters wide pedestrian bridge, which makes the other alternative routes not attractive for the visitors.

Consequently, the congestion inside the pedestrian bridge is very high and the traveling times become long. In addition to the comfort, the overcrowding on the bridge might imply safety issues. This provided motivations for the analysis here discussed, which will explore three main simulation scenarios.

4.2   Experiments

For the experiments performed, the population of agents has been instantiated according to two normal distributions, which split a total of 15,000 pedestrians among the two origin/destination points (blue dots in Fig. 2(b)): the square in front of the train station and the event location. The distribution of agents from the train station has been centered one hour before the other one in the simulation time-line, to achieve an earlier incoming flow towards the event. Both the distributions are configured with a standard deviation of 30 min.

Fig. 3. Satellite view of the area simulated with the microscopic model (picture taken with Google Earth).

The dimensions of the simulated environment brings motivations for the usage of the multi-scale approach: as shown in Fig. 2(b), the surrounding of the pedestrian bridge is represented with the detailed 2-dimensional discrete model as a rectangular area of 100.8×41.2 m^2, since it is the area affected by complex pedestrian flows and interactions. The outer connecting streets, which will not be affected by congestion, have been modeled as 1-dimensional queues, to improve the computational efficiency as well as to simplify the task for the scenario configuration. The dimensions and proportions of the environment, in addition to the roads lengths—also in the Figure—have been extracted with Google Earth software. The pedestrian bridge is composed of a single 35 m long span preceded by two 10 m long runs of stairs at its extremes. The west staircase is perpendicular to the flat way and connected with an additional flat component of 3×3 m^2, while the east run of stairs is parallel and directly linked to the walkway. To improve the understanding of the setting, a satellite picture of the part of the scene represented with the microscopic model is shown in Fig. 3.

In this simulation campaign, two versions of the environment have been designed by means of the microscopic model: a base-line that approximates the real setting and an alternative one that proposes an extension of the handrail along the pedestrian bridge, in order to physically separate the directions of flows. The two environments are used to configure five case studies:

- real world setting, all agents traveling the shortest path;
- real world setting, at the Nash Equilibrium;
- alternative scenario, with shortest path;
- alternative scenario, at the Nash Equilibrium;
- alternative scenario, at the System Optimum;

The simulation of the first two scenarios showed that the performance of the real setting is quite low with the assumed population of agents. The 2-directional flow on the bridge, in fact, starts generating some congestion on the east side access way after around 1 h and 20 min of simulated time (near the peak of the incoming flow to the event). The congestion continues to grow with the increasing

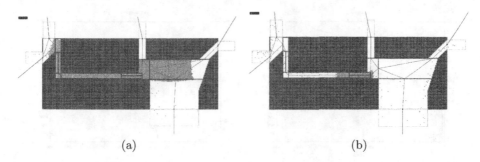

(a)   (b)

Fig. 4. Screenshots from the simulation of the real world setting, with the SP (a) and NE (b) scenario. The blue agents are directed towards the event, while the red ones to the station square. The associated network is superimposed to the scenario. Both screenshots are taken at about 2 h and 10 min of simulated time. (Color figure online)

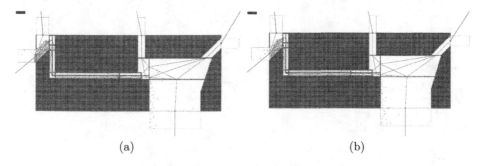

(a)   (b)

Fig. 5. Screenshots from the simulation of the alternative setting, with the SP/NE scenario (a) and the SO one (b). The same color is applied to the agents, regarding their destination. Screenshots are taken at about 2 h and 40 min of simulated time.

Table 1. Average and maximum traveling times of agents in all scenarios.

Scenario name	Routing strategy	Separated flows	Avg. travel time	Max travel time
SP_NONSEP	Shortest path	No	4544 s	13,648 s
NE_NONSEP	Nash equilibrium	No	504 s	4,790 s
SP_SEP	Shortest path	Yes	237 s	1,898 s
NE_SEP	Nash equilibrium	Yes	239 s	2,132 s
SO_SEP	System optimum	Yes	232 s	1,625 s

frequency of arrival of the counter-flow agents, reaching full congestion of the pedestrian bridge and its nearby after about 2 h and 10 min (see Fig. 4(a)). The congestion heavily affects the traveling times and around 3 h are needed to reach a complete discharge of the bridge, achieving the end of the simulation around time 5 h and 30 min.

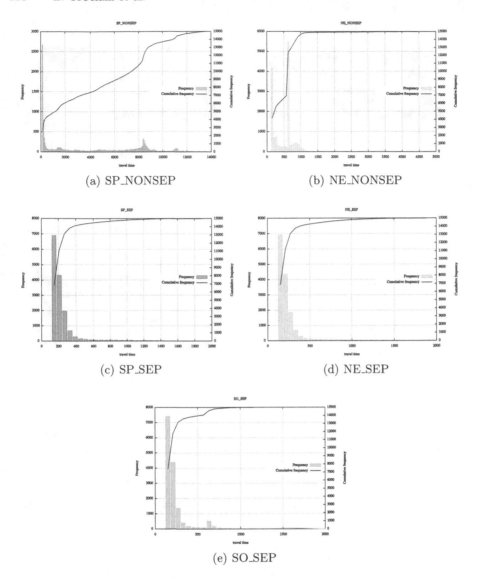

Fig. 6. Travel time histograms for the various scenarios. Note, the scales in (a) and (b) do not match the scale of the other plots.

With the progression of the iterations, the long traveling times induce the choice of the agents to the alternative route, gradually solving the congestion. At the Nash Equilibrium state for this environment, the jamming is almost solved and the average traveling time has been decreased to 504 s (see Table 1). Nonetheless, the maximum traveling time is still relatively high, due to the length of the alternative route not allowing a complete dispersion of the congestion. A comparison of the histograms of Fig. 6(a) and (b) shows that the distribution of traveling times significantly differs: at the Nash equilibrium state two peaks are recognizable, identifying the initial portion of the population that succeeds in performing the plan without encountering congestion and another large part that experience a limited congestion that shifts the traveling times to around 600 s.

The simulation of the second environment shows that the proposed modification that separates the flows is quite effective, despite its simplicity. In this way, the conflicts on the bridge are prevented and jamming arises only in front of the access ramps with minor effects. Thus the longer route has no advantage in terms of travel time and the Nash equilibrium becomes equal to the shortest path solution. The respective traveling times are approximately less than half as long as the ones achieved in the real environment (see the Table 1). The average and maximum traveling times for the Nash equilibrium simulation are higher than for the shortest path solution. This is not a particular finding, but this is due to the stochastic nature of the model. Overall the relative distribution of traveling times (Fig. 6(c) and (d)) share the same trend and data range.

With this configuration of the environment and pedestrian flows, however, the Nash equilibrium state is different from the system optimum. The system optimum results in lower average and maximum travel times. The difference is more perceivable in the histogram of the travel times distribution in Fig. 6(e). Firstly, the number of agents which reached the destination in the box corresponding to the smallest travel time is increased by about 500 individuals. Moreover, there is an additional local distribution peak at around 600 s (probably) generated by the individuals that accepted to take the detour in order to make space for persons behind. This effect is also observable by comparing the screenshots in Fig. 5(a) and (b): a small percentage of agents takes the detour (two are visible in Fig. 5(b)) and induce a small reduction of the congestion in front of the west access staircase.

5   Conclusion

A multi-scale pedestrian and crowd simulation approach has been proposed. The system consists of two simulation models: a microscopic CA based model is combined with a fast mesoscopic queue based simulation model. While the CA is applied to complex situations with high pedestrian interactions (e.g. high density counter-flows), the queue model is employed to the wider area, where pedestrian densities are rather low. By the combination of the two different models it is possible to simulate large and complex scenarios in reasonable time frames.

The performance of the multi-scale simulation approach has been demonstrated based on a real-world scenario. The baseline scenario reproduced the environmental settings as they exist in the real-world. The simulation results in situations of high densities and congestion are similar to what is observed in the real-world. Several improvements to the environment and crowd management strategies have been tested. It has been shown that separating flows in combination with a Nash equilibrium or system optimum routing strategy significantly reduces average and maximum travel time. The Nash equilibrium routing strategy mimics real-world travelers behavior, where travelers iteratively look for faster paths on their regular commutes. While the Nash equilibrium minimizes individual travel times, the system optimum minimizes the average or system travel time. One might argue that an exposition like the "Fuori Salone", even if held annually, is a rather singular event whose attendants change every year and thus do not learn faster ways from their previous experience. In addition, many people may prefer to wait in long queues at high densities and overtaking a long detour without any queue. Moreover, the concept of system optimum is not based on an intrinsic behavior and would have to be enforced externally.

The answer can be that one still learns a lot from the results of the Nash equilibrium and system optimum. E.g. if the results for an optimal crowd management show that that the longer path is currently faster and this could be communicated, then the acceptance would increase. In order to establish such a system one would have to dynamically measure the incoming flow and distribute the crowds dynamically to the different paths.

However, the main insight—and probably also the most obvious one—is that separating flows in a crowded situation significantly improves the overall performance of the system. Indeed, even in the SP_SEP scenario, where everyone uses the shortest path, the average travel time is considerably decreased compared to any scenario with non-separated flows. The smaller average travel time is achieved by a higher average speed. Since there is a one-to-one mapping between speed and density, this also implies a lower average density. A lower average density definitely improves the comfort of the visitors and significantly contributes to safety and security. Finally, it must be stated that in the underlying scenario a rather long detour is required to avoid the crowded bridge. Thus, even for the SO_SEP scenario only a few agents chose the long detour and thus all three scenarios with the separated flows (i.e. SP_SEP, NE_SEP, and SO_SEP) lead to very similar results.

Density aware cost functions for the routing strategies would be an interesting future direction for this research, with a routing solution that avoids densities above a certain threshold as a result. However, as for the system optimum, those routing solutions would have to be enforced by an active crowd management.

References

1. Anh, N.T.N., Daniel, Z.J., Du, N.H., Drogoul, A., An, V.D.: A hybrid macro-micro pedestrians evacuation model to speed up simulation in road networks. In: Dechesne, F., Hattori, H., Mors, A., Such, J.M., Weyns, D., Dignum, F. (eds.) AAMAS 2011. LNCS (LNAI), vol. 7068, pp. 371–383. Springer, Heidelberg (2012). doi:10.1007/978-3-642-27216-5_28
2. Bandini, S., Crociani, L., Vizzari, G.: Heterogeneous pedestrian walking speed in discrete simulation models. In: Chraibi, M., Boltes, M., Schadschneider, A., Seyfried, A. (eds.) Traffic and Granular Flow 2013, pp. 273–279. Springer International Publishing, Switzerland (2015)
3. Blue, V., Adler, J.: Emergent fundamental pedestrian flows from cellular automata microsimulation. Transp. Res. Rec. J. Transp. Res. Board **1644**, 29–36 (1998)

4. Bourr, E., Lesort, J.B.: Mixing microscopic representations of traffic flow: hybrid model based on Lighthill-Whitham-Richards theory. Transp. Res. Rec. **1852**, 193–200 (2003)
5. Burghout, W., Koutsopoulos, H., Andréasson, I.: Hybrid mesoscopic-microscopic traffic simulation. Transp. Res. Rec. **1934**, 218–225 (2005)
6. Burghout, W., Wahlstedt, J.: Hybrid traffic simulation with adaptive signal control. Transp. Res. Rec. **1999**, 191–197 (2007)
7. Burstedde, C., Klauck, K., Schadschneider, A., Zittartz, J.: Simulation of pedestrian dynamics using a two-dimensional cellular automaton. Phys. A Stat. Mech. Appl. **295**(3–4), 507–525 (2001)
8. Cascetta, E.: A stochastic process approach to the analysis of temporal dynamics in transportation networks. Transp. Res. B **23B**(1), 1–17 (1989)
9. Chooramun, N., Lawrence, P., Galea, E.: Implementing a hybrid space discretisation within an agent based evacuation model. In: Peacock, R., Kuligowski, E., Averill, J. (eds.) Pedestrian and Evacuation Dynamics 2010, pp. 449–458. Springer, Berlin (2011)
10. Chraibi, M., Seyfried, A., Schadschneider, A.: Generalized centrifugal-force model for pedestrian dynamics. Phys. Rev. E **82**(4), 46111 (2010)
11. Crociani, L., Lämmel, G.: Multidestination pedestrian flows in equilibrium: a cellular automaton-based approach. Comput.-Aided Civ. Infrastruct. Eng. **31**, 432–448 (2016). doi:10.1111/mice.12209
12. Crociani, L., Manenti, L., Vizzari, G.: MAKKSim: MAS-based crowd simulations for designer's decision support. In: Demazeau, Y., Ishida, T., Corchado, J.M., Bajo, J. (eds.) PAAMS 2013. LNCS (LNAI), vol. 7879, pp. 25–36. Springer, Heidelberg (2013). doi:10.1007/978-3-642-38073-0_3
13. Dada, J.O., Mendes, P.: Multi-scale modelling and simulation in systems biology. Integr. Biol. **3**(2), 86–96 (2011)
14. Dijkstra, E.: A note on two problems in connexion with graphs. Numerische Mathematik **1**, 269–271 (1959)
15. Espié, S., Gattuso, D., Galante, F.: A hybrid traffic model coupling macro and behavioural micro simulation. Annual Meeting Preprint 06–2013, Transportation Research Board, Washington DC (2006)
16. Flötteröd, G., Lämmel, G.: Bidirectional pedestrian fundamental diagram. Transp. Res. Part B Methodol. **71**(C), 194–212 (2015)
17. Gawron, C.: An iterative algorithm to determine the dynamic user equilibrium in a traffic simulation model. Int. J. Mod. Phys. C **9**(3), 393–407 (1998)
18. Helbing, D.: A fluid dynamic model for the movement of pedestrians. arXiv preprint cond-mat/9805213 (1998)
19. Helbing, D., Hennecke, A., Shvetsov, V., Treiber, M.: Micro- and macro-simulation of freeway traffic. Math. Comput. Model. **35**, 517–547 (2002)
20. Helbing, D., Molnár, P.: Social force model for pedestrian dynamics. Phys. Rev. E **51**(5), 4282–4286 (1995)
21. Henderson, L.: The statistics of crowd fluids. Nature **229**(5284), 381–383 (1971)
22. Hoogendoorn, S., Bovy, P.: Dynamic user-optimal assignment in continuous time and space. Transp. Res. Part B Methodol. **38**(7), 571–592 (2004)
23. Krajzewicz, D., Erdmann, J., Behrisch, M., Bieker, L.: Recent development and applications of SUMO - Simulation of Urban MObility. Int. J. Adv. Syst. Meas. **5**(3&4), 128–138 (2012)
24. Kretz, T., Lehmann, K., Hofsäß, I.: User equilibrium route assignment for microscopic pedestrian simulation. Adv. Complex Syst. **17**(2), 1450010 (2014)

25. Lämmel, G., Chraibi, M., Kemloh Wagoum, A., Steffen, B.: Hybrid multi- and inter-modal transport simulation: a case study on large-scale evacuation planning. Transp. Res. Rec. (forthcoming)
26. Lämmel, G., Flötteröd, G.: Towards system optimum: finding optimal routing strategies in time-tependent networks for large-scale evacuation problems. In: Mertsching, B., Hund, M., Aziz, Z. (eds.) KI 2009: Advances in Artificial Intelligence. LNCS (LNAI), vol. 5803, pp. 532–539. Springer, Berlin Heidelberg (2009)
27. Lämmel, G., Flötteröd, G.: A CA model for bidirectional pedestrian streams. Procedia Comput. Sci. **52**, 950–955 (2015)
28. Lämmel, G., Grether, D., Nagel, K.: The representation and implementation of time-dependent inundation in large-scale microscopic evacuation simulations. Transp. Res. Part C Emerg. Technol. **18**(1), 84–98 (2010)
29. Lämmel, G., Klüpfel, H., Nagel, K.: The MATSim network flow model for traffic simulation adapted to large-scale emergency egress and an application to the evacuation of the Indonesian city of Padang in case of a tsunami warning. In: Timmermans, H. (ed.) Pedestrian Behavior, Chap. 11, pp. 245–265. Emerald Group Publishing Limited, UK (2009)
30. Lämmel, G., Seyfried, A., Steffen, B.: Large-scale and microscopic: a fast simulation approach for urban areas. Annual Meeting Preprint 14–3890, Transportation Research Board, Washington, DC (2014)
31. Michon, J.: A critical view of driver behavior models: what do we know, what should we do? In: Evans, L., Schwing, R.C. (eds.) Human Behavior and Traffic Safety, pp. 485–524. Springer, US (1985)
32. Nash, J.: Non-cooperative games. Ann. Math. **54**(2), 286–295 (1951)
33. Raney, B., Nagel, K.: Iterative route planning for large-scale modular transportation simulations. Future Gener. Comput. Syst. **20**(7), 1101–1118 (2004)
34. Simon, P., Esser, J., Nagel, K.: Simple queueing model applied to the city of Portland. Int. J. Mod. Phys. **10**(5), 941–960 (1999)
35. von Sivers, I., Köster, G.: Dynamic stride length adaptation according to utility and personal space. Transp. Res. Part B Methodol. **74**, 104–117 (2014)
36. Taillandier, P., Vo, D.-A., Amouroux, E., Drogoul, A.: GAMA: a simulation platform that integrates geographical information data, agent-based modeling and multi-scale control. In: Desai, N., Liu, A., Winikoff, M. (eds.) PRIMA 2010. LNCS (LNAI), vol. 7057, pp. 242–258. Springer, Heidelberg (2012). doi:10.1007/978-3-642-25920-3_17
37. Weidmann, U.: Transporttechnik der Fussgänger - Transporttechnische Eigenschaftendes Fussgängerverkehrs (Literaturstudie). Literature Research 90, Institut füer Verkehrsplanung, Transporttechnik, Strassen- und Eisenbahnbau IVT an der ETH Zürich (1993)

Communication and Shared Mental Models for Teams Performing Interdependent Tasks

Ronal Singh[(✉)], Liz Sonenberg, and Tim Miller

University of Melbourne, Melbourne, Australia
ronals@student.unimelb.edu.au, {l.sonenberg,tmiller}@unimelb.edu.au

Abstract. Research shows that performance of human teams improves when members have a shared understanding of their task; that is, when teams develop and use a shared mental model (SMM). An SMM can contain different types of information or components and this paper investigates the influence on team performance of sharing different components. We consider two components of an SMM: intentions (e.g. goals) and world knowledge (e.g. beliefs) and investigate which component(s) contribute most to team performance across different forms of interdependent tasks. We performed experiments using a Blocks World for Team (BW4T) testbed for artificial agent teams and our results show that with high levels of interdependence in tasks, communicating intentions contributes most to team performance, while for low levels of interdependence, communicating world knowledge contributes more. Additionally, as is the case with human teams, higher sharedness correlated with improved team performance for the artificial agent teams. These insights can assist in the design of communication protocols that improves team performance when team members are engaged in interdependent tasks and help design artificial agents that can communicate effectively when working with humans as teammates.

Keywords: Task interdependence · Shared mental models · Joint action

1 Introduction

Agents perform tasks that range from independent tasks that does not require interactions with others to highly *interdependent tasks* requiring close and continuous interactions [14]. When faced with interdependent tasks, effective coordination and collaboration of team members become crucial. One of the key foundations of effective coordination and collaboration is having *shared mental models (SMM)*. Shared mental model has been defined as [1]: "knowledge structures held by members of a team that enable them to form accurate explanations and expectations for the task, and, in turn, coordinate their actions and adapt their behaviour to demands of the task and other team members".

More than a decade of research has correlated SMMs with improved team performance in human teams [12]. The basic assumption is that SMMs allow team members to anticipate the needs and actions of other members, thereby

© Springer International Publishing AG 2016
N. Osman and C. Sierra (Eds.): AAMAS 2016 Ws Best Papers, LNAI 10002, pp. 163–179, 2016.
DOI: 10.1007/978-3-319-46882-2_10

increasing team performance. Recent studies in human-agent and artificial agent teams have also found similar correlations [3,5]. SMMs can be broadly classified as either task work model or team work model. Task work concerns the task or job that the team is to perform, while team work concerns what has to be done in order to complete a task as a team [9]. SMMs can also be viewed as having different components [5,9], such as world knowledge and intentions. World knowledge includes knowledge of the current state of the environment and the team while intentions represent what the agents intend to do [4].

Four types of task interdependence have been identified for human activities: pooled, sequential, reciprocal, and team [14,15]. In sequential task interdependence, tasks are performed in a sequential order. For example, in a relay race each runner has to wait for the previous team member to pass on the baton. In reciprocal task interdependence, participants take their turn in completing part of the task. A key property associated with reciprocal task interdependence is interleaved execution: for example, surgical teams often work reciprocally. In team task interdependence, participants execute their individual tasks concurrently and may include *joint actions*. By "action", we mean the atomic actions that make up a task. In joint action, multiple participants execute a particular action concurrently, for example when two people lift a heavy object together. In pooled task interdependence, the participants can successfully execute tasks without any interaction with each other. Due to the simple nature of these tasks, we do not study such tasks in this paper. The four types of task interdependence forms a hierarchy of pooled-sequential-reciprocal-team, with this hierarchy representing increasing levels of dependence between team members as well as increasing needs for coordination [14].

While *sharedness* has been linked with better team performance, central to the notion of SMM is how much and what to share. There has been recent work investigating this question in multi-agent systems research, such as [5,11,17]. However, as far as the authors are aware, with the exception of Li et al. [10], studies in the related work only consider sequentially-interdependent tasks, rather than more tightly linked team and reciprocal tasks. A recent report [16] highlights the need for studies considering other types of interdependence, notably *intensive* task interdependence – a type that we characterise as a *joint action*.

The subject of this paper is the communication content, specifically *what* to share when team members engage in interdependent tasks. We investigate the influence of the two components of the SMM (world knowledge and intentions) on the team performance across different forms of interdependent tasks. We used search and rescue like scenarios for a team of artificial agents for the experiments. The scenarios were generated using a Blocks World for Teams (BW4T) testbed [8]. In BW4T, which is an extension of the classical blocks world domain, the teams' joint task is to find and deliver coloured blocks in a particular order. Using the testbed, we designed and executed two sets of experiments. The first set studies the influence of sharing the two components – world knowledge and intentions – on the team performance for each form of task interdependence. The second set introduces joint actions within sequential and reciprocal tasks and studies the influence of sharing the two components on team performance. Introduction of joint actions allows for a shift from sequential or reciprocal to team task interdependence where members execute individual actions concurrently.

The outline of the paper is as follows. Section 2 introduces SMM, along with related work. Section 3 describes the task and the testbed and provides the details of the artificial agents that we implemented. Section 4 details the experimental setup while Sect. 5 discusses the results. Sections 6 and 7 conclude the paper with a discussion.

2 Background and Related Work

Mental models are simplified representations used by individuals to explain and predict their surroundings [13]. These models comprise content and structure or relationships between the content. In addition, individuals can simultaneously hold multiple mental models. In a team setting, when team members interact, their mental models converge resulting in shared mental models.

To extend the concepts of SMM that has been well studied for human teams [12] to human-agent teams, Jonker et al. [9] proposed mental model ontologies. They view a team as a system. A team performs team activities and has physical components, e.g. team members. A team member is an agent with a mind comprising many mental models: all but one of which represent the mental models of others in the team. Based on this conceptualisation, they proposed a measure that could be used to assess the similarity or the overlap of agents' mental models. We discuss this measure in the next section.

2.1 Measuring SMM

While several methods exist for measuring SMMs for human teams [2], one for teams comprising artificial agents is Jonker et al. [9]. Harbers et al. [5] extended Jonker et al's similarity measure so that it could be applied to teams of agents and performed experiments to show that their similarity measure can be used to predict team performance. We discuss the extended version of the measure next. In the following discussions, similarity refers to the overlap of the mental model contents of the agents. We consider the SMM to be made of two components – world knowledge and intentions.

Figure 1 shows an example of SMM. Assume Bot 1 and Bot 2 are two agents engaged in a joint task. Each has its mental model. While engaged in their task, the agents may communicate their beliefs and goals, making their own beliefs and goals known to others. For example, notice that each agent has it's own as well as others' beliefs and goals, which are shown in italics. The SMM is a theoretical construct that can be used to represent the overlapping content of the mental models of the two agents. In the example, the SMM is composed of the components - world knowledge (beliefs) and intentions (goals).

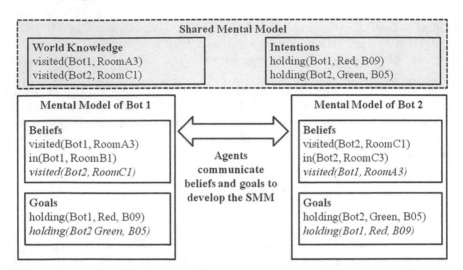

Fig. 1. Example SMM. The beliefs and goals of other agents are shown in italics. An agent has certain beliefs and goals that it is not required to communicate, e.g. *in(agent, room)*, and these may not part of the SMM.

Jonker et al. [9] and Harbers et al. [5] proposed a compositional measure of sharedness. We reproduce their definitions here with some simplifications. They view SMMs as having components, which can include sub-components. For example, Fig. 1 shows an SMM with two components. Examples of sub-components can be found in Sect. 3.3. The (sub)components can be queried by posing questions that all team members should be able to answer. The answers are used to compute the model agreements, which is a measure of the similarity of the answers provided by each agent for each question. Formally, let M be the set of all mental models, Q be the set of all questions, and $ans(m, q)$ be the answer of model $m \in M$ with respect to question $q \in Q$. The agreement between models M for questions Q is:

$$Ag(M, Q) = \frac{1}{|Q|} \sum_{q \in Q} \frac{|\cap_{m \in M} ans(m, q)|}{|\cup_{m \in M} ans(m, q)|} \tag{1}$$

If $|\cup_{m \in M} ans(m, q)| = 0$ then the agreement for question q is 0. Given a set of agents A, a set of mental models M_A (a model for each agent), and questions Q, we say that the model m is shared *to the extent* θ, denoted by $Sh(M, A, Q, \theta)$, with respect Q, iff $Ag(M_A \cup \{m\}, Q) >= \theta$. The compositional measure CS is:

$$CS(M, A, Q) = max\{\theta \mid Sh(M, A, Q, \theta)\}, \text{ if M is not composed}$$
$$CS(M, A, Q) = c(\{CS(m, A, Q) \mid m \in M\}), \text{ if M is composed} \tag{2}$$

where m is a component of M and c is composition function, for example: $\sum_{m \in M} w_m CS(m, A, Q)$. Each component and sub-component can be weighted to model the relevance of each (sub)component. The weight of each (sub)component is $w_m \in [0,1]$ and CS can be normalised to $[0,1]$ by setting $\sum_{m \in M} w_m = 1$.

2.2 SMM and Task Interdependence

Interdependence is the central organising principle of *Coactive Design Method*, from Johnson et al. [7], which is a method aimed at designing systems in which humans and agents collaborate as teammates. They define interdependence as relationships between members of a team, and argue that these relationships determine what information is relevant for the team to complete (interdependent) tasks, and in that sense, the interdependent relationships define the *common ground* that is necessary. A number of studies have considered some of the different forms of task interdependence [5,10,17], and some have also measured sharedness [5,9]. Generally, higher sharedness of mental models produces better team performance. For example, Harbers et al. [5] found higher sharedness correlated with better team performance. In their work, SMM were composed of world knowledge and intentions, which is how we view SMM in this work. Similarly, task interdependence has naturally been part of these studies. However, almost all involve sequentially interdependent tasks. The exception is Li et al. [10], who introduced joint action in sequentially interdependent tasks and Wei et al. [17], who studied tasks that were not very strongly sequential. They did this by creating subtasks that multiple agents could complete simultaneously. None of these have explicitly employed reciprocally interdependent tasks.

Mixed results have been reported for studies involving sequentially interdependent tasks in terms of which type of information or component contributes more to team performance, that is task completion times. Harbers et al. [5] reported that when agents communicated their intentions with others, the team performance improved more than if they shared world knowledge. However, Wei et al. [17] reported that beliefs contributed more to team performance than goals. While [17] did not measure sharedness, they view the agents mental models to comprise of two components, goals (intentions) and beliefs (world knowledge). We perform further experiments involving sequentially interdependent tasks and may help explain the difference between the two studies.

In a separate study, Li et al. [10] introduced joint action in sequentially interdependent tasks. They studied search and retrieval tasks using the BW4T testbed. In one setup, agents collaborated on a task in which some blocks were heavier, and required two agents to collect. The agents exchanged goals, beliefs, and both. Their experiments revealed that with joint actions, exchanging goals improved team performance, measured as completion time, more than sharing beliefs only. When agents shared their goals that fulfil the current team sub-goal with others, the other team members could start on a new task. This allowed the team to finish the team task more quickly.

These works show that sequentially interdependent tasks have been investigated, but other forms of task interdependence have not. This work aims to fill that gap.

3   Scenario: Blocks World for Teams

We used a BW4T testbed [8] for our experiments. As explained next, we modified the testbed to be able to setup tasks with joint actions.

Basic BW4T: In BW4T, teams find and deliver coloured blocks in a particular order. The environment has a set of rooms, each containing coloured blocks, and a drop zone. The agents search the rooms, find the required blocks and drop these in the drop zone. Agents have a map of area but do not know the location of the required blocks. Agents have to go to each room to perceive the blocks that are present in it. Agents cannot see each other but can communicate with others. A simplified map is shown in Fig. 2. Each room has one door. The teams' joint task, i.e. the sequence of colours, is displayed at the bottom left. A black triangle appears on top of a colour if the colour is dropped off. The room above the joint task is the drop zone. The agents are represented by either black squares or the colour the agent is holding, and their names are displayed in red. The basic version is well suited to perform experiments for sequential and reciprocal tasks. However, it does not explicitly support joint actions.

Modified BW4T: To design joint tasks that would be a fair representation of the different forms of task interdependence, we modified the testbed. In the original version, only one agent could be in a room at any one time. To implement joint actions, we follow Li et al. [10] and introduce "heavy blocks", which required two agents to carry to the drop zone. This means in our version, two agents can carry the same block simultaneous, and therefore can be in the same room at the same time. Secondly, for team task interdependence, the blocks could be delivered in any order, that is, we removed the sequential delivery requirement.

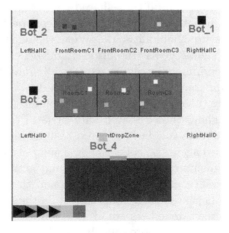

Fig. 2. Sample BW4T environment.

3.1   Task Design

We designed tasks to be able to test the effects of communication content on the team performance for each type of the task interdependence as well as later include joint action within other forms of task interdependence and test the effect of communication content on the team performance for each combination. Variations of two basic joint tasks (Fig. 3) has been used to realise the different forms of task interdependence.

(a) Task 1   (b) Task 2

Fig. 3. Basic joint tasks used to simulate different types of task interdependence. (Color figure online)

Team Task: In team tasks, agents execute their actions concurrently. The joint task had some *heavy* blocks. The heavy blocks required one agent to help the other lift it, and afterwards the first agent delivers it to the drop zone. The act of lifting the heavy block *together* is the joint action. Additionally, the agents could lift any colour. Consider the task shown in Fig. 3a. In this task, agents can lift both colours. The red blocks are heavy blocks. In order to remove the underlining sequential interdependence from this task, the agents could deliver the blocks in any order, for example, the second (red) block can be delivered before the first (yellow) block. Green, pink and red are heavy blocks in Task 2.

Reciprocal Task: In a reciprocal task, each agent takes it's turn in completing part of the task. In this task, the agents deliver a sequence of alternating colour sets in the order the colours appear in the task. Furthermore, each agent can lift colours from only one of the two distinct colour sets. Consider the task shown in Fig. 3a. For this task, one agent would be delivering yellow blocks while the other red ones. The blocks must be delivered in the order they appear. This means that agent delivering the red block now depends on the agent delivering the yellow blocks and vice-versa, making them reciprocally interdependent.

Sequential Task: In sequential task, the first three colours are delivered by one agent while the remaining three by another agent. The blocks must be delivered in the specified order, but the second agent is free to search for its coloured blocks while the first agent is delivering.

3.2   Agent Teams and Agent Behaviours

We had two team compositions; (1) 2-agent team and (2) 4-agent team. The 4-agent team was a 2×2-agent team, i.e. 2 sub-teams of 2 agents each. This composition was required for certain tasks, such as reciprocal tasks in which we needed to have at least one agent for each of the two colour sets.

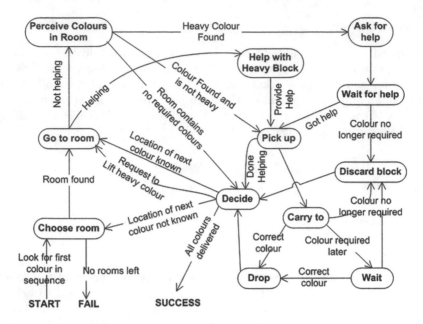

Fig. 4. Abstract decision cycle of an agent.

Agents were programmed in GOAL [6]. The BW4T testbed provides interfaces that enable GOAL agents to interact with it. Using these interfaces, the agents can perceive specific details of the environment, such as the blocks present in rooms, and can perform actions, such as picking up a block. The abstract decision cycle of an agent is shown in Fig. 4. The basic steps each agent takes are: (1) decide the colour to search for; (2) choose a room; (3) go to and search room; (4) if required block is found and is not heavy, pick it up; (5) if required block is found and is heavy, ask for help and wait. When help arrives, pick up the block; (6) deliver the block to the drop zone; (7) if help is requested, go to the particular room and help lift the heavy block.

Initially, agents start searching for the first undelivered colour. However, agents use a two-block look-ahead protocol to determine which colour to deliver. If an agent knows the location of the first undelivered colour and has the intention of collecting it, remaining agents search for the second undelivered colour. If the one or more of the remaining agents know the location of the next required colour, they go to that room. However, only one will be able to collect the block. When the first colour is picked up, one agent collects the second colour while others start searching for the third colour. The aim of this is to ensure that sufficient time is dedicated to search. When required to lift a heavy block, an agent only asks for help when it is physically present at the heavy block. Other (helper) agents could potentially infer that help will be required soon and go to the location of the heavy block before the agent actually asks for help because the agent may tell others that it has the goal of going to the (heavy) block.

However, our agents do not perform this level of reasoning and only go to help when asked. Furthermore, if one agent asks for help, all agents that are waiting to drop a block at the drop zone or those that are currently searching for their block will go to help. If the agent knows that the colour that it is searching for, has the intention of holding or is holding is no longer required, then it will discard the colour and go on to deciding what it will do next. Rooms are chosen randomly and the agents avoid visiting a room more than once unless the room contains multiple required blocks.

While the basic behaviours of agents are almost the same across the different forms of task interdependence, there are differences in the way agents reason about which colour to search for:

(1) Sequential and reciprocal tasks: Agents choose the first undelivered colour. If another agent has the goal of holding this colour, the agent chooses the next undelivered colour.
(2) Team Task: Blocks can be delivered in any order. Therefore, agents do not reason about when the block has to be delivered. Instead agents have to determine whether the block is heavy and ask for help.

While certain aspects of agent behaviours are different because of task interdependence, there are differences because of what the agents share with each other. Therefore, while the basic decision cycle shown in Fig. 4 is used by all agents, there are some variations in their implementation. The implementation has been guided by what the agents actually do with the information they receive and has been described later in Sect. 3.4. Therefore, if only one component is exchanged, the agent performs reasoning described for that component only.

3.3   Communication and SMM

Agents exchange messages that are indicative of the world knowledge and the intentions. To develop the shared mental model, agents communicate as soon as they have the required information. Agents exchange six sub-components, three each of goals and world knowledge. These sub-components were selected based on prior research work [5,10] and preliminary experiments revealed that each sub-component had the potential to improve team performance. The sub-components are communicated as messages, which are discussed next. The keyword *imp* stands for imperative and indicates what the agent intends to do.

The messages indicative of intentions are:

(1) imp(in(Sender, Room)): Sender intends to visit Room.
(2) imp(holding(Sender, Colour, Block)): Sender intends to collect Block of Colour.
(3) delivered(Sender, Colour, Block): Sender has delivered Block of Colour - implies agent has dropped current goal and may have a new goal.

The messages indicative of world knowledge are:

(1) blockLoc(Sender, Block, Colour, Room): Sender has perceived Block of required Colour in Room.
(2) pickedUp(Sender, Colour, Block): Sender has picked up Block of Colour.
(3) visited(Sender, Room): Sender has visited Room. This message is sent irrespective of whether room contains required blocks.

3.4   Using Shared Mental Models

Agents employ the following policies to SMM to choose their activities such that it prevents potential conflicts with the activities of others. The following outlines how the agents use the components of the shared mental model. We chose a straightforward use of each intention and world knowledge, which was sufficient to test the effect of the component on the team's performance and avoids side-effects that would have been introduced because of using more complex mechanisms. The intentions are used as follows:

(1) An agent will not adopt a goal to go to a particular room if another agent has the goal of going to that room. For reciprocal task, this logic applies when both agents are delivering blocks from the same colour set, that is in a 4-agent team and not in a 2-agent team.
(2) An agent will not adopt a goal to hold a block that has been delivered.
(3) An agent will not adopt a goal to hold a block/colour that another agent has the goal of holding — *unless* the block is heavy (both agents need to lift it together). For reciprocal tasks, this logic is applicable in a 4-agent team.

World knowledge is used as follows:

(1) An agent will not search for a colour if this been found by another agent.
(2) An agent will search for the next colour if the currently required colour has been picked up.
(3) An agent will not search a room that another agent has already searched.

Agents employ the above policies to SMM to reduce interference and duplication of effort. However, the agents have their own decision processes and may make decisions simultaneously. This may result in instances where the agents may adopt similar goals, for example to look for the same colour. Like Wei et al. [17], we simply implement a "first-come first-served" policy instead of implementing detailed negotiation mechanisms to assist agents resolve these issues.

4   Experiment Design

We ran a series of simulation experiments, measuring the following:

(1) Completion Time: Time it takes the team to complete the task. We used this measure as a proxy for team performance.

(2) Number of messages: We measured the total number of messages exchanged by the agents. We also counted the number of messages per component. These measures are indicative of the communication cost.

(3) Sharedness: We measured the sharedness of the agents' mental models. This is a compositional measure (see Sect. 2.1) and was calculated at the time any block was delivered to the drop zone. When one agent drops off a correct colour in drop zone, all agents log their belief and goal bases. These logs are then analysed to find the overlapping content, which is used to compute the sharedness values. The two components had a weight of 0.5 and each of the three sub-components had a weight of 0.33. In experiments where only one component was measured, the weight of the component was set to 1, and only questions related to that component were asked.

In case of sub-teams, we also measured the number of messages and sharedness of the agents with each sub-team.

Independent Variable. The independent variable is the component of the SMM. This variable has three values (see Sect. 3.3): (*1*) World Knowledge (WK); (*2*) Intentions (INT); and (*3*) World Knowledge and Intentions (ALL).

Table 1. Experimental setups (S1 – S6) for each type of task interdependence.

	Set 1				Set 2	
Team size	2 agents		4 agents		4 agents	
Map	1	2	1	2	1	2
Setup	S1	S2	S3	S4	S5	S6

Setup. We used two different maps, one for each task outlined in Sect. 3.1. Variations of each task gave us three different task interdependence types. We refer to Task 1 (Fig. 3a) as Map 1 and Task 2 as Map 2. The setups are as shown in Table 1. We had two sets. In set 1, we had four setups (S1–S4) (both maps combined with two team compositions) for each of the three types of task interdependence giving us 12 combinations.

Set 2 has two setups, S5 and S6, representing reciprocal and sequential tasks with joint actions respectively. Here the sub-teams were reciprocally or sequentially interdependent and were required to lift heavy blocks. We tested the effect of the SMM components on completion times by employing three communication strategies: (*1*) ALL-ALL: where agents exchanged the two components with every other agent. (*2*) WK-Within: where agents shared world knowledge within each sub-team but shared intentions with all agents. (*3*) INT-Within: where agents shared intentions within each sub-team but the world knowledge with all agents. For these two setups, we only used a 4-agent team because a 2-agent team would not have enabled us to fully test the effects of the two components. For example, we needed to have at least 2 agents in each sub-team to be able to test the effect of sharing a component within the sub-team. Combining S5 and S6 with the two types of task interdependence (sequential and reciprocal) gave us further 4 combinations, and a total of 16 combinations.

Combining each of the 12 combinations from Set 1 with the three components of the SMM (ALL, INT, WK) and the 4 combinations from Set 2 with the three communication strategies (ALL-ALL, WK-Within, INT-Within) resulted in 48 combinations in total. Each combination was run 30 times resulting in 1440 runs. Each map had 25 blocks pre-allocated to rooms and further 10 blocks were randomly generated giving a total of 35 blocks for each run. Each map had 9 rooms, 1 drop zone and 6 blocks in the joint task. Statistical significance tests were conducted using Wilcoxon rank-sum (WRS) and Kruskal-Wallis (KW) tests.

5   Results

This study was aimed at identifying the components that contributed most to team performance across different forms of task interdependence. Recall that going from sequential to team tasks represents increasing levels of dependence between agents as well as coordination requirements. For simplicity, we collapse the results of the two tasks (shown in Fig. 3) and report the averages.

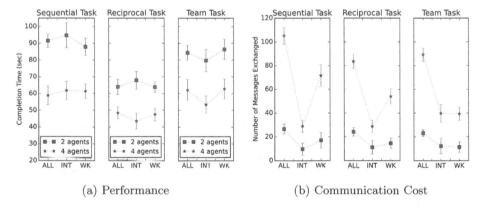

(a) Performance   (b) Communication Cost

Fig. 5. Performance and communication cost for different forms of task interdependence. The communication cost is expressed as the average number of messages exchanged by all team members. Error bars represent on standard deviation.

5.1   SMM Components and Team Performance

Figure 5a shows the average task completion times for the 2-agent and 4-agent teams performing different tasks. These results are for experiments resulting from setups S1-S4. Recall that a 4-agent team comprises 2 sub-teams of 2 agents each. For team tasks, the intentions contributed more to team performance than world knowledge. This finding is significant at 5 % for all except two combinations and consistent for both team compositions. In the team task, some blocks were heavy and the agents could pick any colour. In such scenarios, knowing the intentions of team members allows agents to avoid duplicating their activities, therefore reducing interference. These results are in line with Li et al. [10], who reported that with joint actions, exchanging goals results in improved completion times.

However, for sequential and reciprocal tasks, different trends have been observed between 2-agent and 4-agent teams. For sequential tasks and 2-agent team, the world knowledge contributed significantly more ($p < 0.05$) than intentions in terms of task completion times. In this task setting, the first agent delivered first three blocks while the remaining three by the other agent. Because agents had separate sub-tasks, exchanging world knowledge helped the other agent find it's required blocks faster. However, for reciprocal tasks, this difference was less pronounced. We discuss this more later.

In 4-agent teams performing sequential tasks, no significant difference in terms of completion times were noted between the two components. However, it is worth noting that moving from 2-agent to 4-agent team, the importance of intentions increases. A similar trend occurs for reciprocal and team tasks. In these team settings, the agents within each sub-team could choose conflicting goals, for example, choosing the same block to deliver. By exchanging intentions, agents within sub-teams avoided duplicating their activities, therefore improving the completion times.

To make these trends clearer, we computed *component influence* (CI) for each task. CI is computed based on the difference between the completion times achieved when communicating both components and any one of the two components. To normalise the difference between completion times across different experiments, we used the *tanh* function. The CI for component c is:

$$CI_c = tanh(CompletionTime_{all} - CompletionTime_c)$$

The resulting values were normalised to between 0 and 1 using $CI_{normalised} = (CI - min(CI))/(max(CI) - min(CI))$. Figure 6 for 2-agent teams show that with increasing dependence between agents, that is, going from sequential to team interdependence, the importance of intentions increases while the importance of world knowledge decreases. For 4-agent team, the intentions were almost always more important than world knowledge.

SMM and Joint Actions. Results of experiments relating to setups S5 and S6 indicated that the difference between completion times of WK-Within and INT-Within is significant (p-value = 0.009) in favour of INT-Within. This indicates that sharing intentions within sub-teams and world knowledge with everyone achieves the best team performance. This is consistent with our earlier findings that intentions and team tasks are positively correlated. Also, world knowledge and sequential and reciprocal tasks are positively correlated.

5.2   Communication Performance

Figure 5b shows the communication cost (average number of messages exchanged). The number of intentions exchanged was significantly lower

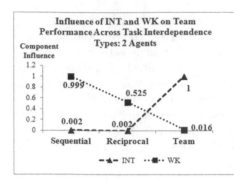 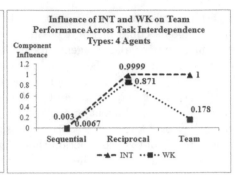

Fig. 6. The two graphs (2 agents and 4 agents) show that intentions become more important more as the level of interdependence increases and as the number of agents in each sub-team increases.

$(p < 0.05)$ than world knowledge for about two-thirds of the combinations. This indicates that agents generally have more information to communicate about the world than their intentions. There was no correlation between the number of messages and team performance. More communication resulted in worst performance in some cases, particularly for larger teams. This is due to the two-block look-ahead policy. When agents exchange information about possible blocks, in larger teams this often results is agents trying to collect the same block/colour and this increases the completion time. When agents only exchange intentions, all agents are required to find the blocks themselves, and so search randomly, thus reducing the number of unnecessary runs for the same block/colour. While it is clear that a mechanism could be designed to improve this by using a different look-ahead policy, we believe our policy is reasonable. Importantly though, this result shows that simply throwing more information towards agents can result in worse performance if significant thought is not given to how that information is used.

5.3   Analysis of Sharedness

We computed the sharedness in relation to each component at the time a block was delivered to the dropzone. Generally, higher sharedness correlates with improved completion times. For simplicity we show the data for team task and note that the results for sequential and reciprocal tasks are similar. For example, Fig. 7 shows the sharedness at the time each correct block is dropped off for team tasks. The plotted delivery times are the time differences between block deliveries. For team tasks, exchanging intentions achieved the best completion times and the sharedness was highest for this component. Notice that in Fig. 7, sharedness of intentions is highest across all six blocks and the delivery times when teams exchange intentions are fastest across most of the six blocks.

Sharedness and Sub Teams. We measured the sharedness of members within each sub-team for tasks solved by 4-agent teams. Sharing intentions resulted

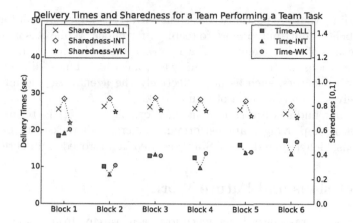

Fig. 7. Sharedness and delivery times for a 2-agent team engaged in a team task.

in the best completion times and the sharedness of intentions was highest for reciprocal and team tasks. For sequential tasks, we noted a significant increase in the importance of intentions compared to 2-agent team. This supports the finding that higher sharedness results in better completion times. The other consistent finding is that in situations where we may have members of sub-teams potentially duplicating their efforts, sharing intentions with each other helps avoid such conflicting actions and therefore, improves the completion times.

6   Discussion

We intended to identify the components contributing most to team performance across the different forms of task interdependence. Our results show that as the interdependence increases, the importance of intentions to team performance also increases. These results are in line with [5,10] who found that when team members exchanged intentions, the team performance improves. In [5], teams were engaged in sequential tasks and their team composition was similar to our 4-agent team while in [10], the authors introduced joint actions in sequentially interdependent tasks.

While our results are in line with the above works, we have observed that when team members can perform their sub-tasks independently, e.g. in 2-agent teams, exchanging world knowledge contributes more to team performance for sequential and reciprocal tasks. This makes sense intuitively: if other members provide potentially useful information, such as location of blocks that one is required to deliver, the team performance improves. This is a form of *soft interdependence* [7] where one team/member 'helps' another voluntarily. In case of 4-agent teams, we found that intentions contributed more to team performance across all forms of task interdependence. This indicates that team composition plays a role in which component is important to team performance.

Our findings that are partially consistent with [17] who found that for sequential tasks, beliefs contributed more to team performance. While this is consistent with the results of our 2-agent team, we noted a marked increase in the importance of intentions when 4-agent team was concerned. These differences may hinge on other factors, such as how effectively the agents use the information that it receives. This is an area of future work.

Finally, our findings are consistent with others (e.g. [5]) in terms the role SMM plays in improving team performance. Across all tasks and both team compositions, higher sharedness of SMM resulted in improved team performance.

7   Conclusions and Future Work

The four types of task interdependence form a hierarchy, from pooled to team, representing increasing levels of dependence between team members as well as increasing needs for coordination. We found that with increasing levels of interdependence, the importance of intentions increases as well. Team composition also plays a role in which component contributes more to team performance. In team compositions, where agents can perform their tasks independently, e.g. in sequential and reciprocal tasks, world knowledge contributed more to team performance. When multiple team members may be engaged in a single sub-task, the potential of interference increases and so does the importance of knowing the intentions of others.

A factor to investigate further is the reasoning capability of the agents; that is, how the agents reason with information that they receive from others. We also have not explicitly analysed the behavioural changes in the agents when agents switch from one task interdependence type to another, making this another opportunity for future investigation.

References

1. Cannon-Bowers, J.A., Salas, E., Converse, S.: Shared mental models in expert team decision making. In: Castellan, J., John, N. (eds.) Individual and Group Decision Making: Current Issues, pp. 221–246. Hillsdale, NJ, Lawrence Erlbaum. (1993)
2. DeChurch, L.A., Mesmer-Magnus, J.R.: Measuring shared team mental models: A meta-analysis. Group Dyn. Theory Res. Pract. **14**(1), 1 (2010)
3. Fan, X., Yen, J.: Modeling cognitive loads for evolving shared mental models in human-agent collaboration. IEEE Trans. Syst. Man Cybern. **41**(2), 354–367 (2011)
4. Harbers, M., Jonker, C.M., Van Riemsdijk, M.B.: Context-sensitive sharedness criteria for teamwork. In: Proceedings of AAMAS 2014, pp. 1507–1508. ACM (2014)
5. Harbers, M., van Riemsdijk, M., Jonker, C.: Measuring sharedness of mental models and its relation to team performance. In: Proceedings of 14th Workshop on COIN, pp. 106–120. Springer, Heidelberg (2012)
6. Hindriks, K.: Programming rational agents in GOAL. In: El Fallah Seghrouchni, A., Dix, J., Dastani, M., Bordini, R.H. (eds.) Multi-Agent Programming, pp. 119–157. Springer, Heidelberg (2009)

7. Johnson, M., Bradshaw, J., Feltovich, P., Jonker, C., Riemsdijk, M.B.V.: Coactive design: Designing support for interdependence in joint activity. J. Hum. Robot Interact. **3**(1), 43–69 (2014)
8. Johnson, M., Jonker, C., van Riemsdijk, B., Feltovich, P.J., Bradshaw, J.M.: Joint activity testbed: Blocks world for teams (BW4T). In: Aldewereld, H., Dignum, V., Picard, G. (eds.) ESAW 2009. LNCS (LNAI), vol. 5881, pp. 254–256. Springer, Heidelberg (2009). doi:10.1007/978-3-642-10203-5_26
9. Jonker, C.M., van Riemsdijk, M.B., Vermeulen, B.: Shared mental models. In: Vos, M., Fornara, N., Pitt, J.V., Vouros, G. (eds.) COIN -2010. LNCS (LNAI), vol. 6541, pp. 132–151. Springer, Heidelberg (2011). doi:10.1007/978-3-642-21268-0_8
10. Li, S., Sun, W., Miller, T.: Communication in human-agent teams for tasks with joint action. In: Proceedings of 9th Workshop on COIN, pp. 111–126 (2015)
11. Manner, M.D., Gini, M.: Improving agent team performance through helper agents. In: Dignum, F., Brom, C., Hindriks, K., Beer, M., Richards, D. (eds.) CAVE 2012. LNCS (LNAI), vol. 7764, pp. 89–105. Springer, Heidelberg (2013). doi:10.1007/978-3-642-36444-0_6
12. Mohammed, S., Ferzandi, L., Hamilton, K.: Metaphor no more: A 15-year review of the team mental model construct. J. Manag. **36**(4), 876–910 (2010)
13. Rouse, W.B., Morris, N.M.: On looking into the black box: Prospects and limits in the search for mental models. Psychol. Bull. **100**(3), 349 (1986)
14. Saavedra, R., Earley, P.C., Van Dyne, L.: Complex interdependence in task-performing groups. J. Appl. Psychol. **78**(1), 61–72 (1993)
15. Singh, R., Miller, T., Sonenberg, L.: A preliminary analysis of interdependence in multiagent systems. In: Dam, H.K., Pitt, J., Xu, Y., Governatori, G., Ito, T. (eds.) PRIMA 2014. LNCS (LNAI), vol. 8861, pp. 381–389. Springer, Heidelberg (2014). doi:10.1007/978-3-319-13191-7_31
16. Smith-Jentsch, K.A.: On shifting from autonomous to interdependent work. Technical Report February, NASA, Houston, Texas (2015)
17. Wei, C., Hindriks, K., Jonker, C.M.: The role of communication in coordination protocols for cooperative robot teams. In: Proceedings of International Conference on Agents and Artificial Intelligence, pp. 28–39 (2014)

An Examination of a Novel Information Diffusion Model: Considering of Twitter User and Twitter System Features

Keisuke Ikeda[1]([⊠]), Takeshi Sakaki[2], Fujio Toriumi[2], and Satoshi Kurihara[1]

[1] The University of Electro-Communications, 1-5-1 Chofugaoka, Chofu, Japan
k-ikeda@ni.is.uec.ac.jp , kuri@is.uec.ac.jp
[2] The University of Tokyo, 7-3-1 Hongo, Bunkyo, Tokyo, Japan

Abstract. Twitter is a popular microblogging service in Japan. People use the Twitter for communicating with friends, and posting tweet daily life events. In addition, Twitter has also been used in an emergency situation, such as the earthquake. In the East Japan great earthquake disaster, people were using Twitter to get refuge and rescue informations. However, spreading false rumor has become a major social problem. We aim to propose suppression scheme of false rumor. Therefore, we propose a novel multiagent-based information diffusion model to reveal the diffusion mechanism of false rumor in this paper. Our model is to focus on the information diffusion behavior of each Twitter user. We consider three elements of each user, "User's diversity", "Life pattern", and "State transition". In addition, our model also takes into account multiple of the information path, which is a feature of Twitter. We evaluate the validity of our model.

Keywords: Twitter · Information diffusion · False rumor

1 Introduction

Twitter is a kind of microblog service, it is a popular communication tool. It is also used in the event of a disaster not only for using in daily life event. In East Japan great earthquake disaster, Japan suffered big damage. Among the confused situation, people were using Twitter to get refuge and rescue information, and communicating each other. Several TV stations and government agencies announced evacuation information and rescue information via Twitter [1]. However, there is demerit when you get these information from Twitter. The demerit is that you may have receive false rumor. Information is rapidly spreading on Twitter. These are an actual example of false rumor in the East Japan great earthquake disaster.

1. A toxic substance attached to clouds by the explosion of Cosmo Oil falls with rain.
2. Drink a bottle of Povidone-iodine will protect you from radioactive damage.

© Springer International Publishing AG 2016
N. Osman and C. Sierra (Eds.): AAMAS 2016 Ws Best Papers, LNAI 10002, pp. 180–191, 2016.
DOI: 10.1007/978-3-319-46882-2_11

We define a false rumor as "information whose correction is announced later, even though this information was not diffused deliberately [2]." When a large-scale disaster, we guess that victims are difficult to ascertain the authenticity of the information. Victims may get a serious damage by the wrong information.

We would like to establish the method of stopping diffusion of false rumor. However, a detailed diffusion mechanism has not been made very clear for either false or corrected rumors. So, in this paper, we will propose a novel multiagent-based information diffusion model (AIDM: Agent-based Information Diffusion Model), based on a multi-agent system. We will evaluate the validity of our model.

This paper is organized as follow: Sect. 2, we introduce related works. In Sect. 3, we describe the problems of information diffusion model that we have previously proposed. Section 4, we propose a new information diffusion model to solve these problems. In Sect. 5, describes the experiment and a method for evaluating our model. Finaly, Sect. 6 concludes our work and describe the future works.

2   Related Works

Recently, there are a lot of research dealing with information diffusion in social media.

We have proposed information diffusion model, hereinafter called "Extended SIR model [2]." Extendet SIR model is an extension of the famous SIR model [3] as epidemiological model. We considered a false rumor as a virus that spreads a disease. However, there are differences in false rumor and virus, we constructed this model considering characteristics of information diffusion. In this model, the state transition of the user is expressed by using the transition probabilities. By using this model, we have succeeded in the reproduction of a particular false rumor diffusion. However, it does not mean that reproduces all of the false rumor that was spreading in the East Japan great earthquake disaster.

Serrano et al. were also carried out the information diffusion studies using the SIR model [4]. They also reproduce the information diffusion by the state transition of the agent. The difference between information diffusion model proposed in this paper is the following two points. First, Serrano et al. are considering the influx of information from other information media. Second, there is a restriction that the user can not tweet about corrected information who has already tweeted false rumor. However, Serrano et al. did not take into account the characteristics of each user.

We propose a new model which considers the characteristics of each user in this paper. From this, we describe the reason to take into account the characteristics of each user. Miura analyzed the contents of tweets on the East Japan Great Earthquake Disaster [5]. She investigated the reason for the increase in communication and negative reason on Twitter. She pointed out that these situations caused a lot of tweet for disaster's stress reduction. As a result, false rumors increased by this action. She also mentioned on feature of Twitter.

The Twitter timeline is different depending on each Twitter user. The information that each user receives is different. We need to change the approach to suit the above purpose.

Takeuchi et al. were studied information diffusion with a focus on user's characteristics [6]. In this information diffusion model, they consider that the user is filtering the information. They considered that whether or not to spread the information by finding value in the information. In addition, they described that another important element is the root of information.

In order to estimate the detailed mechanism of information diffusion, it is necessary to consider knowledge of the Miura and Takeuchi et al. We study the information diffusion phenomenon by focusing on the characteristics of each user and Twitter. In this paper, we propose a new information diffusion model to solve the weak point of "Extended SIR model."

3   Weak Point of Extended SIR Model

This section will explain the four weak points of Extended SIR model.

First, all user agents are the same type for message transmission. It is difficult to representation of diversity. State transition of the agent has been done by the same state transition probability. This condition means that all user's preferences and interests are same. However, each user has different preferences and interests for what information they want to convey. Therefore, it is necessary to take into consideration a user's diversity of communication. In addition, we considered "false rumor" and "corrected information" are different information. The corrected information is the information which denies the false rumor. In short, false rumor and corrected information are same topic. Therefore, the degree of the user's interest isn't different in both information.

Second, users can not tweet more than once on Extended SIR model. The user is expected to tweet more than once to inform the important information to many users. However, it is not possible more than once tweet because our previous model is based on SIR model.

Third, the multiplex path of communication is not taken into consideration. A user agent receives the information only once in our previous model. However, there are some information paths within the Twitter follower network, so that user agent can receive information multiple times.

Fourth, people's life pattern is not taken into consideration. Users don't keep using Twitter during the day As an example, consider a user activity for one day. The user wake up, and eat breakfast in the morning. The user go to work to the company. After the work, go to the home and eat dinner, Sometimes, the user meets with friends. In the night, user go to bed. Thus, the user is doing various activities.

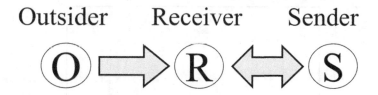

Fig. 1. ORS model

4 Proposed Method

In this section, we describe improvement method of the weak point described by the previous section. Our novel model is a multi-agent model in which a plurality of agents to represent false rumor diffusion phenomenon by interacting. Agents consider elements to be described below.

4.1 State Transition Model

The users are able to more than once tweets the same topic. We propose a new state transition model for representing the above-mentioned. We call the state transition model "Outsider - Receiver - Sender Model (ORS Model)". State transition of "ORS Model" is indicated on Fig. 1. The three states are described below.

- *Outsider*: People who do not know both a false rumor and its corrected information are included in this situation.
- *Receiver*: People who know a false rumor or corrected information are included in this situation.
- *Sender*: People who know a false rumor (or corrected informaiton) and diffused it are included in this situation. "Sender" can return in the state of "Receiver". Therefore, it is possible that the agent multiple times tweets.

4.2 Multiplexing of Information Path

We take into account the multiplexing of information paths. If a user receives a false rumor multiple times, they may tweet uninteresting information. Then, false rumor is spread by the user.

4.3 Life Pattern

By Shahzad et al. study, they have been found that the usage trend of twitter is change by the hour [7]. This work is a study on the usage of Twitter in daily life. However, we target on the use of Twitter in emergency situation. We investigated the usage of Twitter at the East Japan great earthquake disaster. Figure 2 is a plot of the average number of tweets at each time of 7 days

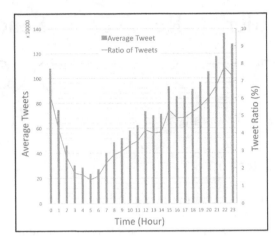

Fig. 2. Average tweet and tweet ratio

(11 March to 17 March 2011). This figure shows the number of daytime posts peak is at 12:00 and 15:00. These hour corresponds to lunch or break time. Tweets are increasing from around 17:00, the number of biggest tweets at 22:00. This time period is after work, users are spending their leisure time. The number of posts is reducing from around 11:00. Around 5:00 in the morning, record the minimum number tweets during the day. This is related at time to fall asleep. In this way, the user's life patterns affect the number of Tweets. Therefore, we have to confine the number of agents to get the information from Twitter, to express "User's Life Pattern."

4.4 User's diversity

In order to take "Users diversity into consideration, we use Endo et al. proposal [8]. They modeled word-of-mouth propagation. They reported two important elements for word-of-mouth propagation. These elements are "the reliability of information sources" and "the value of information contents." For the reliability of information sources, information from experts or specialists have a greater impact on reliability, and more reliable information is more persuasive. For the value of information, in general, the information suits one's interests or hobbies becoming more valuable.

Our model defines the new parameters. These parameters are used as the element of information diffusion.

Degree of Influence: a

The degree of influence a represents the magnitude of the influence of information sources. As an actual example, famous persons have great impact. This value is defined by using a PageRank algorithm. We use this algorithm as the degree of influence a.

Table 1. Setup of tweet ratio

Time	0	1	2	3	4	5
Ratio (%)	6.15	4.26	2.67	1.72	1.62	1.34
Time	6	7	8	9	10	11
Ratio (%)	1.56	2.29	2.78	2.96	3.31	3.55
Time	12	13	14	15	16	17
Ratio (%)	4.18	4.00	4.06	5.32	4.87	4.89
Time	18	19	20	21	22	23
Ratio (%)	5.20	5.53	6.01	6.71	7.78	7.28

Degree of Interest: i

The degree of interest i represents the strength of the interest on the topic of a user. This value expresses the difference in each user's hobbies and diversions. This value becomes large, if the topic suits one's interests and hobbies.

Degree of Sensitivity: s

The degree of sensitivity s represents the degree to which a user tends to believe the information. Endo et al. said that a user judges the truth of information by using their own knowledge and experience. It is necessary to take this into consideration for each user. The this value becomes larger, the more likely it is for the user to be influenced by information.

Our model defines the motivation of tweet (MoT). MoT expresses the desire that a user wants to tweet. If MoT is larger than a threshold value, a user will tweet, and the information will be spread. Below, the method for calculating MoT is shown a formula (1).

$$MoT_{k\beta t} = MoT_{k\beta t-1}e^{-\lambda(t-FG)} + i_{k\beta}s_{\beta}\sum_{n} a_n \qquad (1)$$

In addition, the characters in the formula represent the following. β is users who are wondering whether tweet receives the information. α_n set of users as a source of user β. λ is a forgetting rate, k is topic of received information. t is the present time. FG is the time when the user first receives false rumor information.

Here, we describe the pseudo code (Algorithm 1) the behavior of user. In addition, we explain this pseudo code using a case where the user β has received false rumor tweet. The user β is determined whether receive the false rumor in accordance with the value of Table 1 at the current time. Note that Table 1 shows the rate of users that can be in contact with the information in each time. The user β received a false rumor from one or more users α_n who have followed up on user β. The user β's MoT is calculated by using formula (1). The size of MoT and the threshold value is compared. If MoT is larger than the threshold value, the user β's infection condition is made into "$Sender(FalseRumor)$." If MoT is smaller than the threshold value, the user β's infection condition is made into

---

Algorithm 1. Behavior of agent

1: **if** The agent receives a false rumor according to the ratio of Table 1 at the current
   time &&
   Agent didn't spread same false rumor **then**
2:    MoT is calculated by using formula (1).
3:    **if** MoT > Threshold value **then**
4:       Agent's infection condition is made into *"Sender"*, and spread false rumor to
         agent's follower.
5:    **else**
6:       Agent's infection condition is made into *"Receiver"*.
7:    **end if**
8: **end if**
9: **if** Agent's infection condition is *"Sender"* **then**
10:    Agent's infection condition change to *"Receiver"*.
11: **end if**
   Agent gets new information, repeat the above.

"Receiver(FalseRumor)." Corrected information follows the same idea, too. If MoT is larger than the threshold value, the user's infection condition is made into *"Sender(CorrectedRumor)."* If MoT is smaller than the threshold value, the user's infection condition is made into *"Receiver(CorrectedRumor)."*

5   Experiment

In this section, we describe the experiment for confirming the validity of our proposed model.

Table 2. Parameters for follower network

Number of nodes	100,000
Expectation of numbers of degree	upper limit = 3000
	lower limit = 10
	Pareto index = 0.5
Expectation of possibility of having follower	upper limit = 15.0
	lower limit = 0.05
	Pareto index = 0.5

5.1   Experiment Outline

We use a simulator that included our model. We reproduce an actual false rumor by using the simulator. The actual false rumor was the false rumor information diffused just after the East Japan great earthquake disaster, specifically, a disastrous fire occurred at the Chiba refinery of Cosmo Oil Co., Ltd. in Chiba

Table 3. Setup of each parameter

Degree of Interest:i	Random value of range 0 to 1
Degree of Sensitivity:s	Random value of range 0 to 1
Degree of Influence:a	PageRank value of each node
Forgetting rate λ	1/8
Threshold	5×10^{-7}

prefecture in Japan. At this time, since the false rumor "a toxic substance contained clouds that comes from the Cosmo Oil explosion will fall with the rain" spread as a chain mail and was posted to Twitter after that, the false rumor was spread to many users. Diffusion of this false rumor was 48 hours (from 18 O'clock, 11th March to 18 O'clock, 13th March). In this simulation, we take into account the User's life pattern, we set simulation one step as one hour of real time.

The conditions of a simulation refer to the literature [2]. The simulation procedure is shown in Table 4. The setup of the network used in the simulation is shown in Table 2. The setup of the parameters used within the model are shown in Table 3.

We try the simulation 5000 times. It will result the ones with the smallest "Distance" in the 5000 times simulation (For "Distance", we describe in next section).

5.2   Evaluation Methods

We describe the evaluation method of our model. We use two indicators "Distance" and "Infection Rate".

– Distance

The simulation results are the number of each state in each simulation step. The candidate for comparing the simulation results are real data. The real data[1]

Table 4. Procedure of simulation

Step1 : Construct a follower network depending on the parameters of Table 2
Step2 : Choose one node at random, and change the infection situation to I at time $t = 1$ of the simulation environment.
Step3 : Choose one node at random and change the infection situation to R at time $t = 16$ of the simulation environment.
Step4 : Stop the simulation at time $t = 48$ of the simulation environment

---

[1] Real tweets collected before and after the East Japan earthquake disaster by Toriumi et al. from March 11 to 24, 2011 [9]. Okada et al. extracted these tweets related to false rumors and their corrections.

was obtained as follows. The contents of a tweet in the case of an earthquake disaster were analyzed. The number of people of each time and each infection state is counted. Both real data and simulation results were used to carry out the next processing. Let the sum total of the number of each state in each step be a denominator. The rate of the number is calculated.

The Euclidian distance is used for comparing a simulation result and real data. We usually use Euclidian distance in order to calculate distance. The value that should be calculated is the difference between real data and a simulation result in each step and state. Then, the sum total of the distance is calculated. If the total distance is close to 0, the real data and the simulation result are similar.

The calculation method is described below. First, suppose that there are two kinds of vectors "$X = \{x_1, x_2, \ldots, x_n\}$" and "$Y = \{y_1, y_2, \ldots, y_n\}$". Data are already calculated as a number ratio.

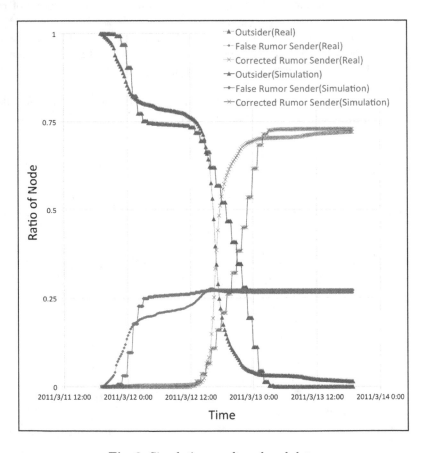

Fig. 3. Simulation result and real data

$$D = \sqrt{(x_1' - y_1')^2 + (x_2' - y_2')^2 + \cdots + (x_n' - y_n')^2}$$

$$= \sqrt{\sum_{i=1}^{n}(x_i' - y_i')^2} \qquad (2)$$

Note that, it defines as one hour to one step in the simulation. However, we were aggregating the actual data every 15 min. Therefore, to simulate one step, comparing the four actual data.

– Infection Rate

The infection rate of the false rumor is found by analysis of the actual data. "Infection Rate" represents probability of how many users infected by the false rumor. By comparing the actual infection rate and our simulation infection rate to measure the validity of the model. The actual infection rate is calculated by our previous work [2]. However, there is missing data in the actual data, it is not perfect. Infection rate can not be calculated accurately. In addition, the scale of simulation network is smaller than the actual follower network. From the foregoing, we determined to be valid unless the extremely greater the simulation result than the actual infection rate.

5.3 Experimental Results

The result of having performed the simulation 5000 times by using the above-mentioned setup is described below. It shows the simulation results of Cosmo Oil's false rumor diffusion in Fig. 3. First, from Fig. 3, the reduction rate of "*Outsider*" resembled the actual false rumor. The increase of the agent ("False Rumor Sender") who spread the false rumor slightly faster than the actual data. The increase of the agent ("Corrected Rumor Sender") who spread the corrected information is a little slower than the actual data. However, it can be seen that the state changes are generally conforming to the actual data. It shows distance in this case in the Table 5.

Next, It shows infection rate in this case in the Table 6. From this table, infection rate of false rumor was close the real data value. Infection rate of corrected rumor has become a value lower than the actual data. However, it is determined that both infection rate values were similar because it is lower than the actual data.

From these results, it can be generally reproduced false rumor spread using our model.

Table 5. Distance

Outsider	Sender(false rumor)	Sender(corrected rumor)	Average
1.613	0.408	1.585	1.202

Table 6. Infection rate (simulation result and real data)

	Real data	Simulation result
False rumor	0.05	0.031
Corrected rumor	0.347	0.076

6　Conclusion

In the East Japan great earthquake disaster, diffusion of false rumor has become a major problem. In order to eliminate the damage caused by false rumor, it must suppress the diffusion of false rumor. For this purpose, it is necessary to clarify the diffusion mechanism of information. In this paper, we propose a novel information diffusion model to reveal the information diffusion mechanism on Twitter.

Our model considers four elements, "State Transition", "Multiplexing of information path", "Life Pattern", and "User's diversity". Therefore, this model can be expressed more finely diffusion phenomenon. We reproduced the actual false rumor spreading to evaluate our model. As a result, actual false rumor could be reproduced using our model, and the validity of the model was proved.

As future work, we will verify also possible this model is applied to other false rumors. Finally, we will propose a diffusion control method.

References

1. Ministry of Internal Affairs and Communications, Japan, "WHITE PAPER 2011 (2011). http://www.soumu.go.jp/johotsusintokei/whitepaper/eng/WP2011/2011-index.html
2. Okada, Y., Ikeda, K., Numao, M., Toriumi, F., Sakaki, T., Shinoda, K., Kazama, K., Noda, I., Okada, S.: SIR-extended information diffusion model of false rumor and its prevention strategy for Twitter. J. Adv. Comput. Intell. Intell. Inf. **18**(4), 598–607 (2014)
3. Kermack, W.O., McKendrick, A.G.: A contribution to the math-ematical theory of epidemics. In: Proceedings of the Royal Society of London A: Math-Ematical, Physical and Engineering Sciences, vol. 115(772). The Royal Society (1927)
4. Serrano, E., Iglesias, C.Á., Garijom M.: A Novel agent-based rumor spreading model in Twitter. In: Proceedings of the 24th International Conference on World Wide Web Companion. International World Wide Web Conferences Steering Committee (2015)
5. Miura, A.: Social psychology of online communication on 3.11 disasters in Japan (3. Diversification of Distribution Means of Disaster Information, Special Issue Disaster Recovery Activities from the Great East Japan Earthquake and Teachings Obtained from the Disaster). J. IEICE **95**(3), 219–223 (2012). (In Japanese)
6. Takeuchi, S., Kamahara, J., Shimojo, S., Miyahara, H.: Human-network-based filtering: the information propagation model based on word-of-mouth communication. In: Proceedings of IEEE Symposium on Applications and the Internet (2003)

7. Shahzad, B., Alwagait, E.: Best, the worst times to Tweet: an experimental study. In: WSEAS, Proceedings of 15th International Conference on Mathematics and Computers in Business and Economics (MCBE 2014) (2014)
8. Endo, H., Noto, M.: A word-of-mouth information recommender system considering information reliability and user preferences. In: 2003 IEEE International Conference on Systems, Man and Cybernetics, vol. 3. IEEE (2003)
9. Toriumi, F., Shinoda, K., Kurihara, S., Sakaki, T., Kazama, K., Noda, I.: Disaster changes the social media. In: JWEIN 2011, pp. 41–46 (2011). (In Japanese)

Author Index

Printed in the United States
By Bookmasters